PROFESSOR BERNHARDI

AND OTHER PLAYS

D1479131

Studies in Austrian Literature, Culture, and Thought

Translation Series

Arthur Schnitzler

Professor Bernhardi

and

Other Plays

Translated by G. J. Weinberger

Afterword by Jeffrey B. Berlin

ARIADNE PRESS

Ariadne Press would like to express its appreciation to the Austrian Cultural Institute, New York and the Austrian Ministry of Education and Art, Vienna for their assistance in publishing this book.

Library of Congress Cataloging-in-Publication Data

Schnitzler, Arthur, 1862-1931.
    Professor Bernhardi and other plays / Arthur Schnitzler; translated by G.J. Weinberger ; afterword by Jeffrey B. Berlin.
        p.   cm. -- (Studies in Austrian literature, culture, and thought. Translation series)
        Contents: Professor Bernhardi -- Comedy of words -- The Hour of recognition -- The Big scene -- The Bacchanale -- Fink and Fliederbusch.
        ISBN 0-929497-70-8
        I. Title. II. Series.
    PT2638.N5A28 1993
    832'8--dc20   93-7274
                                            CIP

Cover Design:
Designer: David Hubbell
Art Director: George McGinnis

Copyright ©1993
by Ariadne Press
270 Goins Court
Riverside, CA 92507

Printed in the United States of America.
ISBN 0-929497-70-8

In Memory
of
my Mother
JULA WEINBERGER
(1916-1992)

CONTENTS

ACKNOWLEDGMENTS

I wish to thank my friend and colleague, Professor Jeffrey B. Berlin, currently Associate Academic Dean at Holy Family College in Philadelphia, for his original suggestion that I undertake to translate *Professor Bernhardi*, for his agreeing to provide this collection with an afterword, and for his readiness, over the years, always to share both his knowledge and his vast collection of secondary sources with me.

I am also indebted to Professor Donald G. Daviau for his kindly given and helpful suggestions for revisions.

I wish also to acknowledge the assistance and courtesies extended to me by colleagues, administrators and the inter-library loan staff at Central Connecticut State University, and to thank Ms. Carol Sessions, English Department secretary, for her kind willingness to type the occasional introduction or afterword on short notice. In addition, I am indebted to Reinhard Urbach's *Schnitzler-Kommentar zu den erzählenden Schriften und dramatischen Werken* (München: Winkler, 1974) for providing the basic source for my annotations of *Professor Bernhardi*.

As always, I am most indebted to my wife, Jill, for her support and encouragement. Had unhappy circumstances not intervened yet again, I would gladly have dedicated this volume to her with the epigraph, "Jeder Druck der Hände. . . ."

New Britain, Connecticut
November, 1992

iii

PROFESSOR BERNHARDI

A Comedy in Five Acts

CHARACTERS

DR. BERNHARDI, *Professor of Internal Medicine, Director of the Elisabethinum*
DR. EBENWALD, *Professor of Surgery, Vice-Director*
DR. CYPRIAN, *Professor of Nervous Disorders*
DR. PFLUGFELDER, *Professor of Ophthalmology*
DR. FILITZ, *Professor of Gynecology*
DR. TUGENDVETTER, *Professor of Dermatology*
DR. LÖWENSTEIN, *Instructor in Pediatrics*
DR. SCHREIMANN, *Instructor of Laryngology*
DR. ADLER, *Instructor in Pathological Anatomy*
DR. OSKAR BERNHARDI
DR. KURT PFLUGFELDER
DR. WENGER, *Tugendvetter's assistant*
DR. HOCHROITZPOINTNER, *Resident*
LUDMILLA, *nurse*
PROFESSOR DR. FLINT, *Minister of Education*
THE HON. DR. WINKLER, *on the staff of the Education Ministry*
FRANZ REDER, *priest at the church of St. Florian*
DR. GOLDENTHAL, *defense attorney*
DR. FEUERMANN, *district physician in Oberhollabrunn*
KULKA, *a journalist*
SERVANTS *at Bernhardi's, at the Elisabethinum, and at the Ministry of Education*

Vienna around 1900

FIRST ACT

A modest anteroom leading to a ward. To the right a door to the hallway. In the back the door to the ward. To the left a rather wide window. In the center, towards the left, an oblong table on which lie a thick logbook as well as folders containing case histories, documents, and all manner of papers. Next to the entry a clothes tree. In the corner right an iron stove. Next to the window a wide étagère, on its top shelf a stand with test-tubes next to some medicine bottles. On the lower shelves books and periodicals. On either side of the center door a closed cupboard. A white smock, an overcoat, and a hat hang on the clothes tree. Above the étagère a fairly old photograph representing the senior staff. A number of chairs as needed.

The NURSE, SISTER LUDMILLA, *around 28, fairly attractive, pale, with large, sometimes watery eyes, occupied at the étagère.* HOCHROITZPOINTNER *emerges from the ward. He is a pale young man of 25, of medium height, heavy, with a small mustache, smartly styled hair, and a dueling scar, wearing a pince-nez.*

HOCHROITZPOINTNER The Professor not here yet? They're taking a long time down there today. *At the table, opening one of the folders* Third autopsy in a week now. Quite a bit for a ward with twenty beds. And tomorrow we'll have another one.

NURSE Do you think so, Doctor? The sepsis?

HOCHROITZPOINTNER Yes. By the way, have the authorities been notified?

NURSE Of course, Doctor.

HOCHROITZPOINTNER Nothing could be proven, of course. But I'm sure it was an illegal operation. I tell you, Sister, all sorts of things happen in the world out there. *He notices an open package lying on the table* Ah, here are the invitations to our ball. *Reads* Under the patronage of the Princess Stixenstein. Well, Sister, are you coming to our ball too?

NURSE *smiling* I don't think so, Doctor.

HOCHROITZPOINTNER Are you forbidden to dance, then?

NURSE No, Doctor. We are not a religious order, you know. We're not forbidden anything.

HOCHROITZPOINTNER *with a sly glance at her* So, nothing at all?

NURSE But it really wouldn't be seemly. And besides, we don't have a mind for that in our profession.

HOCHROITZPOINTNER But why not? What should we say, then, we doctors? Take Doctor Adler, for example. He's an anatomical pathologist and yet, a very jolly fellow. Personally, I'm never in a better mood than when I'm in the dissecting room.

DR. OSKAR BERNHARDI *enters from the right, 25 years old, quite elegant; of obliging but somewhat insecure conduct.*

OSKAR Good morning.

HOCHROITZPOINTNER AND NURSE Good morning, Doctor.

OSKAR Father will be here right away.

HOCHROITZPOINTNER So, finished downstairs already? What was the diagnosis, if one may ask?

OSKAR The tumor originated in the kidney and was quite sharply defined.

HOCHROITZPOINTNER So you could still have operated in fact?

OSKAR Yes, could have.

HOCHROITZPOINTNER If Professor Ebenwald had thought so too —

OSKAR — we'd have had the autopsy a week earlier. *At the table* Ah, here are the invitations for our ball. Why the people send this here. . . ?!

HOCHROITZPOINTNER This year's Elisabethinum ball promises to be one of the most elegant events of the carnival season. Says so in the paper already. And I hear you've even dedicated a waltz to the committee.

OSKAR *with a self-deprecating gesture* Go on — *towards the ward* Anything new in there?

HOCHROITZPOINTNER With the sepsis case it's almost over.

OSKAR Oh, well . . . *regretfully* There was nothing to be done.

HOCHROITZPOINTNER I've given her a camphor injection.

OSKAR Oh yes, the art of prolonging life, that we understand especially well.

PROFESSOR BERNHARDI *enters from the right; over fifty, with a full beard tinged with gray, smooth, not excessively long hair. His bearing is more that of a man of the world than a scientist.* DOCTOR KURT PFLUGFELDER, *his assistant, 27, with a mustache and wearing a pince-nez; he is both lively and somewhat severe in his manner. Mutual greetings.*

BERNHARDI *still at the door* But —

NURSE *takes his overcoat, which he had draped around his shoulders, and hangs it on a hook.*

KURT I tell you, I can't help myself, Professor. Doctor Adler really would have preferred it if Professor Ebenwald's diagnosis had been right.

BERNHARDI *smiling* But my dear Doctor Pflugfelder! You smell treason everywhere. Wherever will you end up with your suspicions?

HOCHROITZPOINTNER Good morning, Professor.

BERNHARDI Good morning.

HOCHROITZPOINTNER I've just heard from Doctor Oskar that we turned out to have been right.

BERNHARDI Yes, Doctor. But "we" turned out to have been wrong at the same time as well, didn't we? Or aren't you attending Professor Ebenwald's lectures any longer?

OSKAR Doctor Hochroitzpointner attends lectures in almost every department.

BERNHARDI You must have a large stock of loyalties, then.

HOCHROITZPOINTNER *purses his lips.*

BERNHARDI *kindly, placing his hand lightly on his shoulder* Well, then, what's new?

HOCHROITZPOINTNER The sepsis case is doing very badly.

BERNHARDI So the poor girl is still alive?

KURT Her they could just as well have kept in the gynecological department.

OSKAR They happened not to have a bed free the day before yesterday.

HOCHROITZPOINTNER What are we actually going to give as the cause of death?

OSKAR Well, blood-poisoning, naturally.

HOCHROITZPOINTNER And the cause of the blood-poisoning? Since it was most likely an illegal operation —

BERNHARDI *who has in the meantime signed a few papers which the nurse placed before him at the table* We were unable to prove that. We could not demonstrate any injury. The report has been filed; with that the matter is finished for us. As it was for the poor person in there. . . some time ago. *He stands up and goes towards the ward.*

PROFESSOR EBENWALD *enters; a very tall, slim man of around 40, his overcoat draped over his shoulders, with a small beard and eyeglasses. He speaks honestly and with an occasionally overdone colloquial accent.*

EBENWALD Good morning. By any chance is — Ah, here you are, Director.

BERNHARDI Good day to you, Doctor.

EBENWALD Do you have a minute?

BERNHARDI Right now?

EBENWALD *closer to him* If possible. It's about the replacement in Tugendvetter's department.

BERNHARDI Is it all that urgent? If you'll come to my office in half an hour, perhaps —

EBENWALD That would be fine, if I weren't lecturing just then.

BERNHARDI *after a moment's reflection* I won't be long in there. If you'll wait out here for a moment.

EBENWALD Yes, thank you. Thank you.

BERNHARDI *to Oskar* Have you given Doctor Hochroitzpointner the autopsy report yet?

OSKAR Yes, right. *Takes it out of his pocket* Perhaps you'll be so kind and enter it right away.

HOCHROITZPOINTNER Of course.

Bernhardi, Oskar, Kurt, and the Nurse go into the ward.

HOCHROITZPOINTNER *sits down and prepares to write.*

EBENWALD *has gone to the window, looks down, and polishes his eyeglasses.*

HOCHROITZPOINTNER *officiously* Wouldn't the Professor like to take a seat?

EBENWALD Don't let me bother you, Hochroitzpointner. Well, how's it going?

HOCHROITZPOINTNER *getting up* Thank you very much, Professor. As one might expect a couple of weeks before the last exam.

EBENWALD Oh, don't worry, nothing will happen to you, the way you apply yourself.

HOCHROITZPOINTNER Yes, on the practical side I feel fairly secure, but all that dull theory, Professor.

EBENWALD Is that it? Well, it wasn't my strong suit either. *Closer to him* If it'll make you feel any better, I even flunked physiology myself. You see, it doesn't harm one's career particularly.

HOCHROITZPOINTNER *who has sat back down, laughs with pleasure.*

EBENWALD *looking over his shoulder* Autopsy report?

HOCHROITZPOINTNER Yes, Professor.

EBENWALD Great joy in Israel, what?

HOCHROITZPOINTNER *unsure* How do you mean, Professor?

EBENWALD Well, because Bernhardi's department triumphed.

HOCHROITZPOINTNER Ah, the Professor means because the tumor was defined.

EBENWALD And because it did actually originate in the kidney.

HOCHROITZPOINTNER But that could not, in fact, have been diagnosed with absolute certainty. It was more of a guess, if I may say so.

EBENWALD But Hochroitzpointner, a guess! How could you! Intuition is what we call that! Diagnostic insight!

HOCHROITZPOINTNER And it was no longer operable in any case.

EBENWALD Out of the question. They can afford to get involved in that sort of experiment across the way, at the state hospital, but we, in a relatively new, as it were private institute. You know, my dear fellow, there are always these cases where only the internists are in favor of operating. Conversely, we're always operating too much for them. But don't let me interrupt your writing.

HOCHROITZPOINTNER *begins to write.*

EBENWALD Oh, right, excuse me for disturbing you again. You're still attending lectures in Tugendvetter's department, of course?

HOCHROITZPOINTNER Yes, Professor.

EBENWALD The thing is, I want to ask you in confidence, how are Doctor Wenger's lectures, actually?

HOCHROITZPOINTNER Doctor Wenger?

EBENWALD Well, yes, he does often stand in for the old man when he just happens to get an urgent summons to a hunt or to a sick prince.

HOCHROITZPOINTNER Yes, certainly, Doctor Wenger lectures then.

EBENWALD Well, how does he lecture?

HOCHROITZPOINTNER *unsure* Actually, quite well.

EBENWALD So.

HOCHROITZPOINTNER Perhaps somewhat too — too scholarly. But very lively. Certainly — but, perhaps I shouldn't allow myself— about a future Head —

EBENWALD Why future Head? That has by no means been determined yet. There are others too. And besides, this is a private conversation. We could just as well be sitting and chatting across the street at the Riedhof. Well, go on, tell me. What have you got against Doctor Wenger? Vox populi, vox dei.

HOCHROITZPOINTNER Well, actually, I have very little against his lectures, it's more his entire manner. You know, Professor, a bit obtrusive is what he is.

EBENWALD Aha. My dear fellow, the thing you're alluding to is probably identical with what my cousin so accurately called "the jargon of the soul" in Parliament recently.

HOCHROITZPOINTNER Ah, very good. Jargon of the soul. *Encouraged* But he's got the other one too, the Doctor.

EBENWALD That doesn't mean anything. We simply happen to live in a nation of dialects.

Bernhardi, Oskar, Kurt and the Nurse enter from the ward.

BERNHARDI So, here I am, Doctor.

NURSE *places a sheet of paper before him for his signature.*

BERNHARDI What is it? Something else? Ah, so. Excuse me for just another moment, Doctor. *While he is signing* It really is amazing how it works time and again. *To Ebenwald* You know, we have a patient with sepsis lying in there. Eighteen-year-old girl. Completely conscious. Wants to get up, go for a walk, thinks she is perfectly well. And her pulse can't even be counted any more. It could be all over in an hour.

EBENWALD *matter-of-factly* We see that frequently enough.

HOCHROITZPOINTNER *officiously* Shall I give her another camphor injection perhaps?

BERNHARDI *looking at him calmly* You could have spared yourself the trouble of giving her the last one. *Calming him* But, then, maybe you've allowed her to experience the happiest hour of her life. Yes, I know, that wasn't your intention either.

HOCHROITZPOINTNER *irritated* But why not, Sir? One isn't a butcher in the end, either.

BERNHARDI I do not recall having reproached you for being one. *Hochroitzpointner and Ebenwald exchange a glance.*

BERNHARDI *to the nurse* Does she have family?

NURSE No one has been here these three days.

BERNHARDI Not her lover either?

KURT He'd be the last one.

OSKAR She hasn't even mentioned him. Who knows whether she knows his name.

BERNHARDI And this too was called love's bliss once. *To Ebenwald* Well, I'm at your disposal, Doctor.

OSKAR Excuse me, father, are you coming up again afterwards? Because she did so beg you to.

BERNHARDI Yes, I'll look in again.

KURT *has gone to the étagère and busied himself with two test-tubes.* OSKAR *goes up to him, they speak to each other and soon after go back into the ward.*

NURSE *to Hochroitzpointner* I'm going over now to get His Reverence.

HOCHROITZPOINTNER Yes, you just run along. If you come too late it's no tragedy either. NURSE *exits.*

HOCHROITZPOINTNER *takes a few case histories out of a folder and goes into the ward.*

EBENWALD *who has grown very impatient* So, the thing is this, Director. I've received a letter from Professor Hell in Graz. He would be inclined to accept his selection as Tugendvetter's successor.

BERNHARDI Ah, he would be inclined.

EBENWALD Yes, Director.

BERNHARDI Has anyone asked him?

EBENWALD I took the liberty — as an old friend and schoolmate.

BERNHARDI But you did write him in a private capacity?

EBENWALD Of course, since we've reached no decision for the time being. Still, I felt entitled to do so, all the more since I know that Professor Tugendevetter also views Hell's candidacy with some favor.

BERNHARDI *somewhat sharply* Professor Tugendvetter is not assuming his position at the state hospital before the beginning of the summer semester. Our discussion of this subject and, if I may be allowed to observe, my dear colleague, your exchange of letters with Professor Hell as well, strike me, therefore, as a bit premature. And we have all the less need to act rashly in this matter as Doctor Tugendvetter's current assistant, Doctor Wenger, has already demonstrated on several occasions and in excellent fashion that he is qualified to serve at least as a temporary replacement.

EBENWALD I do not wish to fail, in this connection, to state my opposition in principle to provisional appointments.

PROFESSOR TUGENDVETTER *enters right. Around fifty, gray hair, mutton chops. His demeanor is somewhat jovial, purposely humorous, but also insecure and approval seeking; in all, he resembles less a scientist than a stockbroker. He enters wearing his hat which he does not remove for a few seconds.*

TUGENDVETTER   Good morning. Hi, Bernhardi. Hello, Ebenwald. I was looking for you upstairs, Bernhardi.

EBENWALD I'm in the way perhaps —

TUGENDVETTER Not at all. No secrets.

BERNHARDI So, what's up? You want to talk to me?

TUGENDVETTER Well, you see, His Excellency, the Minister of Education, has asked me if I would be in a position to take charge of the clinic over there right away.

BERNHARDI Right away?

TUGENDVETTER As soon as possible.

BERNHARDI But they said Brunnleitner would continue to head the clinic until the beginning of the summer semester.

TUGENDVETTER He applied for vacation. Poor devil. Six percent sugar. Last days of Pompeii, right?

He has the habit of adding an unthinking, questioning "Right" at the end of some sentences, especially quotations.

BERNHARDI Where did you hear that? Is it reliable?

TUGENDVETTER   Reliable? If Flint himself told me. I happened to be at the Ministry yesterday. They're supposed to build me a new wing. I'll get it, too. By the way, he sends his regards.

BERNHARDI Who sends his regards?

TUGENDVETTER   Flint. We spoke of you a good deal. He holds you in high esteem. He still remembers with pleasure the time you were both Rappenweiler's assistants. His words. Some career, what? The first instance in human memory, at least in Austria, of a clinical professor's becoming Minister of Education!

BERNHARDI   He was always a good politician, your latest friend Flint.

TUGENDVETTER He's very much interested in our — in your — no, for now still our Institute.

BERNHARDI That is not exactly news to me. At one time he was on the verge of ruining it out of sheer interest.

TUGENDVETTER That wasn't him. That was the entire board. It was the battle of the old against the young. And anyway, that was over long ago. I assure you, Bernhardi, his position towards the Elisabethinum is one of utmost sympathy.

BERNHARDI With which, if need be, we can live without these days, thank God.

TUGENDVETTER I want my Spaniard proud, right?*

BERNHARDI For the time being I am only interested in how you responded to his inquiry.

TUGENDVETTER I had absolutely no response. *Humorously* It's for the Director to decide. Only after you've given me your consent in private will I submit my request to the Board of Directors. You require something in writing too, you pedant, right?**

BERNHARDI Naturally we won't keep you a day longer than you want to stay. I promise you I'll take care of the matter as quickly as possible. Fortunately, you have a very able assistant who, for the time being, will lead your department in your spirit.

TUGENDVETTER Little Wenger, yes. Able fellow. Yes. But surely you won't let him take my place for long?

EBENWALD I took the liberty just now of observing that I generally consider provisional appointments to be unhealthy, and to report on a letter I received from Professor Hell in Graz, who would be prepared —

TUGENDVETTER Oh. He's written to me already as well.

---

* *I want my Spaniard proud*: from Schiller's *Don Carlos* 3. 10, "Stolz will ich den Spanier."

** *You require something in writing too, you pedant*: from Goethe's *Faust I*, "Studierzimmer," l. 1716.

BERNHARDI He does seem to be quite an active gentleman.

TUGENDVETTER *with a brief glance at Ebenwald* Look, Bernhardi, Hell would be an excellent acquisition for your Institute.

BERNHARDI Then he seems to have developed rather brilliantly in Graz. As long as he was in Vienna people considered him a quite incompetent fellow.

TUGENDVETTER Who?

BERNHARDI You, for instance. And we do all know to whom he owed his appointment to Graz at the time. Certain influences from above.

EBENWALD But really, it's no disgrace if one has restored a prince to health.

BERNHARDI Nor do I hold it against him. But his entire career should not be built upon a single case such as that. And his scientific contributions —

TUGENDVETTER Excuse me, but in this area I might really be the better informed. He's published several excellent articles.

BERNHARDI That's as may be. In any case, I gather from all this that you yourself would rather propose Hell as your successor than your assistant and pupil Wenger.

TUGENDVETTER Wenger is too young. I'm convinced he himself isn't giving it a thought.

BERNHARDI That would be a mistake. His last paper on serum caused some excitement.

EBENWALD A sensation, Director. That is not the same thing.

TUGENDVETTER He has talent. Without a doubt, he has talent. But as far as the reliability of his experiments is concerned —

EBENWALD *simply* There are people who hold him to be — let's say a quixotic dreamer.

TUGENDVETTER That's going too far. Besides, I cannot prevent anyone from announcing his candidacy. Neither Hell nor Wenger.

BERNHARDI But let me point out to you that you will have to decide for one of them.

TUGENDVETTER Surely it doesn't depend on me? I'm not going to name my successor, after all.

BERNHARDI But you will take part in the voting. The fate of your former department and of our Institute will still interest you to that extent, I hope.

TUGENDVETTER I should say so. Not bad, not bad at all. We did found it, the Elisabethinum, *to Ebenwald* Bernhardi, I, and Cyprian. All in green went three knights riding — right?* How long has it been now?

BERNHARDI It's been fifteen years, my dear Tugendvetter.

TUGENDVETTER Fifteen years. A beautiful time. By God, it's not going to be easy for me. Say, Bernhardi, couldn't something be worked out in the beginning, so I could attend both here and at the General Hospital —

BERNHARDI *determined* Absolutely not. It goes without saying, on the day you take up your position over there I will entrust your present assistant to take your place.

EBENWALD Then I would ask that our meeting concerning the permanent replacement be scheduled within the next few days.

BERNHARDI Why, if I may ask? That would almost look as if we wanted to prevent Wenger from proving his ability to teach over the next few months.

EBENWALD I doubt whether the Elisabethinum was founded to serve as a lecturing school for young instructors.

---

* *All in green went three knights riding*: Schnitzler's line, "Es ritten drei Reiter zum Tore hinaus" (Three riders rode out through the gate) is cited from a folk song. The line provided in the translation is adapted from e. e. cummings's "all in green went my love riding."

BERNHARDI   You may leave everything to me in all confidence, my dear Ebenwald. You will admit, I'm sure, that nothing has ever been put off without cause in our Institute up to now, but also that nothing has ever been done with frivolous haste.

EBENWALD   The insinuation that I may have called for haste, or even frivolous haste, is one I must reject as untrue.

BERNHARDI   *smiling* Duly noted.

EBENWALD   *looking at his watch* I have to go to my department. My pleasure, gentlemen.

BERNHARDI   I must be getting to my office too. *Lets Ebenwald go ahead* Please, Doctor, your audience is waiting.

TUGENDVETTER   To make a third, he join'd the former two — right?[*]

EBENWALD   *meets Doctor Adler in the doorway* Good day. *Exits.*

Dr. ADLER *enters; short, dark, fresh, lively, sparkling eyes, dueling scar, around thirty years old, wearing white overalls.*

ADLER   Gentlemen.

BERNHARDI   What brings you into the realm of the living, Doctor?

ADLER   I wanted to look up something else about your case in the file, Professor.

BERNHARDI   Everything's at your disposal.

ADLER   A pity by the way, Director, that you weren't downstairs just now. A case from Cyprian's department. Imagine, besides the consumption of the spinal cord, which

---

[*] *To make a third, he join'd the former two*: adapted from the last line of Schiller's ballad, "Die Bürgschaft."

had been diagnosed, the beginnings of a tumor in the cerebellum that hadn't shown up at all.

BERNHARDI My, my, when one thinks that some people never get around to experiencing all their sicknesses, so to speak, one might not know what to make of providence.

OSKAR *coming from the ward, to Tugendvetter* Good day, Professor.

TUGENDVETTER Hello, Oskar. I've heard. Musician. "Racing Pulses." Dedication waltz.

OSKAR Oh, please, Professor —

BERNHARDI What's this, you've composed something again and I don't know anything about it? *Pulls him playfully by the ear* Well, are you coming along?

OSKAR Yes. I'm going to the lab.

TUGENDVETTER Fathers and Sons — right?

Tugendvetter, Bernhardi, and Oskar exit. Hochroitzpointner enters from the ward.

HOCHROITZPOINTNER Morning, Doctor.

ADLER Hello there. I wanted to ask you if I could take another look at that case history.

HOCHROITZPOINTNER Please.

He takes the page out of a folder.

ADLER Thank you very much Doctor Hochroitz — how?

HOCHROITZPOINTNER Hochroitzpointner.

ADLER *sits down at the table* Some name you have.

HOCHROITZPOINTNER Not beautiful perhaps?

ADLER *looking at the case history* Oh, but this is splendid. Right away it makes one think of mountain peaks and treks on glaciers. You're from the Tyrol, Doctor, aren't you?

HOCHROITZPOINTNER Yes, I am. From Imst.

ADLER Ah, from Imst. As a student, I started out on a marvelous excursion from there. Up to the Wetterfernkogel.

HOCHROITZPOINTNER They threw up a refuge hut there last year.

ADLER They're building huts all over the place nowadays. *Again looking at the case history* No albumen the entire time?

HOCHROITZPOINTNER Absolutely not. We looked for it every day.

KURT *has come from the ward* Albumen showed up during the final few days. In considerable quantities, I might add.

HOCHROITZPOINTNER Yes, of course, in the last three days, to be sure.

ADLER Aha, here it is.

HOCHROITZPOINTNER Naturally, it says so right there.

ADLER *to Kurt* How is your father? He doesn't come down to see us at all. *Referring to the case history* So, you only had him here for a week?

HOCHROITZPOINTNER Yes. Before that he was in Professor Ebenwald's department. But since it was an inoperable case —

ADLER As a diagnostician he is really first rate, your Chief, one can say what one wants.

KURT *smiling* What is it one wants to say?

ADLER How's that?

KURT Well, since you said, one can say what one wants.

ADLER *in a somewhat saccharine tone* Why are you so severe with me, Doctor Pflugfelder? I simply meant that your main strength lies in diagnosis and not so much in therapy, where you do a damned lot of experimenting around, in my less than authoritative opinion.

KURT Yes, but tell me, Doctor, what else should we do in Internal Medicine. We do have to try new remedies if the old ones no longer work.

ADLER And by tomorrow the new will be the old again. You can't help it, I know. I went through it once too, you know. But it really is depressing at times to have to grope around in the dark like that. That's the reason I fled to pathological anatomy. There one can be the master, as it were.

KURT Excuse me, Doctor, there is still one other above you.

ADLER But that one has no time to concern himself with us. He is too busy with another faculty. *Referring to the case history* So, radiation too? Say, do you really believe that in cases like this —

KURT We feel obligated to try everything, Doctor. Especially where there is nothing more to lose. This has nothing to do with quixotic dreams or a craving for publicity, as is maintained in some quarters, and one should not hold it against the Professor.

ADLER Who holds it against him? Not I, certainly.

KURT I know, Doctor, not you. But there are people.

ADLER Everyone has his enemies, that's all.

KURT And people who envy him.

ADLER Naturally. Whoever works and achieves anything. Many enemies, much honor. Bernhardi really has nothing to complain about. Practice in the highest circles and in certain other ones, which fortunately pay better. Professor, Director of the Elisabethinum —

KURT Well, who else should be, if not him? He's fought enough battles for the Institute.

ADLER I know, I know. I'm the last person who'd want to downplay his merits. And for him to have come so far, especially with today's political climate — I have a certain right to speak of that since I myself have never made a secret of my Jewish ancestry, even if I'm descended from an old middle-class Viennese family on my mother's side. In my student days I even had occasion to bleed for the other half.

KURT We all know, Doctor.

ADLER To tell you the truth, Doctor, I'm glad you too give our Director his just due.

KURT Why are you glad?

ADLER You were a German-National fraternity brother, weren't you?

KURT And an anti-Semite, yes indeed, Doctor. Still am, actually. Except I've also become an anti-Aryan since then. I find human beings in general to be quite a deficient lot, and I cling to the few exceptions here and there.

PROFESSOR CYPRIAN *enters from the right. A small, elderly man with long, almost still blond hair. He has a somewhat drawling, sing-song manner of speaking and always lapses into lecturing without being aware of it, speaking as to an audience.*

CYPRIAN Good day to you, gentlemen. *Mutual greetings* Is Doctor Adler here by any chance? Ah, there you are. I was looking for you downstairs. Can I depend on it, Doctor Adler, that today's skull won't disappear on me again like the paralytic's the other day?

ADLER The attendant has been instructed, Professor —

CYPRIAN The attendant is nowhere to be found. Probably in the bar again. You will yet go through what I did in Prague at the time I was working there under Heschel. We also had an alcoholic attendant employed in the pathological-anatomical institute. That fellow gradually guzzled up all the alcohol from our specimen jars.

ADLER Ours prefers brandy for now, Professor.

CYPRIAN So, I'd like to come down this evening. When will you be there?

ADLER I've been working until around midnight usually.

CYPRIAN Fine, then I'll come after ten.

Bernhardi and Oskar enter from the right.

BERNHARDI Good day. Hello, Cyprian. Are you looking for me?

CYPRIAN Actually, I had something to discuss with Doctor Adler. But I'm very glad to have run into you. I wanted to ask you when you might have time to come to the Ministry of Education with me.

BERNHARDI Why, what's the matter?

They stand alone together. Oskar goes into the ward at once.
The others stand aside, in conversation.

CYPRIAN There's nothing particularly the matter at all. But I think we should strike while the iron is hot.

BERNHARDI Really, I don't know what you're talking about.

CYPRIAN Now is the most propitious moment to gain something for our Institute. For a physician, a clinical professor to find himself in a key position, this is a situation we must take advantage of.

BERNHARDI You're all remarkably optimistic with regard to Flint.

CYPRIAN With good reason. I prophesied his career when we worked together in Brücke's lab almost thirty years ago. He is an administrative genius. I've already outlined a memorandum. What we are going to ask for is first of all a government subsidy so that we will no longer be dependent on the somewhat demeaning private fund raising. Further —

BERNHARDI You are forgetting one crucial point. Flint is our bitterest enemy.

CYPRIAN Oh, please, that's over and done with. His position towards the Elisabethinum today is one of greatest sympathy. Doctor Winkler told me so again yesterday. Quite of his own accord.

BERNHARDI Well.

OSKAR *comes from the ward and goes quickly up to Bernhardi* Say, father, I think that if you still want to speak to her —

BERNHARDI Excuse me, my dear Cyprian. If you'll be patient for five minutes. *Exits.*

OSKAR *to Cyprian* A dying woman, Professor.
Follows his father into the ward.

KURT *casually* A blood-poisoning case. Young girl. Abortion.

HOCHROITZPOINTNER *to Adler* For tomorrow, Doctor.

CYPRIAN *in his monotonous manner* When I was still an assistant under Skoda, we had a department head in the hospital, I won't mention his name, who asked us, us assistants I mean, to call him to every death-bed if at all possible. He wanted to write a psychology of dying moments, allegedly. Right away I said to Bernitzer, who was an assistant along with me, something here isn't right. He's not concerned with psychology. Well, just imagine, one day the department head suddenly disappeared. A married man with three children. The next night they found a ragged fellow stabbed to death in some out-of-the-way street. Well, I'm sure you can guess the point, gentlemen. It turns out that the department head and the stabbed bum are one and the same person. For many years he had led a double life. During the day he was a busy doctor, at night he was a regular in all sorts of suspicious dives, a fancy man.

THE PRIEST *enters, a young man of 28 with energetic, intelligent features. The sacristan with him remains standing at the door.*

ADLER *officiously* Good day to you, Reverend.
PRIEST Good morning, gentlemen. I hope I haven't come too late.
KURT No, Reverend. The Professor is just now with the patient. *He introduces himself* Assistant Dr. Pflugfelder.
PRIEST So you've not given up all hope yet?
OSKAR *enters from the ward* Good morning, Reverend.
KURT We have, Reverend. It's a totally hopeless case.
OSKAR Please, Reverend, would you like —
PRIEST Perhaps I'll wait until the Professor has left the patient. *The sacristan withdraws, the door closes.*
HOCHROITZPOINTNER *moves a chair over for the priest.*
PRIEST Thank you, thank you. *He does not sit down at first.*
CYPRIAN Oh, yes, Reverend, if we only attended those patients whom we could still help. But sometimes we can do nothing better than comfort them.
KURT And lie.

PRIEST *sits down* You use a somewhat harsh word there, Doctor.

KURT I'm sorry, Reverend. Naturally it applies only to us doctors. I might add, it's precisely this that is sometimes the most difficult and the noblest part of our profession.
Bernhardi appears at the door. The priest stands up. The Nurse follows Bernhardi into the room.

BERNHARDI *somewhat surprised* Oh, Reverend.

PRIEST We are relieving each other, Professor. *He extends his hand to him* I trust I'll find the patient still conscious?

BERNHARDI Yes. One could even say, in a heightened state of consciousness. *More to the others* Absolute euphoria has set in. *Explaining to the priest* She feels well, so to speak.

PRIEST Well, that really is splendid. Who knows! Just recently I had the pleasure again of meeting a perfectly healthy young man in the street who a few weeks earlier, fully prepared for death, had received extreme unction from me.

ADLER And who knows whether it wasn't just the Reverend who gave him back the strength, the courage to live.

BERNHARDI *to Adler* The Reverend has misunderstood me, Doctor. *To the priest* What I meant is that the patient is totally oblivious. She is doomed, but she thinks she has recovered.

PRIEST Truly.

BERNHARDI And I'm almost afraid that your appearing, Reverend —

PRIEST *quite mildly* Have no fear for your patient, Professor. I haven't come to pronounce a death sentence.

BERNHARDI Of course, but all the same —

PRIEST Perhaps the patient could be prepared.

NURSE *unnoticed by Bernhardi, in response to a barely noticeable sign from the priest, goes into the ward.*

BERNHARDI That would not make it any better. As I've already said, Reverend, the patient is totally oblivious. And she expects anything but this visit. On the contrary, she is under the happy illusion that someone close to her will show up in the next few hours to fetch her and take her away with him again — to life and happiness. I believe, Reverend, it would be no good deed, I'd almost dare say not a deed pleasing to God, if we were to awaken her from this last dream.

PRIEST *after a brief hesitation, with more resolve* Is there any possibility, Professor, that my appearance would affect the course of her illness in an unfavorable —

BERNHARDI *quickly interrupting* It would not be impossible for it to hasten the end, perhaps only by a matter of minutes, but nonetheless —

PRIEST *more lively* Once again: can your patient still be saved? Does my appearance constitute a danger in this sense? If so, I would of course be prepared to withdraw at once.

ADLER *nods in approval.*

BERNHARDI She is beyond help. Of that there can be no doubt.

PRIEST Then I see absolutely no reason —

BERNHARDI I'm sorry, Reverend, for the time being I am still here in my capacity as her physician. And part of my responsibility, when nothing else lies within my power, is to provide a happy death for my patients, at least as far as possible.

CYPRIAN *shows slight impatience and disapproval.*

PRIEST A happy death. It is likely, Professor, that we understand different things by that. And from what the nurse told me, your patient requires absolution more urgently than some others.

BERNHARDI *with his ironic smile* Aren't we all sinners, Reverend?

PRIEST I'd say that is not relevant here, Professor. You cannot know whether in precisely these final moments which are still granted her, somewhere in the depths of her soul, which God alone can see, there doesn't stir a longing to unburden herself of all her sins through a last confession.

BERNHARDI Must I repeat it again, Reverend? The patient does not know that she is lost. She is cheerful, happy and — without remorse.

PRIEST All the heavier the guilt I would take on myself if I budged from this place without having administered to the dying woman the consolations of our sacred religion.

BERNHARDI Both God and every earthly judge will absolve you of this guilt, Reverend. *In response to a movement from the priest* That's right, Reverend. Because I as a physician cannot allow you to approach this patient's bed.

PRIEST I was called here. Thus, I must ask —

BERNHARDI Not by my orders, Reverend. And I can only repeat that as a physician to whom the well-being of his patients remains entrusted until the last moment, I must unfortunately forbid you to enter this room.

PRIEST *stepping forward* You forbid me to?

BERNHARDI *lightly touching his shoulder* Yes, Reverend.

NURSE *hurrying out of the ward* Reverend —

BERNHARDI You were in there?

NURSE You'll be too late, Reverend.

KURT *rushes into the ward.*

BERNHARDI *to the nurse* You told the patient that His Reverence is here?

NURSE Yes, Director.

BERNHARDI I see. And — now answer me calmly — how did the patient take it? Did she say anything? Go on. Well?

NURSE She said —

BERNHARDI Well?

NURSE She got a bit frightened.

BERNHARDI *not angrily* Do speak, won't you! What did she say?

NURSE "Must I really die, then?"

KURT *coming from the ward* It's over.
Short pause.

BERNHARDI Don't be frightened, Reverend. It's not your fault. You only wanted to do your duty. I did too. I'm sorry enough that I didn't succeed.

PRIEST It is not for you, Professor, to grant me absolution. The poor creature in there passed away in sin and without the consolations of religion. And that is your fault.

BERNHARDI I'll take it upon myself.

PRIEST It remains to be seen, Professor, whether or not you'll be able to do that. I bid you good day, gentlemen. *He exits. The others remain behind, agitated and in some embarrassment. Bernhardi looks at them one after the other.*

BERNHARDI So, tomorrow morning, my dear Doctor Adler, the autopsy.

CYPRIAN *to Bernhardi, unheard by the others* It wasn't right.

BERNHARDI How do you mean, not right?

CYPRIAN And besides, it'll remain an isolated case. You won't change anything in the thing itself.

BERNHARDI In the thing? Between doctors and priests? That wasn't my intention.

ADLER I would consider it dishonest, Director, if I didn't state at once that I am unable to take your side in this matter.

BERNHARDI And it would be dishonest of me, Doctor, if I didn't assure you that I could have figured that out right away.
Cyprian and Adler exit.

OSKAR *bites his lip.*

BERNHARDI Well, son, it won't damage your career, I hope.

OSKAR Really, father.

BERNHARDI *takes his head tenderly* Come on. I didn't mean to offend you.

NURSE Professor, I thought —

BERNHARDI What did you think? Well, what's the use, it's all over now.

NURSE We've always — and — *indicating Hochroitzpointner* the Doctor —

HOCHROITZPOINTNER Well, naturally, I didn't forbid her —

BERNHARDI Obviously, Doctor Hochroitzpointner. You probably attend lectures in the church too, what?

HOCHROITZPOINTNER We live in a Christian state, Director.

BERNHARDI Yes. *Looks at him a long time* May God forgive them, they know damned well what they're doing. *Exits with Kurt and Oskar.*

HOCHROITZPOINTNER But child, what are you thinking of to apologize? You've only done your duty. But what's with you — Now you're even starting to cry. Don't you go getting hysterical again.

NURSE *sobbing* But the Director was so angry.

HOCHROITZPOINTNER And what if he was angry — the Director. Well, he'll not stay Director for long now. This will break his neck!

Curtain

SECOND ACT

Professor Bernhardi's consulting room. The main entrance to the right; on the left a door to the adjacent room and a medicine cupboard. The entire back wall is taken up by bookshelves, partly covered by a green curtain. On the stove in the right corner a bust of Aesculapius. A desk with chairs. A small table next to the desk. Along the desk, facing the audience, a divan. Chairs.
On the walls photographs of various scientists.

DR. OSKAR BERNHARDI *is sitting at the desk, entering something in an open log-book, after which he rings.* SERVANT *enters.*

OSKAR No one else waiting?
SERVANT No, Doctor.
OSKAR Then I'll go out now. If my father should come home — *the outside bell rings* Oh, see who that is.
SERVANT *exits.*
OSKAR *closes the log-book, puts the desk in order.*
SERVANT *enters, bringing a calling card.*
OSKAR Wants to speak to me?
SERVANT The gentleman asked if the Professor is in. But —
OSKAR But he'll make do with me. All right, show him in.
SERVANT *exits.*

DR. FEUERMANN *enters; a young, short excited man with a black beard and glasses, wearing a frock coat and gloves. Hat in hand.*

OSKAR *goes towards him.*
FEUERMANN I don't know if you'll still remember me —

OSKAR But Feuermann, if I still remember you! *Shakes hands.*

FEUERMANN It's been eight years since —

OSKAR How time flies. Well, won't you sit down? You wanted to speak to my father?

FEUERMANN Yes, I —

OSKAR I'm covering for him today. He was called to Prince Konstantin in Baden.

FEUERMANN He does have a wonderful practice, your father. *He sits down.*

OSKAR Well, and how are you doing? You haven't come as a patient, I imagine. Where is your practice, by the way?

FEUERMANN In Oberhollabrunn.

OSKAR Yes, right. So, what brings you here? Are you opening a sanatorium, maybe, or going somewhere as a spa doctor? Or do you want to turn Oberhollabrun into a health resort?

FEUERMANN Nothing like that. It's a horrible story. You haven't heard anything yet?

OSKAR *shakes his head.*

FEUERMANN I've already written your father about it.

OSKAR He gets so many letters.

FEUERMANN If you would also put in a good word for me —

OSKAR But what is this all about?

FEUERMANN You know me, Bernhardi. We were in school together, you know I've never lacked in industry and conscientiousness. An accident like this can happen to anyone who is forced to go into practice directly from the university. Not everyone has it as good as you, for example.

OSKAR Well, being the son of a famous father has its down side too.

FEUERMANN I'm sorry, I didn't mean it that way. But it really is invaluable to be able to continue training in the hospital, to hear lectures at the bosom of the alma mater —

OSKAR *somewhat impatiently* So, what actually happened?

FEUERMANN I'm under indictment for criminal negligence. I may lose my license. Alleged malpractice. I won't even claim that I'm entirely without blame. If I had practiced at the obstetrics clinic here for another year or two, then I'd have probably pulled the woman through. You can only imagine conditions in a nest like that. No assistance, no proper antiseptics. Ah, what do you know here in the big city? How many people's lives I saved, no one takes that into account. One has bad luck just once and he may as well put a bullet through his head.

OSKAR But Feuermann, you needn't talk of the worst right off. You haven't been convicted yet, have you? The expert witnesses will have something to say yet.

FEUERMANN Yes, the expert witnesses. Well, that's actually the reason, that is why I wanted your father — he knows me too, perhaps he'll still remember me, I even took a course on diseases of the heart from him once —

OSKAR Now that —

FEUERMANN He is surely very friendly with Professor Filitz, who heads the gynecological department at the Elisabethinum, and Filitz has been proposed as expert witness. And so I wanted to ask your father, if he couldn't put in — Oh, I don't want anyone pulling strings, but —

OSKAR I'll tell you, my dear Feuermann, whether my father's intercession — The fact is, he is not on such especially good terms with Filitz as you seem to assume.

FEUERMANN Your father is Director of the Elisabethinum —

OSKAR Well, yes, but circumstances here aren't so simple. It's a long story. Then again, you people out in Oberhollabrunn probably can't have any accurate picture of these conditions. There are currents and undercurrents and crosscurrents. So, whether any intervention on my father's part might not have precisely the opposite effect —

FEUERMANN If he could intercede for me in a different way, perhaps! Your father writes so brilliantly. His articles on professional questions always hit the nail on the head. It would simply be a matter of establishing a general perspective for my case. Of pointing out the root cause of the mischief. The disastrous material circumstances of young physicians, the difficulties of a country practice, the hostilities, the rivalries, and so on. Oh, that would be a topic for your father — and could I put material at his disposal.

Servant enters with a calling card.

OSKAR Oh, Fil — *he stands up* You'll have to excuse me, Feuermann. Have him come in.

SERVANT *exits.*

FEUERMANN Did I hear you say Filitz?

OSKAR I —

FEUERMANN Yes, you said it.

OSKAR Surely you don't want to — now. Please, I beg of you, perhaps through this door —

FEUERMANN Oh no. You can't ask that of me. This a sign from heaven.

FILITZ *enters. Forty years old, a handsome blond man wearing a pince-nez.*

FILITZ Good afternoon, my young colleague.

FEUERMANN Would you be so kind, my dear friend, as to introduce me to the Professor?

OSKAR *with an embarrassed smile* I imagine the Professor will want to speak with —

FEUERMANN *introduces himself* Doctor Feuermann. You see, Professor, I take it as a sign from heaven that at this very moment you — that I have the good fortune — I am a general practitioner in Oberhollabrunn — Doctor Feuermann. An indictment has been brought against me.

FILITZ Feuermann. Oh, yes. I know. *Amiably* You dispatched one to the other side, a teacher's wife.

FEUERMANN *horrified* The Professor has been falsely informed. When you've first — if you'll have the great kindness to look into the case in detail — it was a sequence of disastrous coincidences.

FILITZ Yes, it's always like that. But such coincidences would not occur if the young people didn't rush out into practice without any proper training. One gets through his few exams amid moaning and groaning and thinks God will help along with the rest. But occasionally he just happens not to help and with good reason.

FEUERMANN Please, Professor, if you'd allow me. I passed all my examinations with distinction, including in obstetrics. And I had to go into practice because I'd have starved otherwise. And that this poor woman bled to death after giving birth, I'll venture to say it could have happened to her with a professor too.

FILITZ There are all sorts of professors.

FEUERMANN But if it had been a professor, they wouldn't have indicted him, instead — instead it would have been attributed to God's inscrutable decree.

FILITZ Ah, you think so. Well, yes. *Stands in front of him and fixes him with his glance* I suppose you are also one of those young gentlemen who think they owe it to their scientific dignity to act the atheist?

FEUERMANN Oh, Professor, I am truly —

FILITZ Entirely as you wish, Doctor. But I assure you, faith and science get along very well. I would even go so far as to assert that science without faith must always remain an uncertain endeavor, if only because it will then lack its moral foundation, its ethos.

FEUERMANN Certainly, Professor. Please, my earlier remark —

FILITZ As to where this nihilistic arrogance leads, there is no lack of examples. And I hope it will not be your ambition, Doctor Feuerstein —

FEUERMANN *shyly* Feuermann —

FILITZ — to offer your shocked contemporaries a new example. Anyway, I have your file at home. Why don't you come over tomorrow morning at eight, we'll discuss the matter further.

FEUERMANN *as if intoxicated by this new turn* You will permit me to? Oh, I am infinitely grateful. If I could give you the material. You see, my very existence is at stake. I have a wife and two children. There would be nothing left for me but to kill myself.

FILITZ I would appreciate it, Doctor, if you abstained from that sort of sentimental observation. If you really have nothing to reproach yourself with there is no need for such silliness, at least not with me. So, until tomorrow, Doctor.

OSKAR You will excuse me if I don't see you out, dear Feuermann.

FEUERMANN Oh. I thank you very much. *Exits.*

OSKAR I want to apologize on his behalf, Professor, for his somewhat tactless remarks. You can understand his agitation.

FILITZ Classmate?

OSKAR Yes, Professor. And I should observe at once, a very industrious and conscientious student. I know that during the first few years he had to live on fifteen or twenty gulden a month, which he earned by giving lessons.

FILITZ That alone proves nothing, my dear colleague. My father was a millionaire and I turned out quite well too. Oh well. Your father is out of town?

OSKAR Not out of town, Professor, he is only in Baden at Prince Konstantin's.

FILITZ Ah.

OSKAR Actually, he wanted to be back in time for his office hours.

FILITZ *looking at his watch* Well, I'm afraid I can't wait much longer. Perhaps you'll be so kind and give your father a message which may be of some interest to you too, namely that my wife was not received by the Princess Stixenstein today.

OSKAR *not understanding entirely* So. Perhaps the Princess was not at home?

FILITZ My wife had an appointment for one o'clock, my dear colleague, in her capacity as President of the Honorary Ball Committee, with the ball's patroness and wife of the President of our Board, the Prince Stixenstein. I believe this fact speaks volumes.

He fixes his glance on Oskar in his usual way.

OSKAR *somewhat embarrassed.*

SERVANT *enters with a calling card.*

OSKAR Excuse me, Professor. It's Professor Löwenstein.

FILITZ Don't let me bother you. Anyway, I have to —

OSKAR *to the servant* Show him in.

FILITZ *gives the appearance of being ready to leave.*

LÖWENSTEIN *enters. Around forty, of medium height, somewhat hurried, with small eyes which he sometimes opens very wide. Eyeglasses. He likes to stand across from the person he is speaking to with a slightly lowered left shoulder and slightly bent knees while occasionally running his hand through his hair.*

LÖWENSTEIN Good afternoon. Oh, Professor Filitz. You were leaving? Stay for another minute. This will interest you. Here, Oskar, read this. *He gives him a letter* I'm sorry, Professor Filitz, he has to read it first as a member of the Ball Committee. The Princess Stixenstein has resigned her sponsorship of the ball.

OSKAR *has skimmed the letter, hands it to Professor Filitz* Without specifying any grounds?

LÖWENSTEIN She didn't find it necessary.

FILITZ Especially as they are so clear to everyone.

OSKAR Has this — this story become that public already? Within a week?

LÖWENSTEIN Dear Oskar, I didn't have a moment's doubt on that score. When they told me about what happened I said right away, this will be quite a tidbit for certain people, this will get blown up out of all proportion.

FILITZ Excuse me, dear Doctor Löwenstein, nothing has been blown up here, nor did anything need to be blown up here. The entire episode, in all its plain and unsettling clarity. But I prefer to express my opinion of it to my friend Bernhardi in person.

OSKAR I imagine I need hardly tell you, Professor, that in this entire affair I stand completely on my father's side.

FILITZ Of course, of course, that is your duty.

OSKAR It is also my conviction, Professor.

LÖWENSTEIN As it is mine, Professor. And I will say, categorically, that only ill will can attempt to turn a totally harmless incident into something like an affair. And, to put it quite plainly, that not a soul would attempt to do so if Bernhardi didn't happen to be a Jew.

FILITZ Well, there you are again with your fixed idea. Am I an anti-Semite too, maybe? I, who always have at least one Jewish assistant? Against decent Jews there is no anti-Semitism.

LÖWENSTEIN Fine, fine, I would maintain precisely —

FILITZ If a Christian had behaved like Bernhardi it would also have turned into an affair. You know that perfectly well, dear Löwenstein.

LÖWENSTEIN Fine. Possibly. But this Christian would then have had thousands or hundreds of thousands backing him who now are doing nothing or who will even stand up against Bernhardi.

FILITZ Who?

LÖWENSTEIN The German-Nationals and naturally the Jews — a certain sort, I mean, who don't let any opportunity pass by to flee to the protection of the powers that be.

FILITZ I'm sorry, dear Löwenstein, that borders on paranoia. And I want to say right here that it is precisely people like you, my dear Löwenstein, with your ridiculous sniffing out of anti-Semites under every rock, who are most to blame for the regrettable intensification of the antagonisms. And it would be a hundred times better —

BERNHARDI *enters.*

BERNHARDI *obviously in a good mood, with his slightly ironic smile, greeting and shaking hands* Well, gentlemen. What's the matter? Has the Institute burned down? Or has someone given us a million?

OSKAR *giving him the letter* The Princess has withdrawn her patronage of our ball.

BERNHARDI *skimming the letter* Well, so we'll just look for another patroness. *Playfully, to Oskar* Or are you perhaps going to resign your presidency too, my son?

OSKAR *somewhat offended* Father.

LÖWENSTEIN Dear Bernhardi, your son has just now solemnly declared that he stands entirely on your side.

BERNHARDI *gently stroking Oskar's head* Well, of course. I hope you don't take it the wrong way, Oskar. And you, Löwenstein, I don't even have to ask. But what's the matter with you, Filitz? You really do look as if we had burned down.

OSKAR I'm going now. *Smiling* It so happens that we have a meeting of the Ball Committee at six. Good day, Professor, good day, Löwenstein. *Both shake hands with him* Oh, right, Father, Doctor Feuermann was here. He says he wrote to you.

BERNHARDI Oh, yes.

FILITZ Don't worry about this Feuerstein. If it is possible, somehow, I'll pull him out of it, *with a triumphant glance at Löwenstein* in spite of his being a Jew.

OSKAR I really believe, Professor, that he's not an unworthy —

FILITZ Certainly, certainly. Good day, my dear colleague.

OSKAR *exits.*

BERNHARDI Was it on account of this Feuermann —

FILITZ Oh no. I only met him here by chance. I came here in order to inform you that my wife was not received by the Princess Stixenstein this noon.

BERNHARDI And?

FILITZ Not received! Not only did the Princess withdraw her patronage, she also refused to see my wife.

BERNHARDI Really, that's the reason you've come to see me?

FILITZ What are you playing the innocent for, my dear Bernhardi! You know very well that all this, as meaningless as it may be in itself, is most indicative of the interpretation placed in influential higher circles on a matter not entirely unfamiliar to you.

BERNHARDI *very cheerful* For my part, I can offer you entirely different indications from perhaps still higher circles. I'm just now coming from Prince Konstantin who naturally has already heard the story too, and who seems to have a totally different opinion of it than Her Highness the Princess Stixenstein.

FILITZ Please, Bernhardi, don't start with this Prince Konstantin. Being a liberal is a sport for him, like shooting pigeons is for others of his class.

BERNHARDI Nonetheless —

FILITZ And as far as I'm concerned, I don't care what Prince Konstantin's opinion of this business might be. For my part, I take a totally different view of your actions, that is to say, of your behavior in the matter in question.

BERNHARDI I see. Has your wife sent you here to reprimand me?

FILITZ *very angry* I have absolutely no right, and far be it from me besides — In a word, I am here to ask how you intend to give satisfaction to my wife for the affront she has suffered.

BERNHARDI *truly astonished* Oh. Say, you don't seriously mean —

CYPRIAN *enters.*

CYPRIAN Good evening, gentlemen. I beg your pardon that I've — unannounced. But I can imagine — *shakes hands with everyone.*

BERNHARDI Have you also come because the Princess Stixenstein has withdrawn her patronage of our ball?

CYPRIAN The ball is secondary.

FILITZ *looking at his watch* I have no more time, unfortunately. You will excuse me, Cyprian. I'll only repeat my question to you one more time, Bernhardi, how do you intend to obtain satisfaction for my wife for *with a glance at Cyprian* not being received by Princess Stixenstein.

LÖWENSTEIN *looks at Cyprian.*

BERNHARDI *very calmly* Tell your esteemed wife, dear Filitz, that I took her to be too intelligent to allow myself to assume that she would be seriously offended for so much as a second that the salon of a most serene goose remained closed to her.

FILITZ Well, your attitude certainly saves me the trouble of any further discussion. It's been a pleasure, gentlemen. *Exits quickly.*

CYPRIAN You shouldn't have said that, Bernhardi.

LÖWENSTEIN Why shouldn't he have?

CYPRIAN Quite aside from the fact that there are certain people one should not irritate unnecessarily, he is wrong. The

Princess is anything but a goose. She is in fact a very intelligent person.

BERNHARDI Intelligent? Babette Stixenstein?

LÖWENSTEIN Limited, narrow-minded, bigoted is what she is.

CYPRIAN There are things about which the Princess must not even think, otherwise she would be as degenerate as you if you did not think about them. We need to understand these people. It's part of our nature. And they must not understand us in the least, which, in turn, is part of their nature. And by the way, this is only the beginning. It goes without saying that the Prince will draw his own conclusions as well — that means the Board will in all likelihood resign as a body.

LÖWENSTEIN That would be truly monstrous.

BERNHARDI *who had been walking up and down, stops in front of Cyprian* Excuse me, Cyprian. The Board consists of Prince Konstantin, Bishop Liebenberg, Prince Stixenstein, Bank Director Veith and Councilor Winkler. And aside from the Prince, I guarantee you —

CYPRIAN Better not guarantee anything.

BERNHARDI I spoke to the Prince not an hour ago.

CYPRIAN I suppose he expressed his appreciation?

BERNHARDI He was the soul of amiability. And that he had me summoned just today speaks volumes, since there's not the least thing wrong with him. He called me only in order to discuss the matter with me.

CYPRIAN He brought it up?

BERNHARDI Naturally.

LÖWENSTEIN What did he say?

BERNHARDI *smiling in a somewhat self-satisfied manner* That a couple of hundred years ago I'd have probably ended up at the stake.

CYPRIAN And you interpreted that as agreement?

BERNHARDI I haven't told you yet what he added: "Me too, probably."

LÖWENSTEIN Ha!

CYPRIAN Which doesn't keep him from attending Mass regularly and from voting against marriage law reforms in the Upper House.

BERNHARDI There are official obligations.

CYPRIAN Well, and did you at the same time happen to inquire of the Prince what the other Board members think about all this?

BERNHARDI The Prince volunteered a remark of the Bishop's.

LÖWENSTEIN Well?

BERNHARDI "I like that man."

LÖWENSTEIN You like the Bishop?

BERNHARDI No, he likes me.

CYPRIAN Well, I've already heard about that comment too, only they didn't suppress the second half for me.

BERNHARDI The second half?

CYPRIAN The complete remark runs like this: "I rather like this Bernhardi, but he's going to regret it."

BERNHARDI And from whom did you learn this so precisely?

CYPRIAN From Councilor Winkler, from whose office I've just come, and who also gave me to understand that the Board is going to resign.

BERNHARDI Oh, please. The Councilor is on the Board himself, and surely he won't desert us.

CYPRIAN He wouldn't have any choice. He can't remain as the only Board member if the others all go.

BERNHARDI Why not? If he is the man we always took him for —

LÖWENSTEIN Oh, please, a councilor —

CYPRIAN Of what use would it be if he were the only one to take your side? Can you ask him, for your sake —

BERNHARDI It's not a question of me, you know that very well.

CYPRIAN Exactly right, not of you. You said it yourself. It is a question of the Institute. Of our Institute. And if the Board goes, then it's all over for us.

BERNHARDI Go on, really!

LÖWENSTEIN But how? Neither your Prince Konstantin nor His Eminence either has ever distinguished himself through any particular generosity.

CYPRIAN But I'll name you a dozen Jews who give us anything at all only because a prince and a bishop sit on the Board. And if we don't get any more money we may as well close up.

BERNHARDI And all this is supposed to happen because I did my duty as a doctor —

LÖWENSTEIN It's monstrous, monstrous. So let it collapse, our Institute. We'll found another one, a better one, without the Filitzes and Ebenwalds and their clan. Ah, Bernhardi, how I warned you against these people. But you, with your blind confidence. This will have taught you, I hope.

CYPRIAN *who has sought in vain to silence him* Won't you let someone else finally get a word in? For the time being the Institute is still standing. And we even have the Board still, for the time being. It hasn't resigned so far. And possibly some way will be found to prevent this somewhat painful step.

BERNHARDI Some way?

CYPRIAN Even the Councilor, who, you will not deny, is a very intelligent, enlightened individual, and really well-disposed towards you, is of the opinion —

BERNHARDI What opinion? Do get to the point, Cyprian.

CYPRIAN That you would not be compromising your dignity in the least, Bernhardi, if you, in some suitable form —

LÖWENSTEIN *interrupting* He should apologize?

CYPRIAN Who's talking about apologizing? Nobody said anything about him doing penance in a hair shirt at the church door. Or about recanting anything or swearing allegiance to some dogma. *To Bernhardi* It will be quite enough if you express your regret —

BERNHARDI I have nothing to regret.

LÖWENSTEIN Quite the contrary.

CYPRIAN All right, not your regret. Let's not quibble about words. But you can issue a statement, without compromising yourself in the least, that it was the last thing on your mind to offend anyone's religious sensibilities. After all, you really didn't want to do that.

BERNHARDI But everybody knows that.

CYPRIAN As if that were the point. You always talk as if you were dealing exclusively with honest people. Of course everybody knows it, and those people who want to twist this affair into a noose for you know it best of all. But nevertheless, I foresee, and there are signs already, that they'll try to portray you as a deliberate offender against religion and accuse you of having mocked a holy sacrament.

BERNHARDI Go on!

CYPRIAN Depend on it. And there will be no one, no one, who will stand up for you.

BERNHARDI No one?

CYPRIAN And you will have to get through the entire affair not only to the malicious howling of both your age-old and your newly acquired enemies, but also to the embarrassed silence or disapproving murmuring of the indifferent world and even of your friends. And naturally there will be no lack of accusations that you of all people should have guarded against such carelessness because you lack certain prerequisites which first make a person capable of grasping the profound meaning of the Catholic sacraments.

BERNHARDI But just tell me —

CYPRIAN I've already heard it all, my friend, from benevolent, from so-called enlightened people. So you can get an idea of what you may expect from the others.

LÖWENSTEIN And because of this rabble —

CYPRIAN Stop with this moral-ethical indignation all the time. Yes, the people are a rabble, but we have to take that into account. And — *to Bernhardi* since it is neither your intention nor your inclination to get involved with the rabble, and since you will not effect the least little change in the people or in the state of affairs by your obstinacy, I advise you again most urgently to do everything possible to calm the threatening storm and for now simply to make a statement, as I suggested before. The opportunity is there. We have a meeting tomorrow concerning the replacement in Tugendvetter's department.

BERNHARDI Right, right. Actually, it would be more important to talk about that than about this whole damned —

CYPRIAN I think so too. No one expects you to deny your convictions, you know. As I said, a simple statement would be sufficient.

BERNHARDI And you think that with that —

LÖWENSTEIN You're not really going to do that, Bernhardi, are you? If you do, then I'll take the whole thing upon myself, I'll answer for it. As if I myself had kept His Reverence —

CYPRIAN Don't let yourself be stirred up by this man, Bernhardi. Just think it over! Would you hesitate for even an instant to sacrifice so small a part of your vanity if, for example, it were a question of your Oskar's future? And in the end, a creation such as the Elisabethinum is not much less than a child. It is principally your creation, even if I stood at your side. Just remember the attacks against which you defended it, how you worked for it, fought for it.

BERNHARDI *continually pacing back and forth* There is a good deal of truth in that. They truly were years of battle, especially the first few. I do have to admit, it was no small thing what I —

CYPRIAN And now that we've brought the Institute so far, is it to be this seriously threatened or even destroyed in the end on account of such a trifle? No, Bernhardi, this must not happen. You have better things to do than to exhaust your strength in a fruitless and rather ridiculous battle. You are a doctor. And a human life saved is worth more than a banner held high.

LÖWENSTEIN Sophistry!

CYPRIAN We are at a turning point. It depends on you alone, Bernhardi, and our Institute will go forward into a brilliant future.

BERNHARDI *remains standing, astonished.*

CYPRIAN The fact is, you don't even know the most important thing yet. I also had occasion to speak to Flint.

BERNHARDI You spoke with him about this matter?

CYPRIAN No, not a word about that. I avoided it on purpose, as did he. I went to see him about the criminal-anthropological exhibition which is supposed to take place in the Fall. But naturally, we also got to talking about the Elisabethinum, and I can assure you, Bernhardi, that he really has entirely changed his opinion of us.

LÖWENSTEIN Flint is a climber, a prattler.

CYPRIAN He has his faults, we all know that, but he is an administrative genius; he intends great things, is planning reforms in all kinds of areas, especially in medical education and public hygiene, and for that — these are his own words — he will need individuals, not bureaucrats. Individuals like me and you —

BERNHARDI So? Individuals he needs. He may even have believed it at the moment he said it to you.

CYPRIAN Yes, he catches fire easily, we know that. But the idea now is to keep him warm. Then we'll be able to get a good deal out of him. And he really values you, Bernhardi. He was downright moved when he spoke of your time together as Rappenweiler's assistants. He is genuinely sorry you've drifted apart, and he hopes, in his own words, that you will find each other again at the peak of your careers.

What reason would he have to say something like that if he didn't mean it?

BERNHARDI Mean it — At that instant. I do know him. Had you stayed a quarter of an hour longer he would have convinced himself that I had been his best friend. And in just that way, ten years ago, if you'll remember, he called the Elisabethinum the center of an epidemic in the midst of the city, and us a questionable clique of all too ambitious young university lecturers.

CYPRIAN He has grown older and more mature since then. Today he knows what the Elisabethinum signifies, and we have a friend in him. Believe me, Bernhardi.

BERNHARDI *after a short pause* We still have to get together today in any case, if only on account of the replacement business.

CYPRIAN Yes, of course. I'll telephone Tugendvetter too.

LÖWENSTEIN He won't come.

BERNHARDI Well, if it's all right with all of you, let's meet at the Riedhof at nine-thirty, and we can have another word about the form of this so-called statement.

LÖWENSTEIN Bernhardi —

BERNHARDI The thing is, I really have no desire to play the hero at all costs. That I am a man who accomplishes what he wants in serious matters — that I have demonstrated any number of times. So, perhaps some form will find itself —

CYPRIAN I'm not worried about the form. I'm sure you'll find the right one after your fashion, slightly ironic if you like, but only slightly. In the end, your smile will probably suffice, which, after all, need not be reported to the Princess.

LÖWENSTEIN Some men you are!

CYPRIAN Calm down, Löwenstein, you really are only a kibbitzer, for whom no stake is high enough.

LÖWENSTEIN I am not a kibbitzer, I'm a player on my own account.

CYPRIAN Well, see you later, Bernhardi, at nine-thirty. And you'll bring a draft.

BERNHARDI Yes, one that won't offend your religious feelings either, Löwenstein.

LÖWENSTEIN Oh, that's terrific!

BERNHARDI *shakes hands with both of them and they exit.*
Bernhardi remains alone, paces back and forth a few times, then he looks at his watch, shakes his head, takes out a notebook, looks inside and then puts it back in his pocket with a gesture that says, "That can wait." Then he sits down at the desk, takes a sheet of paper out of a folder and begins to write, seriously at first, but soon an ironic smile crosses his mouth. He continues to write. The SERVANT *enters, hands him a calling card.*

BERNHARDI *surprised, hesitant — then* Show him in.

EBENWALD *enters.*

EBENWALD Good evening.

BERNHARDI *goes up to him and shakes hands* Good evening, Doctor. To what do I owe the pleasure?

EBENWALD If it's all right with you, Director, I'd like to get right to the point, without preamble —

BERNHARDI Of course. Please. *Invites him to sit down.*

EBENWALD *sits down in a chair next to the desk.*

BERNHARDI *sits down in his desk-chair.*

EBENWALD The thing is, Director, I consider it my duty to inform you that something is afoot against you, that is, against our Institute.

BERNHARDI So, is that it? I think I can set your mind at ease there, Doctor, the matter will be smoothed over.

EBENWALD Which matter, if I may ask?

BERNHARDI You are talking about the rumored impending resignation of the Board, aren't you?

EBENWALD So, the Board wants to resign? Well, yes, that is fairly — but I'm only just learning that from you. I've come for a totally different reason. As I hear from parliamentary circles, there is supposed to be an interpellation introduced concerning a matter not unfamiliar to you.

BERNHARDI Oh! Well, we may assume that this interpellation will be stopped too.

EBENWALD I beg your pardon, Director, of course I have no idea how you intend to influence the undesirable if not entirely incomprehensible attitude of certain personalities in this disagreeable affair in a way favorable to us all; but whether the danger posed by this interpellation can without further ado be deflected from your head, that is to say, from our heads — on that score I cannot, unfortunately, be as optimistic as you.

BERNHARDI We'll just have to wait and see.

EBENWALD That too is a point of view. But this is not a question involving you alone, Professor, but our Institute.

BERNHARDI I'm aware.

EBENWALD And thus it would certainly be advisable to think of some means by which this interpellation could be prevented.

BERNHARDI I don't see that as being so easy, because the gentlemen concerned will in any case raise the issue out of conviction — in the name of the religion I insulted. And what on earth could induce staunch men to back off again from a purpose they perceive as right and necessary?

EBENWALD What could induce these people to back off again? Well, if they came to understand that you meant no harm, at least not to the extent they assumed at first, if they arrived at the conviction that you have no inclination, how shall I say, to take up an anti-Catholic position —

BERNHARDI Do these people actually have to be told this?

EBENWALD No, not told, since telling them is easy. One would have to prove it.

BERNHARDI This is beginning to get interesting. How do you envision such proof, Doctor?

EBENWALD If one were to hit upon a concrete occasion, perhaps, out of which the inference I've suggested would grow, so to speak, unambiguously —

BERNHARDI *impatiently* One would absolutely have to invent an occasion like that.

EBENWALD Not at all. The occasion is at hand.

BERNHARDI How so?

EBENWALD The replacement in Tugendvetter's department is supposed to be decided tomorrow.

BERNHARDI Ah!

EBENWALD *coolly* Yes. There are two candidates.

BERNHARDI *very firmly* One who deserves the position and one who does not deserve it. I know no other differences worthy of consideration.

EBENWALD It may be that both candidates deserve it, and I do not know, Director, if you've studied dermatology sufficiently to decide in this case —

BERNHARDI Of course, I've read through the publications of both candidates in the last few weeks. It is simply ludicrous - and you know it as well as I do — even to name the two people together in the same breath. Your Doctor Hell has written a couple of case histories, in pretty questionable German, by the way, while Wenger's articles are extraordinary, groundbreaking.

EBENWALD *very calmly* On the other hand, in the opinion of others, Hell's case histories are excellent and of enormous importance for the practical physician, while Wenger's articles, though certainly ingenious, are viewed by specialists as being not especially reliable. And as far as his personality is concerned, his preponderant and otherwise also not very agreeable character enjoys only slight sympathy even among his friends. And in my opinion, a doctor, especially the head of a department, should —

BERNHARDI *increasingly impatient* This discussion strikes me as pointless. It's not my decision to make but the entire board's.

EBENWALD But in a tie vote, Director, you will decide. And a tie vote is a foreseeable certainty.

BERNHARDI Why?

EBENWALD Well, voting for Wenger will be Cyprian, Löwenstein, Adler and, naturally, the old liberal Pflugfelder.

BERNHARDI And Tugendvetter.

EBENWALD You yourself don't believe that, Director.

BERNHARDI Has he promised you his vote already?

EBENWALD That would prove nothing. But you know as well as I do he will not vote for Wenger. And that his own teacher could deny him his vote should cause you some doubt too —

BERNHARDI *pacing back and forth in his fashion* You know perfectly well, Professor Ebenwald, why Tugendvetter is against his student. Simply put, because he is afraid to lose some of his practice to him. Moreover, you know as well as all the rest of us that Tugendvetter's last few articles were not his but Wenger's.

EBENWALD Please, Director, won't you tell Professor Tugendvetter that in person?

BERNHARDI Let me worry about that, Professor. It has always been my habit to tell people to their face what I think. And thus I'm telling you, Professor, that you are agitating for Hell only because he is not a Jew.

EBENWALD *very calmly* I could reply, with just as much right, that your position in favor of Wenger —

BERNHARDI You forget that three years ago I voted for you, Professor Ebenwald.

EBENWALD But a little against your better judgment, isn't that so? And that's how it would be for me with Wenger. And for that reason I won't do it. One always regrets something like that. And even if I had a higher opinion of Wenger, I assure you, Director, in a corporation it does not depend solely on the talent of any individual —

BERNHARDI But on character.

EBENWALD On the atmosphere, I was going to say. And here we've arrived back at the starting point of our conversation. It really is terrible that here in Austria all personnel questions end up becoming political. But we simply have to learn to live with that. Look, Director, if Hell were an idiot then I would naturally not vote for him, nor expect it of you. But after all, he will cure people just as well as Wenger. And if you consider that by the adoption of a certain position on your part all the inconvenient consequences of that other affair could possibly be avoided as well — I can't undertake to guarantee anything, of course, since it is only an idea of mine.

BERNHARDI Ah!

EBENWALD Of course. But it would be worth the effort in any event, Director, if you would think it over free of anger or bias. We can talk about it again tomorrow, before the meeting.

BERNHARDI That would probably be superfluous.

EBENWALD As you wish, Director. But if I may say something, you shouldn't, through any false pride — all this will remain between you and me, of course —

BERNHARDI I have no reason whatever to request your discretion, Professor. Tell the gentlemen who sent you here —

EBENWALD Oho!

BERNHARDI That I will not enter into deals of that sort and —

EBENWALD Excuse me, no one sent me here; I am not therefore in a position to accept messages. My visit here was a completely unofficial one. Please keep that in mind. I've come neither as an ambassador nor on my own behalf, since I feel no inclination whatever to share the responsibility for your behavior vis-a-vis His Reverence, but in the interest of our Institute and in your own, Director. You have scorned the proffered hand of friendship —

BERNHARDI And you're departing as my enemy. I prefer that. It's the more honest role.

EBENWALD As you wish, Director. Good day to you.

BERNHARDI Good evening.

Accompanies him to the door. Ebenwald exits. Bernhardi alone, walks up and down a few times, picks up the sheet of paper on which he had begun to write earlier, reads it, then tears it in pieces. Looks at his watch again and gets ready to go out. The servant enters.

BERNHARDI What's the matter?

SERVANT *hands him a calling card.*

BERNHARDI What? In person? I mean, His Excellency himself is here?

SERVANT Yes, Professor.

BERNHARDI Show him in.

SERVANT *exits.*

Immediately thereafter FLINT *enters; tall, slim, past fifty, hair cut short, small mutton chops, a not entirely unstudied diplomat's mask, very amiable, often with sincere warmth.*

BERNHARDI *still at the door* Excellency? *With his slightly ironic smile.*

FLINT *shaking his hand* We haven't seen each other in a long time, Bernhardi.

BERNHARDI We did only recently, at the Medical Society.

FLINT I mean privately, like this.

BERNHARDI Yes, that certainly. Won't you sit down?

FLINT Thank you, thank you. *He sits down, Bernhardi does so soon after.* You're surprised to see me here?

BERNHARDI I am — pleasantly surprised, and don't want to miss the opportunity to congratulate you on your new honor.

FLINT Honor! You do know that I don't see my new position that way. But all the same, I accept your congratulations with particular satisfaction. Of course, as you may imagine, I didn't come only to collect these congratulations in person.

BERNHARDI Of course.

FLINT *beginning* Well, my dear Bernhardi, I need hardly tell you that I don't intend to use my portfolio as a soft cushion, but that I'm determined to use what may be the scant measure of time granted me in this office to carry out all manner of reforms which, as you may remember, have been close to my heart since my youth. Reforms in the areas of medical instruction, of social hygiene, of universal public education — well, and so on. For this, the people which the government has put at my disposal, honest, but with a somewhat conventional world view, will obviously not suffice. For this I will need a staff, as it were, a volunteer staff, naturally, of independently thinking, unbiased men. We have no lack of efficient bureaucrats here in Austria, you know, and especially in the Ministry of Education; but what I need to carry out my plans are human beings. And I've come to ask you, dear Bernhardi, if I can count on you.

BERNHARDI *after hesitating briefly* Perhaps you will be so kind as to express yourself more precisely.

FLINT Still more precisely? Hmm — well— I was prepared to find you coy.

BERNHARDI No, not at all. I only want you to explain yourself in more detail. After all, I can't, beforehand — I do have to know in which area you require my cooperation. *With his ironic smile* In medical instruction, in social hygiene, in public education. Have I left anything out?

FLINT Still the same old fellow. But it's for that very reason I place particular hope in you. There may still be a few things to be cleared up between us, although I do not rightly know —

BERNHARDI *seriously* I'll tell you what it is, Flint; the friendship of youth and — what became of it afterwards.

FLINT *cordially* But what became of it, Bernhardi? We simply drifted apart a bit over the years, the result, perhaps of our respective spiritual development.

BERNHARDI My view entirely.

FLINT Are you bearing a grudge, Bernhardi?

BERNHARDI I only have a good memory.

FLINT That could be a defect, Bernhardi, if it prevents a clear understanding of present circumstances. Actually, I thought we had buried the hatchet and forgotten the years of battle.

BERNHARDI Battle? Truly a noble word for a not particularly noble business.

FLINT Bernhardi!

BERNHARDI No, my friend, it was not pretty! And it would strike me as a betrayal of my own past if I could laugh it off so easily. *He has gotten up* Oh, with what weapons you fought against us back then, you and the other professors; by what means you tried to undermine our newborn undertaking! What all you made up to lower people's opinion of us, how you cast suspicion on us and persecuted us! We were accused of creating our Institute in order to take money from the general practitioners, of contaminating the city, of wanting to establish a second medical faculty —

FLINT *interrupting him* My dear Bernhardi, all these accusations could, in a certain sense, still be made today, if the good that you accomplish in the scientific and humanitarian fields had not long since made up for the less positive aspects of your undertaking. We realized this, I most of all, dear Bernhardi, and for this reason, only for this reason, we changed our attitude towards you. And you can believe me, the Elisabethinum possesses no warmer friend today than I. Aside from which, personal motives never influenced my position towards you, and it was only out of conviction that —

BERNHARDI Yes, one always tells oneself that in the growing bitterness of battle. The conviction!

FLINT Excuse me, Bernhardi. We all have our faults, you know. You most likely as well as I. But if there is one thing I can affirm it is this, that I never, not even in the least thing, spoke or acted against my convictions.

BERNHARDI You're quite sure of that?

FLINT Bernhardi!

BERNHARDI Think about it carefully.

FLINT *somewhat unsure* I may have made mistakes in my life like all of us, but against my convictions — No!

BERNHARDI Well, I know of one case in which you acted against your conviction in a quite demonstrable way.

FLINT Then I must —

BERNHARDI And your acting in that way even resulted in the death of a human being.

FLINT That really is a bit strong. But now I must insist —

BERNHARDI Please, please. *He paces up and down a few times, stops suddenly, very lively* We were Rappenweiler's assistants at the time. We had a patient in the clinic, I still see him before me, I still remember his name even, Engelbert Wagner, a government clerk, whom our chief, and all the rest of us, had diagnosed incorrectly. When it came to the autopsy it became apparent that the patient could have been saved by means of another, anti-syphilitic, treatment. And as we stood down there and the thing became clear, you whispered to me, "I knew it all along." Do you remember? You had known what was wrong with the patient, you had made the correct diagnosis —

FLINT The only one.

BERNHARDI Yes, the only one. But you carefully avoided breathing any hint of it while the patient was alive. And why you avoided it, that is a question that you can answer for yourself. I assume it couldn't have been out of conviction.

FLINT Damn, you have a good memory. I remember the case too, and it's true, I did in fact keep to myself my thought that a different treatment was not only more promising of success but indicated. And let me confess to you freely, I kept silent only to avoid injuring Rappenweiler's feelings, who, as you know, didn't like it when his assistants were smarter than he. And so, you may be quite right in throwing up to me that I sacrificed a human life. Only, you're mistaken about the reasons, the deeper reasons. This one sacrifice, Bernhardi, had to be made for the benefit of hundreds of other human lives which were to be entrusted to my medical skill later on. I could not yet do without Rappenweiler's influence entirely back then, and I had my eye on that professorship in Prague.

BERNHARDI You think that Rappenweiler would have dropped you if you —

FLINT It's very likely. You overestimate humanity, Bernhardi. You have no idea how narrow-minded people are. Naturally, it would not have cost me my career, but no doubt it would have meant a delay. And it was important to me to get ahead quickly, in order to gain the necessary free play for my talents, which even you will not deny I have. That is why, my dear Bernhardi, I let the government clerk Engelbert Wagner die, and I feel unable even to regret it. Because it does not mean much, dear Bernhardi, to behave correctly or, if you will, to keep faith with one's convictions in some insignificant individual instance, it's a question of being faithful to the immanent idea of one's own life. I find it most interesting that you've summoned poor Engelbert Wagner from his grave again in the course of our conversation, because it's just hit me now, the profound spiritual difference between you and me, and — perhaps this will astonish you, Bernhardi — our ability to complement each other. Perhaps you are, more so than I, what people call a decent human being. You're more sentimental in any case. But whether you'd be capable of accomplishing more than I for the general good, that seems to me very questionable. What you lack, Bernhardi, is an eye for the essential, without which all your faithfulness to convictions continues to be only dogmatism. Because it's not a question of being right in the individual instance but of being effective on a large scale. And to sacrifice the possibility for such effective action for the somewhat paltry consciousness of having done the right thing in some indifferent instance strikes me not only as petty, but also, in a higher sense, as immoral. That's right, my dear Bernhardi. Immoral.

BERNHARDI *recollecting himself* You now have something quite specific in mind, evidently, if I interpret your tone of voice correctly.

FLINT My field of vision, so to speak, has shifted while I was talking.

BERNHARDI And have we not now, quite unexpectedly, come upon the actual purpose of your visit?

FLINT Not the actual one, but still a not entirely incidental one.

BERNHARDI And for that reason you're making the effort —

FLINT For that reason too. Because I foresee with some certainty that the business we are both now thinking about might create additional ripples. Obviously, you did not anticipate this. In keeping with your charming but sometimes unfortunate tendency, you failed, in the unquestionably noble excitement of the moment, to look ahead. And thus, in your behavior towards His Reverence you forgot one trifle, namely that we live in a Christian state. — I don't know what there is to smile about.

BERNHARDI You will wonder at my good memory once again. I recall an article you wanted to write as a young man. It was supposed to be entitled: "Houses of God — Houses of Healing."

FLINT Hmm!

BERNHARDI You wanted to argue that we should build more hospitals instead of so many churches.

FLINT Ah, one of the many articles I wanted to write and never wrote.

BERNHARDI And never will write.

FLINT Certainly not that one. Today I know they can exist very well side by side, the houses of God and the houses of healing, and that some ailments are cured in the churches which we in the hospitals, dear Bernhardi, are still powerless to cure. But let's not get lost in political discussions, all right?

BERNHARDI All the less since I could hardly keep up with you in that field.

FLINT Well, yes, you may be right. So, let's confine ourselves to the particular case, rather.

BERNHARDI Yes, let's do that. I am very curious about what proposal His Excellency the Minister of Education and Religion has to convey to me.

FLINT Proposal? I have nothing specific. Only I can't conceal from you that the general attitude towards you wherever one hears anything, including in circles where you wouldn't even suspect it, is highly unfavorable, and I wish wholeheartedly for your sake and your Institute's that this entire affair could be done away with, insofar as that's still possible.

BERNHARDI I wish that too.

FLINT What's that you say?

BERNHARDI I have lots of far more important things to do, you know, than to occupy myself much longer with this business.

FLINT Are you serious?

BERNHARDI How can you doubt it? I can even tell you that not an hour ago I consulted with Cyprian and Löwenstein about a statement with which the allegedly offended parties will surely be satisfied.

FLINT Why, that would — that would really be splendid. But I fear under the present circumstances we could not quite make do with that.

BERNHARDI How come? What then should I do?

FLINT If perhaps you — in my opinion you would not be compromising yourself in the least, all the less so since to my knowledge no charge has been officially lodged yet, if by means of a personal visit to His Reverence you —

BERNHARDI What?

FLINT It would make a most excellent impression. Since you did commit the, let's call it indiscretion of preventing His Reverence more or less by force —

BERNHARDI By force?

FLINT That's too strong a word, of course. But still, you did, at least people say —

BERNHARDI What do they say?

FLINT — push him away from the door somewhat forcefully.

BERNHARDI That's a lie. Surely you'll believe me —

FLINT Then you did not push him away?

BERNHARDI I barely touched him. Whoever says I used force is a deliberate liar. Oh, I know who these people are. But they will not — Now I myself will —

FLINT Calm down, Bernhardi. Officially, not the least charge has been filed. But if you've decided to make a statement, then it would really be the easiest thing to use the occasion explicitly to mention that all these rumors —

BERNHARDI Excuse me, dear Flint, you're mistaken. To be sure, I had a statement in mind which I wanted to make at tomorrow's meeting first of all, but circumstances have arisen in the meantime that make my delivering such a statement absolutely impossible.

FLINT What's the matter now? What circumstances?

BERNHARDI Compelling ones, you may believe me.

FLINT Hmm. And you can't reveal them to me in more detail? I would be very much interested —

BERNHARDI *smiling again* Tell me, my dear Flint, did you really come here only to help me out of a predicament?

FLINT If it were of no importance to me how this business turned out for you, and for your Institute, then I would certainly not need to concern myself any further. To say the least, you've behaved improperly enough that it would bother my conscience very little to let you face the music, if I didn't feel sorry for you and your Institute.

BERNHARDI In short, you would like for my sake that I — save you from a parliamentary interpellation.

FLINT To be sure. There's not much good can come of it. You simply happened not to have conducted yourself absolutely correctly towards the priest. And as an honest man one would be obligated at least to admit that, even if for the rest, one could vouch for the purity of your intentions, for your importance as a man of science —

BERNHARDI My dear Flint, you probably have no idea how much you overestimate your power.

FLINT Hmm —

BERNHARDI Clearly you fancy that it still rests with you to prevent such an interpellation.

FLINT It rests with you. I can assure you.

BERNHARDI With me, yes. You have no idea how right you are. With me alone. Half an hour ago I had it in my power to avert the danger of this interpellation from your head and mine.

FLINT You had —

BERNHARDI Yes, in the easiest way in the world. We're choosing a new head for Tugendvetter's department, as you know. We're having a meeting tomorrow. If I had pledged, in case of a tie, to vote not for Wenger but for Hell, everything would be in order.

FLINT Pledged? How? To whom?

BERNHARDI Ebenwald was just here. He delivered the proposal to me.

FLINT Hmm. Do you really think?

BERNHARDI At any rate, I had the impression that Ebenwald had full authority to conclude the deal, even if he did deny it. And maybe I was only supposed to fall into a trap, and the interpellation would have followed even if I had voted for Hell.

FLINT *pacing back and forth* Our colleague Ebenwald is very friendly with his cousin, Representative Ebenwald. He is one of the leaders of the Clericals, and if he doesn't want the interpellation it would certainly not take place. I do believe that in this instance our colleague Ebenwald proceeded honestly, as it were. Well, how did you respond to his proposal?

BERNHARDI Flint!

FLINT Well, yes, I suppose you consider Wenger the more eminent dermatologist.

BERNHARDI And so do you. You know as well as I do that Hell is a cipher. And even if both were equally qualified, Ebenwald, by his request, would have made it simply impossible for me to vote for anyone but Wenger.

FLINT Well, Ebenwald certainly didn't manage this very cleverly.

BERNHARDI Not cleverly?! and that's all you have to say? I find you somewhat mild, my dear Flint.

FLINT My good Bernhardi, politics —

BERNHARDI What do politics concern me?

FLINT They concern all of us.

BERNHARDI And you think that because such infamies occur every day in your so-called politics I should put up with this latest one with a smile, as perfectly normal, and actually take this disgraceful bargain into consideration?

FLINT You know, it's possible that the question won't involve you at all, that there will be no tie vote, and that Hell or Wenger will be elected without your participation.

BERNHARDI Oh, my dear Flint, the thing will not be made
that easy for you.

FLINT For me? I think —

BERNHARDI *warmly* Flint, even if you are a Cabinet Minister
today, you are, when all is said and done, a doctor too, a
man of science, a man of truth. How did you yourself put it
before? It's a question of keeping the essential in view. Well,
what is essential here? Don't you see it? That we give the
department to the most qualified man, for whom it will then
be possible to accomplish something of consequence for sick
people and for science. That's the point, isn't it? That's
what's essential. Not that you or I be spared the
inconvenience of an interpellation, which we could respond
to pretty well if necessary.

FLINT Hmm. I certainly wouldn't be worried about an answer.

BERNHARDI I didn't think so.

FLINT Tell me, Bernhardi, could you put it in writing — I
mean, could you write me a letter presenting this entire
business concisely and to the point, so that I, if need be —

BERNHARDI If need be?

FLINT In any event, I want to have it in hand, in black and
white. Maybe it won't be necessary to read the letter. I could
respond rather reservedly, at first, if they interpellate, I
mean. But then, if they don't keep quiet, then I could come
out with your letter.

Gestures, as if pulling the letter from his breast pocket.

BERNHARDI No doubt your parliamentary experience will
show you the right way to proceed here.

FLINT Experience? Probably more my intuition for now. But
I don't believe it would get that far — to the reading of your
letter, I mean. Right from my first words they would notice,
from my tone of voice, that I am holding something in
reserve. They would all notice it. Because I'll have them
where I want them, Bernhardi, as soon as I start to speak, I'll
have them all. I have the gentlemen in Parliament, exactly as

I had my students at the clinic. Recently there was a short debate about the new amendment to the school laws; I only intervened in an incidental way, but you couldn't imagine the breathless silence in the house, Bernhardi. To tell the truth, I didn't say anything particularly important. But I had their ear at once. And that's what it comes down to. They listen to me. And if one will only really listen to another person, he can no longer treat him entirely unjustly.

BERNHARDI Certainly.

FLINT And at the risk of your taking it as vanity on my part, Bernhardi, I'm almost beginning to hope that those rascals do interpellate.

BERNHARDI Flint!

FLINT Because it would give us a real opportunity to get into some general questions. I mean, I see in this individual case a symbol of our entire political situation.

BERNHARDI Which it is.

FLINT It always happens this way with me — even with apparently quite insignificant single instances. Every one of them becomes a symbol for me somehow. I suppose that's what it is that predestines me for a political career.

BERNHARDI To be sure.

FLINT And that's why I believe we could use the occasion to get into some general questions.

BERNHARDI Aha, Houses of God — Houses of Healing.

FLINT You're smiling. I am unfortunately not capable of taking such things lightly.

BERNHARDI But my dear Flint, after everything you've said now, one might almost get the impression that you would be inclined to take my side in the matter.

FLINT That doesn't take much acumen. I want to confess to you: at the outset I was not so entirely — because I find, now as before, that your conduct towards the priest was not especially correct. But this Ebenwald deal, this puts everything in an entirely different light. The only important thing, of course, is that this remain a secret between the two of us. I mean, that you mustn't say a word about this Ebenwald business to your friends either. Because if those people get wind of my intentions they could change their minds in the end and desist from their interpellation. So, naturally, you'll keep a copy of the letter, but its contents will remain a secret until the moment I place it on the table. *Gestures without exaggeration.*

BERNHARDI It is highly gratifying to me that you are so — but I want to give you still another thing to consider. The party against whom you would have to take the floor is very strong, very ruthless, and the question is whether you'll be able to remain Minister without them —

FLINT It would have to be put to the test.

BERNHARDI Still, if you should prefer your office —

FLINT Over you —

BERNHARDI Over the truth, which is the only thing that counts, then I'd rather you not get involved in the matter, then I'd rather you didn't stand up for me.

FLINT For you? I'm not doing that at all. For the truth, for the just cause.

BERNHARDI And are you now quite convinced now, Flint, that this trivial affair is worthy of your involvement?

FLINT This trivial affair? Bernhardi! Don't you realize yet that we're talking about far higher values here than may appear at first glance? That here, in a sense, the eternal battle between light and darkness. But that sounds like phrase-making.

BERNHARDI A battle in any event, my dear Flint, the outcome of which is fairly uncertain under present conditions, and in which all your ministerial glory —

FLINT Let me worry about that. However it turns out, I can imagine no more beautiful death than for a just cause and for one who — admit it — was still my enemy an hour ago.

BERNHARDI Your enemy I wasn't. And in any case, I'll gladly apologize to you if I should have done you an injustice. But this I want to tell you, Flint: even if all this does not turn out entirely well for you, I will not suffer any pangs of conscience. Because you know where justice lies in this case, and I refuse in advance to, let's say, admire you for doing what is in fact your duty.

FLINT Nor should you, Bernhardi. *He shakes his hand* Farewell. *As lightly as possible* I was looking for a human being, I've found him. Good-bye!

BERNHARDI Good-bye. *Hesitating* I thank you.

FLINT Oh! You mustn't do that either. Our friendship must rest on firmer ground. *He exits.*

BERNHARDI *remains standing in thought awhile* Well, we'll see, won't we?

Curtain

THIRD ACT

Conference room in the Elisabethinum. Furnished in the usual way. Long green table in the center, cupboards, two windows at the rear center. Photographs of famous doctors, a portrait of the Empress Elisabeth over the entrance left. It is evening; artificial lighting. A chandelier with a large green shade, not fully turned on at first. A small table along the wall on the right side.

HOCHROITZPOINTNER, *sitting over a large log book, copying from another page.*
Assistant Professor Dr. SCHREIMANN *enters. He is tall, bald, and has a small military mustache and a dueling scar on his forehead, and wears glasses. He speaks in an honest, deeply resounding German in a strong Austrian dialect with suddenly intruding Jewish accents.*

HOCHROITZPOINTNER *leaps up* Good afternoon, Capt — Doctor.
SCHREIMANN Hi. So, slept off the ball, Hochroitzpointner?
HOCHROITZPOINTNER I didn't even lie down, Professor. It wasn't worth the effort any more.
SCHREIMANN *noticing Hochroitzpointner is still standing at attention* At ease, at ease.
HOCHROITZPOINTNER *in a more comfortable position* I danced until seven, by eight I was already at Internal Medicine, by ten in Surgery, at noon —
SCHREIMANN *interrupting him, sits down at the table* Cut it out, will you, I know you're everywhere. And now you've made a fair copy of the minutes of the last meeting?
HOCHROITZPOINTNER Didn't get to it sooner, unfortunately, Sir.

SCHREIMANN But — But it's not even your job. In my capacity as Secretary, I thank you. Were you able to read everything all right? *Goes up to him and reads, murmuring* "The ballot — four votes for Senior Professor Hell of the University of Graz, four for Doctor S. Wenger" — *turning to Hochroitzpointner* Samuel —

HOCHROITZPOINTNER But that doesn't get written out.

SCHREIMANN I'd like to know why. My grandfather, for instance, was named Samuel and always wrote it out, and I'm named Siegfried and always write it out.

HOCHROITZPOINTNER *dumbly* Yes, Captain, Sir.

SCHREIMANN But look here, I'm not your Regimental Officer any more. *He continues reading* "The Director made use of his statutory right to cast the deciding ballot in case of a tie and voted for Assistant Professor Doctor Wenger, whereby the latter is elected Head of the Department of Dermatology and Syphilis." *Short pause* So, are you satisfied with your new Chief?

HOCHROITZPOINTNER *involuntarily clicking his heels together* Certainly.

SCHREIMANN *laughing, putting his hand on Hochroitzpointner's shoulder* But what are you doing, Hochroitzpointner? You're no longer a military cadet under my command, you know.

HOCHROITZPOINTNER Unfortunately, Sir. Those were good times.

SCHREIMANN Oh, we were simply younger. But tell me, Hochroitzpointner, as long as we're at it, when are you thinking of taking your last exams?

EBENWALD *enters.*

EBENWALD Yes, that's what I'm always asking him too.

HOCHROITZPOINTNER Good afternoon, Professor.

EBENWALD Hi, Schreimann.

SCHREIMANN Hi.

EBENWALD You know what, Hochroitzpointner, you should take a vacation from the various departments sometime soon and cram. Understand? Cram, so you'll finally get done. By the way, what are you doing in the conference room?

SCHREIMANN The Doctor was kind enough to make a fair copy of the minutes for me.

EBENWALD So, that too. Whatever would the Elisabethinum do without Hochroitzpointner! And last night at the ball you were the leading dancer?

HOCHROITZPOINTNER *dumbly* Leading and following, Professor.

SCHREIMANN And didn't even go to bed.

EBENWALD Ah yes, the young people! So, how was it?

HOCHROITZPOINTNER Awfully crowded. Very exciting.

EBENWALD *to Hochroitzpointner* Do you know where you danced last night, Hochroitzpointner? Atop a volcano.

HOCHROITZPOINTNER It was very hot, too, Professor.

EBENWALD *laughs* Ha! So, take a vacation, pass your exams, and no more dancing on volcanoes! Not even on extinct ones. So long! *Shakes his hand in farewell.*

SCHREIMANN *does the same.*

HOCHROITZPOINTNER *again clicks his heel together.*

EBENWALD Like a lieutenant!

SCHREIMANN I just told him.

HOCHROITZPOINTNER *exits.*

EBENWALD So, His Excellency the Minister of Education was there too?

SCHREIMANN Yes, and he even chatted with Bernhardi for at least half an hour.

EBENWALD It really is odd.

SCHREIMANN Oh, please, at a ball.

EBENWALD But he must be aware that the Board resigned.

SCHREIMANN What if it did? There was even a member of the Board at the ball.

EBENWALD Who?

SCHREIMANN Councilor Winkler.

EBENWALD He's always in some sort of opposition.

SCHREIMANN Besides, it's not official yet.

EBENWALD It may as well be. At any rate, today's meeting has been called on account of the resignation. So — *hesitating* can I depend on you, Schreimann?

SCHREIMANN *lightly* I find that a rather strange question.

EBENWALD Come on, stop it, we're no longer students, you know.

SCHREIMANN You can always depend on me, if I agree with you. And since that is fortunately the case most of the time —

EBENWALD But there may be questions in which going along with me might cause you certain misgivings.

SCHREIMANN I've told you once already, dear Ebenwald, that in my view this entire affair is not to be seen from some religious or denominational standpoint but rather from one of tact. Thus, even if I identified with the Jews, I would take a position against Bernhardi in this case. But aside from that, let me call to your attention once more that I am as much a German as you. And I assure you, for someone of my ancestry to identify himself as a German and a Christian nowadays requires more courage than to remain what he was born. As a Zionist I'd have had it easier.

EBENWALD It may well be. You'd have been assured a professorship in Jerusalem.

SCHREIMANN Stale jokes.

EBENWALD Go on, Schreimann, you do know how I feel about you, but you must, on the other hand, understand that we live in such a muddled time — and in such a muddled country —

SCHREIMANN Hey, don't start again with those anonymous letters.

EBENWALD Ah, you still remember those? Actually, they weren't anonymous at all. They were signed with full names, by good old friends from my student days. Naturally, they wondered that I supported you to such an extent. You mustn't forget, dear Schreimann, at the university and later as a graduate I was a leader of the most extreme German nationals. And you know what that means: Watch on the Rhine — Bismarck's eagle — Waidhofner resolution — no satisfaction to be given to Jews, including those of Jewish extraction —*

SCHREIMANN Still, it didn't work out any other way sometimes, in spite of the strictest observance. The dueling scar here I got as a Jew.

EBENWALD So, do we not live in a muddled country? To this day you're still more proud of your Jewish scar than of all your Germanness.

PROFESSOR PFLUGFELDER *enters; 65, scholarly expression, wearing glasses.*

PFLUGFELDER Good evening, gentlemen. Have you heard yet? The Board resigned!

EBENWALD That's the reason we're here, esteemed Professor.

PFLUGFELDER So, what do you say to that?

---

* *Watch on the Rhine*: anthem of the German-Nationals, adopted a generation later by the Nazis as one of their anthems. *Waidhofner resolution*: passed in 1896 by a number of German-National Austrian student organizations to the effect that Jews were disqualified from seeking satisfaction by force of arms (i.e., in a duel) for any insult offered them.

EBENWALD You seem surprised. We were prepared for it, generally speaking.

PFLUGFELDER Surprised? Not a whit. Oh, you know, I left off being surprised a long time ago. But not being disgusted, unfortunately. Disgust I have up to here.

SCHREIMANN Disgust?

PFLUGFELDER You will have to admit, gentlemen, that the agitation now being staged against Bernhardi is without any intrinsic justification.

EBENWALD I am not aware of any agitation.

PFLUGFELDER Ah! You're not aware of anything? I see, I see. And that your cousin, Ottokar Ebenwald, is the principal instigator, you don't know that either?

EBENWALD I must ask you —

PFLUGFELDER But of course, I don't want to identify you with your cousin. You will reject, quite justifiably, the notion that you have anything in common. Because it turns out, precisely on this occasion, that your cousin, who started out so gloriously as a German-National, now merely lends himself to manage the affairs of the clericals. And you're not a clerical, Ebenwald, are you? You are German, an old German student. And what are the German virtues, Ebenwald? Courage, loyalty, firmness of conviction. Have I left any out? Doesn't matter. We'll make do with these for the time being. And I hope, therefore, that you are of one mind with me: today we will solemnly express our support of our Bernhardi.

EBENWALD Support? But for what? What's happened to him? Up to now nothing except that the Board resigned. And we can close up shop because we don't know where we're going to get money from. Whether that is exactly the right reason to applaud our Director, who has placed us in this situation through his not very tactful behavior —

PFLUGFELDER Ah, I see — well, yes. You simply are what you are, Ebenwald. I would let myself be operated on only by you. Because that you know how to do, yes. But you, Schreimann? You are silent? Against Bernhardi too? Also outraged that he begged the priest to let a poor, sick mortal die in peace? Understandable, understandable. One has to be especially careful of such new-found religious feelings.

EBENWALD *calmly* Don't let him goad you, Schreimann.

SCHREIMANN *very calmly* I was just saying to my colleague Ebenwald earlier, Professor, it's not my religious feelings that were offended, but my sense of good taste. You see, I find that a sick-room is not the right place to play politics.

PFLUGFELDER Politics! Bernhardi played politics! You're not going to try to convince me that you believe that yourself. That is really —

FILITZ *enters. Greetings.*

FILITZ Good evening, gentlemen. I want to tell you right away what I'm thinking of doing. You may take it as you will. For my part, I'm going to follow the good example of the Board and resign.

EBENWALD What?

PFLUGFELDER Ha!

FILITZ I wouldn't know what would be the right thing to do otherwise, if one didn't actually intend to declare his solidarity with the behavior of our Director, which need not be characterized more closely here, and —

EBENWALD Excuse me, Professor, I do not share your view at all. Surely there is another way of proving that we haven't the least intention of expressing solidarity with our Director. We must not leave our Institute in the lurch now, especially not now. Rather, we must try to move the Board to rescind its resignation.

FILITZ That will never happen as long as Bernhardi is at the top.

SCHREIMANN Quite right. As long as he's at the top.

FILITZ As long as —
PFLUGFELDER Oh, have you come that far already, gentlemen! This does exceed —

ADLER *enters.*

ADLER Good evening, gentlemen, have you read it yet?
EBENWALD What?
ADLER The interpellation.
SCHREIMANN In the Bernhardi affair?
FILITZ It's happened already?
ADLER It's in the evening paper.
EBENWALD *rings a bell* We've read nothing. *To Filitz* I thought not until tomorrow.
SCHREIMANN You see, we doctors have no time to sit in the coffee-house in the afternoon.
ATTENDANT *enters.*
EBENWALD Be a good fellow, go across to the tobacco shop and buy an evening paper.
FILITZ Bring three.
SCHREIMANN Six!
EBENWALD *to the attendant* May as well bring a dozen. But fast!
ATTENDANT *exits.*
SCHREIMANN *to Adler* Is it very severe, the interpellation?
PFLUGFELDER Is there no one here yet who knows the wording?

DR. WENGER *enters; a small person, depressed, insecure but still at times overly loud; wearing glasses.*

WENGER Good evening, gentlemen.
SCHREIMANN Give it here, Doctor Wenger. *Pulls a newspaper from his breast pocket* He's got one.

WENGER But Doctor!

EBENWALD This is nice, that you brought us this right away.

WENGER What did I bring? Ah, so! Is that the custom, that the junior member always brings the evening paper to the meetings?

EBENWALD *with the newspaper* Here it is!
The others, except Adler and Wenger, try to look in the paper with Ebenwald.

ADLER *to Wenger* What do you say to that?

WENGER Well, what should I say? I don't understand anything about politics. And I wasn't there.

SCHREIMANN *to Ebenwald* None of us can see anything this way. Read it to us.

EBENWALD Very well, gentlemen, the interpellation reads as follows: "The undersigned take it to be their duty —"

PFLUGFELDER It's leaving you breathless! Let Professor Filitz read! He is sonorous and rhetorical and has the true ring of conviction.

EBENWALD I've got that too, but Professor Filitz certainly reads better. So, please.

FILITZ *reads* "The undersigned take it to be their duty to make known to the government the following incident which took place on the fourth of February at the Elisabethinum" — and so on and so forth. "His Reverence Franz Reder, Parson at the Church of St. Florian, was summoned by the secular Sister Ludmilla to the deathbed of the seriously ill, unmarried Philomena Beier in order to administer to her the holy sacrament of extreme unction. In the anteroom of the ward, His Reverence found a number of doctors gathered, among them Professor Bernhardi, head of the department in question and Director of the Institute, who in rude fashion asked His Reverence to desist from his purpose, on the grounds that the excitement might prove deleterious to the health of the dying woman."

PFLUGFELDER No, no!

THE OTHERS Quiet!

FILITZ *continues reading* "Professor Bernhardi, as a member of the Mosaic confession, was then advised by His Reverence that he had appeared for the fulfillment of a sacred obligation, one all the more urgently indicated in this instance since the patient's condition was the consequence of a criminal operation for which she herself was to blame, in response to which Professor Bernhardi, in mocking fashion, emphatically stressed his control as Head of the Institute over all the rooms, which were of course built and are maintained by the financial support of noble donors. Then, as His Reverence, declining to engage in any further discussion, desired to enter the ward, Professor Bernhardi blocked the door, and at the moment His Reverence grasped the door handle in order to set foot in the sick-room in the exercise of his sacred duty, Professor Bernhardi gave him a shove —"

ADLER An absolute lie!

PFLUGFELDER Infamous!

SCHREIMANN Were you there?

FILITZ As if it were a question of the shove.

EBENWALD There are witnesses.

PFLUGFELDER I know your witnesses.

ADLER I was there too.

PFLUGFELDER But you weren't questioned.

WENGER Questioned?

PFLUGFELDER By a certain commission. Or are you perhaps unfamiliar with the commission as well, Professor Ebenwald?

SCHREIMANN On with the reading!

FILITZ *reads* "During this confrontation in the anteroom, the patient passed away, without having partaken of the consolations of religion for which, as Sister Ludmilla has testified, she longed. In making this incident known to the government, we direct to the government, in particular to His Excellency the Minister of Education and Religion the question, what measures he proposes to obtain satisfaction for the most grievously offended religious sensibilities of the Christian population of Vienna; further, what steps His Excellency proposes to take in order to prevent a repetition of such a shocking incident; and, finally, in view of this incident, whether it does not appear to His Excellency advisable, in filling public positions in the future, to exclude once and for all individuals who by reason of ancestry, education and character are not in a position to show the requisite understanding for the religious feelings of the native Christian population." Signed . . . *Stirring among the men.*

EBENWALD Well, a fine mess we're in now.

WENGER Why we? It doesn't say a word against the Institute.

SCHREIMANN Quite right!

EBENWALD Bravo, Wenger!

WENGER *encouraged* The Elisabethinum stands spotless and pure.

PFLUGFELDER And the Director?

WENGER He too, of course, if he succeeds, which I don't doubt for an instant, in refuting the aspersions contained in the interpellation.

PFLUGFELDER Aspersions? You call those aspersions? But my dear colleague, this interpellation — do you really have to be told that this interpellation signifies nothing other than a political maneuver by the united clerical and anti-Semitic parties.

FILITZ Nonsense!

EBENWALD That old spirit of '48!

WENGER Excuse me, for me there are no religious and no national differences at all. I am a man of science. I abhor —

SCHREIMANN We all abhor!

BERNHARDI *and* CYPRIAN *enter.*

BERNHARDI *in high spirits, his manner of speaking even more humorous and ironic than usual, but not entirely ingenuous.*

As he enters he takes the newspapers from the servant who opened the door for him. Good evening, gentlemen. Here, please, help yourselves. I beg your pardon for being a bit late, I hope the gentlemen amused themselves in the meantime.

General greetings. Bernhardi immediately takes his place at the upper end of the table, the others gradually sit down. Some of them smoke.

BERNHARDI I call the meeting to order. Before I proceed to the agenda, I want, in the name of the Elisabethinum, to extend a most cordial welcome to our new member, who is attending his first staff meeting today, and an extraordinary one at that. Permit me at once to express the hope that Doctor Wenger will feel comfortable in our midst, that he will find further occasion to demonstrate his proven loyalty in his new, more responsible position, and that he will develop into what every single one of us is, a shining light of our Institute. *The jest meets with no response* Doctor Wenger, once again, on behalf of everyone here, I bid you a cordial welcome.

WENGER Most esteemed Director, most esteemed colleagues! It would be immodest of me to lay claim to your valuable time with a long speech —

EBENWALD and SCHREIMANN Quite right!

WENGER So I will content myself with expressing my most heartfelt thanks for the high honor — *Unrest.*

SCHREIMANN *stands up* In view of the late hour, I move that our esteemed colleague, Doctor Wenger, postpone his doubtlessly very substantial speech of thanks until our next meeting so we can proceed to our agenda immediately.

THE OTHERS Agreed! Right!

SCHREIMANN *shakes Wenger's hand, a few others do likewise.*

BERNHARDI Gentlemen, I have taken it upon myself to convene this extraordinary meeting and must, first of all, ask you to excuse my having done so at such short notice; all the more reason for me to express my satisfaction that the gentlemen have all come.

ADLER Löwenstein's missing.

BERNHARDI I hope he will still come. I see in this new evidence of the great, I might say patriotic interest which all of you bring to our Institute, evidence of our cohesion as colleagues, which endures regardless of occasional differences concerning details of the sort which, after all, are not entirely to be avoided in larger bodies, all the less so the more the body is composed of prominent individuals. *Unrest* But that we are of one mind in essential questions, that has already been demonstrated more than once and will hopefully be proven in the future as well, to the joy of our true benefactors and the frustration of our enemies! As you know, we have those too. Gentlemen, I don't think I need fear your reproach that I am torturing your curiosity since you all know why I took it upon myself to call you here. Still, it is my obligation to read to you a letter which was delivered to me this morning via registered mail, return receipt requested.

FILITZ Listen!

BERNHARDI *reads* "Highly esteemed —" etc., etc. "I have the honor of informing you that the members of the Board —" etc., etc.— "have resolved unanimously to resign their honorary positions. In informing you of this resolution, most esteemed Director, I also request that you bring it to the notice of the esteemed members of the senior staff and the faculty. Permit me —" etc. etc. — "Councilor Winkler as Secretary."

EBENWALD *bends over the letter.*

BERNHARDI Please. *The letter is passed around, Bernhardi smiles* Gentlemen, I hope you'll be satisfied that I've not suppressed a single syllable of this most interesting document. The Board has resigned, and the agenda of our meeting today reads, logically: the position of the Directorate and the

Plenary Committee in response to this fact. Professor Ebenwald desires the floor.

EBENWALD I ask the Director if he knows the reason which induced the Board to resign, a question all the more justified in that the Board kept completely silent about it in its letter.

PFLUGFELDER *disgusted* Ecch!

BERNHARDI I could respond with another question, does Professor Ebenwald or any of the other gentlemen not know the reason? But since we all have a number of things to do outside this room —

CYPRIAN Quite right!

BERNHARDI — and the discussion should not be dragged out unnecessarily, I will respond to Vice-Director Professor Ebenwald's inquiry with due brevity: Yes, I know the reason. The reason lies in that same incident of which you read a description in the evening papers just now, with greater or lesser pleasure, in the form of a so-called interpellation.

SCHREIMANN The interpellation is not relevant here.

BERNHARDI Quite right. In my view it's not relevant in Parliament either —

PFLUGFELDER Very good.

BERNHARDI Since this interpellation, pertaining to an incident, gentlemen, witnesses to which are present here, and for which I bear full responsibility, distorts that incident in a factional manner and for the purposes of a certain party —

FILITZ What party?

PFLUGFELDER The anti-Semitic clerical party —

FILITZ Nonsense!

BERNHARDI A certain party, over whose character none of us here are in doubt, however varied our feelings towards it —

PFLUGFELDER Very good!

BERNHARDI — distorts it in a factional manner. I might add that I am not here to justify myself, no matter to whom; rather I stand before you as Director of this establishment for the purpose of asking you how we are to respond to the fact of the Board's resignation. Professor Cyprian has the floor.

CYPRIAN *beginning in his monotonous manner* A few years ago, I happened to be on a vacation trip in Holland, I was standing in an art museum — *unrest* What's the matter, gentlemen?

SCHREIMANN In view of the late hour I would like to ask Professor Cyprian most urgently not to tell anecdotes today but rather to get to the point as quickly as possible.

CYPRIAN It wasn't going to be an anecdote, it was in the profoundest sense — But, as you wish, gentlemen. So, the Board has resigned. We all know the reason, or rather the excuse, since we all know that Bernhardi, when he denied the priest entry into the sick-room, acted solely in the exercise of his duty as a doctor. All of us would have acted exactly the same in a similar situation.

FILITZ Oho!

EBENWALD You at any rate have not done so yet.

SCHREIMANN It was the first time for Director Bernhardi too, as far as we know.

FILITZ Very true.

CYPRIAN If we've never done it, gentlemen, it is only because so acute a situation as the one in which Professor Bernhardi found himself recently seldom presents itself. It would not occur to anyone to deny that countless faithful souls awaiting death have found peace and strength in the sacrament of extreme unction or that even skeptics have found these in the consoling words of a kind priest; and in no case where a priest is desired by the dying person or his relatives has a doctor ever denied him access.

FILITZ Not bad!

CYPRIAN But the priest's appearing at the sick-bed against the will of the dying patient or against the well-founded objections of those responsible for him in his last hours must be termed at least an inadmissible encroachment of pastoral care, the averting of which is not only permitted in certain cases but may, indeed, become an obligation. And such a case, gentlemen, is the one we are confronted with here. And therefore I repeat with total conviction: We would all have acted like Bernhardi — you too, Professor Ebenwald — you too, Professor Filitz.

FILITZ No!

CYPRIAN Or, more precisely, we would have had to, at least if we had yielded to our basic impulses. Only secondary considerations of the possible consequences would have induced us to let the priest in. Bernhardi's mistake, if we even want to call it that, consisted, then, only in his not thinking about the consequences, in his following medical and human impulses, which all of us must approve, as doctors and as human beings. As a result, only one reply to the Board's letter strikes me as suitable, that is, unanimously to express our fullest confidence in our Director, Professor Bernhardi.

PFLUGFELDER Bravo!

ADLER *nods, but somewhat undecidedly.*

WENGER *glances at Adler, then at the others.*

BERNHARDI Vice-Director Ebenwald has the floor.

EBENWALD Gentlemen, let's not fool ourselves. As matters stand today, the Board's resignation is pretty much the worst thing that could happen to our Institute. I do not hesitate to call it a catastrophe. Yes, indeed, gentlemen, a catastrophe. Whether the Board had the right, in an ethical sense, to resign is something I would rather not get into. We have not met here to treat religious questions, as Professor Cyprian found it necessary to do, or to criticize Prince Konstantin, or His Eminence, or Bank Director Veith and so on. We are simply faced with the fact that the patrons of our Institute, to whom we are so indebted for their help, both tangible and intangible, and on whose continued tangible and intangible support we are dependent, *objections* — we are, gentlemen

— and that these patrons have turned their backs on us; and we are faced with the additional indisputable fact that our esteemed Director, Professor Bernhardi, bears the sole responsibility for this misfortune.

BERNHARDI I'll bear it.

EBENWALD And I feel we would be not only acting with a complete lack of gratitude towards the Board, but also downright undermining our Institute if we declared our solidarity with the Director's conduct at a time when, certainly without ill intent but in a most unthinking fashion nonetheless, he has brought the Elisabethinum to the edge of the abyss. *Uproar* I repeat, to the edge of the abyss. I am, therefore, not only against Professor Cyprian's proposed vote of confidence in Professor Bernhardi but, rather, move that we give suitable expression to our regrets concerning the said incident and emphasize that we most sharply disapprove of the Director's conduct towards His Reverence. *He shouts over the increasing noise* I move further that the Board be informed of this resolution in an appropriate manner and that it be requested, in consideration thereof, to withdraw its resignation. *Great uproar.*

BERNHARDI Gentlemen! *Disturbance. He begins again* Gentlemen! In order to prevent any misunderstanding, let me state at once not only that motions of censure will, in light of their predictability, have no effect on me, but also that I am in the pleasant position of being able to dispense with official indications of confidence. Still, to save you from taking steps which you may well regret afterwards, I would like to tell to you that before long we will probably not need a board any more. We are fairly assured of receiving a government subvention of considerable size in the very near future and, what is probably of even greater importance in the long run, the nationalization of our Institute is receiving the most serious consideration by the relevant authorities, as His Excellency gave me to understand again only yesterday.

EBENWALD Ballroom conversation.

CYPRIAN *stands up* I must say, a few days ago His Excellency also told me —

FILITZ None of that is relevant here.

SCHREIMANN Idle speculation!

EBENWALD A subvention now, after this business!

FILITZ After this interpellation! *Considerable uproar.*

BERNHARDI *strongly* You forget, gentlemen, that this interpellation will be suitably answered. And how this answer will turn out, of that we can admit no doubt, that is, without it signaling our mistrust of the Minister of Education, who has most likely been informed about the machinations which led up to this interpellation.

FILITZ Not from one side, I hope.

SCHREIMANN The interpellation is not on the table.

FILITZ Quite right. There is a motion before us.

SCHREIMANN Put it to a vote!

CYPRIAN *to Bernhardi, softly* Yes, put it to a vote first.

BERNHARDI Gentlemen! There are two motions before us. The one by Professor Ebenwald to the end —

LÖWENSTEIN *enters.*

LÖWENSTEIN Gentlemen, I've just come from Parliament. *Stirring* The interpellation has been answered.

EBENWALD I ask for the vote, Mr. Director.

CYPRIAN I thought we had sworn off these parliamentary games, gentlemen. Surely we all want to know —

SCHREIMANN *who has noticed Löwenstein's bewildered expression* I believe I'm speaking for everyone present if I ask the Director to suspend the official meeting for a few minutes to give our colleague Löwenstein the opportunity of giving us a more detailed report about the answer to the interpellation.

BERNHARDI   The gentlemen are all in agreement? Then I'll suspend the meeting for a short while.   *Humorously* Löwenstein, you have the floor.

LÖWENSTEIN   There is — there will be an investigation launched against you for obstructing religion. *Corresponding stirring.*

PFLUGFELDER   But that's impossible!

CYPRIAN   Löwenstein!

SCHREIMANN   Oh!

ADLER   Obstructing religion?

CYPRIAN   Tell us, won't you?

EBENWALD   Doctor Löwenstein will perhaps be so kind as to give us more precise information.

BERNHARDI   *stands motionless.*

LÖWENSTEIN   What is there to inform? The investigation is to be launched! A disgrace! You've gotten what you wanted.

FILITZ   No invectives, dear Löwenstein.

CYPRIAN   So talk!

LÖWENSTEIN   What could possibly be of further interest to you, gentlemen? You'll read the particulars in the papers tomorrow morning. The essential part of the debate was the conclusion, and now you know what that was. That His Excellency was obviously driving at something completely different in the beginning, that's incidental.

CYPRIAN   Driving at what?

SCHREIMANN   My dear colleague, do try, if possible, in a coherent way —

LÖWENSTEIN   Very well, I assure you, gentlemen, in the beginning one had to have the impression that the gentlemen raising the issue were about to suffer a humiliating defeat. The Minister spoke of our Director's great merits and explicitly emphasized that there could be absolutely no question of any intent on his part, that Professor Bernhardi is a complete stranger to political activity, that there exists no reason to staff public positions other than according to worth and merit. And at this point there were already interruptions: "Sure, if that's how it were!" and "Jewification of the university!" and the like. With that the Minister drifted from his theme somehow, became as it seems angry and confused. Then he arrived somehow at the need for religious education, at the connection between a Christian world view and scientific progress, and he concluded suddenly — to his own surprise, I'm convinced — as I've already told you, with the information that he will enter into communication with his colleague, the Minister of Justice, *in a mocking tone* about whether the latter might not find cause to undertake a preliminary investigation of Professor Bernhardi for the offense of obstructing religion, and in this way — this is more or less how he put it — to accomplish, in a totally irreproachable manner, a clarification of the specific incident censured by the gentlemen, one satisfactory in equal measure to all parties in the House and to the population at large.

PFLUGFELDER Disgraceful!

FILITZ Oho!

CYPRIAN And how did the House respond?

LÖWENSTEIN Quite a lot of applause, no objections as far as I heard — the speaker was congratulated.

ADLER It's not possible that you heard wrong, Löwenstein?

LÖWENSTEIN Please, you needn't believe me, you know.

CYPRIAN Nor does it concern us, basically.

FILITZ Well!

EBENWALD I think we can resume the meeting.

BERNHARDI *controlled* I believe I'm speaking for everyone here in expressing our thanks to Doctor Löwenstein for his kind report. I ask you gentlemen to calm down, and I call our meeting to order again. Gentlemen, as you rightly pointed out earlier, the interpellation is not on the table, nor is the reply. There are two motions before us.

EBENWALD I withdraw my motion.

Stirring. Adler brings Löwenstein up to date in a whisper.

EBENWALD That is, I make it part of another motion which strikes me as necessary to the interests of our Institute in view of the state of affairs resulting from the Minister's response.

CYPRIAN The Minister's response is not relevant here.

PFLUGFELDER The answer doesn't concern us at all.

EBENWALD So, I move for the suspension of our esteemed Director from the administration of the Elisabethinum pending the conclusion of the criminal investigation against him. *Great uproar.*

PFLUGFELDER You should be ashamed of yourself, Ebenwald!

CYPRIAN You don't even know if any charge will be brought.

LÖWENSTEIN Unheard of!

CYPRIAN If you withdraw your first motion, mine still remains in effect, namely that we express our confidence —

PFLUGFELDER *interrupts* What do the interpellation and the reply to it concern us? It's an external affair.

EBENWALD *bellowing* Will you keep in mind that we are in danger of making ourselves ridiculous in front of the entire world if we continue with out deliberations and resolutions here, in the face of the possibility that all our resolutions will be nullified at the first opportunity by a higher court?

CYPRIAN Excuse me, Ebenwald, that is nonsense.

ADLER Who has the right to nullify our resolutions anyway?

LÖWENSTEIN Professor Bernhardi is and remains Director of the Elisabethinum. No one can remove him.

FILITZ He no longer is for me!

CYPRIAN *to Bernhardi* Put my motion to a vote.
Stirring.

BERNHARDI I will duly — *Disturbance.*

ADLER *very agitated* Gentlemen, let me say just a few words. If the investigation which the Minister of Education and Religion made more likely should result in a trial, my testimony, among others, will be indispensable, since I was a witness to the incident. And not only I, but everyone here knows that the incident in question was described by the interpellating gentlemen in a manner not entirely corresponding to the truth. But precisely because I am convinced to the depths of my soul of Professor Bernhardi's innocence, indeed, can attest to it —

BERNHARDI I thank you.

ADLER — precisely for that reason I welcome — and all of us, regardless of party affiliation, must welcome the fact —

SCHREIMANN There is no party affiliation!

ADLER — that this matter is to be cleared up before the general public through an official investigation. And we, here, should not create the impression that we are anticipating the final verdict by means of any premature partisanship prior to the conclusion of the judicial investigation, a verdict which we know cannot turn out other than favorably for Professor Bernhardi. If, therefore, I support the motion of the Vice-Director, Professor Ebenwald, for the suspension of the Director — *Disturbance.*

FILITZ Bravo!

ADLER — I beg you all, and above all the esteemed Professor Bernhardi, to view this as proof of my confidence in him — and of my conviction that Professor Bernhardi will emerge untainted from the investigation instituted against him.

CYPRIAN But Doctor Adler, by doing that you're admitting the justification for such an investigation being instituted in the first place.

FILITZ Who doesn't admit that?

LÖWENSTEIN On the basis of a denunciation like that —

FILITZ That remains to be seen.

PFLUGFELDER The Minister's obsequiousness! He crawls before the clericals!

LÖWENSTEIN It's not the first time either!

CYPRIAN *to Bernhardi* Call for the vote on my motion!

BERNHARDI Gentlemen! *Disturbance.*

SCHREIMANN Can this still be called a meeting? A coffee house without the billiards!

FILITZ Professor Ebenwald's motion is the more far-reaching, it has to be voted on first.

BERNHARDI Gentlemen! I have a question to direct to Vice-Director Professor Ebenwald.

SCHREIMANN What's the meaning of this?

FILITZ This is inadmissible under the rules of order.

PFLUGFELDER Childish parliamentary games!

BERNHARDI It will be the business of Professor Ebenwald to answer my question or not.

EBENWALD Please.

BERNHARDI I ask you, Professor Ebenwald, if it is known to you that this interpellation, the response to which on the part of the Minister causes you to move for my suspension — if you know that I could have prevented this interpellation?

LÖWENSTEIN Listen!

SCHREIMANN Don't answer!

BERNHARDI If you are a man, Professor Ebenwald, then you will answer. *Stirring.*

EBENWALD Gentlemen, Professor Bernhardi's question comes as no surprise to me. Actually, I've been expecting it during this entire remarkable meeting. But you will not hold it against me if, in light of the peculiar tone which the Director is pleased to adopt towards me, I decline to answer him directly but, instead, provide you all with information as to what lies behind this somewhat insinuating inquiry. *Unrest, tension* So, gentlemen, shortly after that incident which put our Institute in such an awkward position, I took the liberty of calling upon the Director to express to him my fear that Parliament might perhaps use the opportunity to take up this incident in a manner most detrimental to the interests of our Institute. You know our Institute has always had enemies, and it has even more today than some of you suspect. Because there are still a few among you, gentlemen, who do not know how to reckon with the shifting currents of time and public sentiments, and in public establishments one must reckon with them, whether one finds these currents to be legitimate from a philosophical standpoint or not. The fact is there are many people who do not find it proper that in an institute where a Prince and a Bishop are trustees, and where statistically eighty-five percent of the patients are Catholic, a majority of the attending physicians belong to another confession. That simply makes for bad blood in certain circles.

LÖWENSTEIN But the money we get, eighty percent of that also comes from that other confession.

EBENWALD That is besides the point. The main thing is the patients. So, as you know, there was the question recently of who should get Professor Tugendvetter's department. Professor Hell from Graz or Assistant Professor Wenger. I may speak of it, I assume, in spite of our esteemed colleague's presence, since he knows this himself. Hell is above all an able general practitioner, our colleague Wenger has worked primarily in the theoretical area. Naturally he could not have as much practical experience yet as Hell; that too will come in time. So, now picture this, gentlemen, a good friend comes to one —

PFLUGFELDER Or a cousin —

EBENWALD — can be a cousin too — and tells him: "Say, this will attract attention, your voting a Jew into the Elisabethinum again, especially now after this embarrassing incident that all Vienna is talking about. And it could happen to you that Parliament will attack you." Well, gentlemen, do you find it all that blameworthy if one then goes to the Director, as I did, and tells him, let's take Hell, rather, who is no dog, after all, in order to avert potential trouble?

WENGER Quite right! *Laughter.*

EBENWALD See, you can hear it yourselves! Perhaps I would have done better by going to Doctor Wenger and asking him to withdraw his candidacy. But I don't like subterfuge. And so I went straight to the Director. So, that is what's behind Professor Bernhardi's question to me, which was most likely supposed to make me sink into the ground. And it is true that we might have been spared the interpellation if Hell were sitting here today instead of Wenger. Well, I don't want to say it would have been too good to be true, but it was not to be. And now we're in a pretty mess. That's all I have to say.

PFLUGFELDER Bravo, Bernhardi!

BERNHARDI Gentlemen, Professor Ebenwald has, following some well-known models, answered my question more in a popular than in a pertinent way. However, each of you will know what to think about the affair. To defend myself for not having agreed to the deal proposed to me —

SCHREIMANN Oho!

BERNHARDI I take the liberty of calling it a deal with at least as much right as my conduct towards His Reverence is called obstructing religion.

PFLUGFELDER Very good.

BERNHARDI But, be that as it may, I must plead guilty — guilty that I, as Director of the Institute, did not do everything possible to prevent an interpellation that seems designed to disparage the reputation of our Institute among all hypocrites and fools. And, in order to accept the consequences voluntarily, as well as to prevent further delay, I hereby resign the direction of the Institute!

A great commotion.

CYPRIAN Are you crazy?

LÖWENSTEIN You mustn't do that!

PFLUGFELDER It has to be put to a vote.

BERNHARDI What for? In favor of the suspension are Professor Ebenwald, Professor Filitz, the Assistant Professors Schreimann and Adler —

LÖWENSTEIN That's only four.

BERNHARDI And I want to spare Doctor Wenger any crisis of conscience. He would support me out of gratitude, perhaps, because I recently voted for him, and I do not wish in the end to be beholden to a motive of that sort for what is the not quite unquestionable honor of remaining your Director for the future.

SCHREIMANN Oho!

FILITZ That is going too far!

CYPRIAN But what are you doing?

PFLUGFELDER This is your fault, Adler.

LÖWENSTEIN It has to be put to a vote.

PFLUGFELDER It would be desertion!

BERNHARDI Desertion?

CYPRIAN You have to wait for the vote.

LÖWENSTEIN I call the question!

BERNHARDI No, I will not permit a vote, I will submit to no judgment.

FILITZ Especially since it has already been pronounced.

SCHREIMANN Has Professor Bernhardi resigned the Directorship or not?

BERNHARDI Yes.

SCHREIMANN Consequently, in accordance with the bylaws, Professor Ebenwald, as Vice-Director, has now to take over the running of the Institute and, above all, the running of this meeting as well.

LÖWENSTEIN This is unheard of!

FILITZ Of course.

PFLUGFELDER Does one have to put up with this?

CYPRIAN Bernhardi! Bernhardi!

EBENWALD Since Professor Bernhardi has, to our regret, resigned his position as Director, in accordance with paragraph 7 of our bylaws, I hereby take over the direction of the Elisabethinum and, at the same time, the chair of the meeting still in progress. I ask you, gentlemen, for the same confidence which you showed the departing Director in such copious measure. I hope to prove myself worthy of the same, and give the floor to Professor Filitz.

LÖWENSTEIN Infamous!

PFLUGFELDER You are not the Director, Professor Ebenwald, not yet! *Disturbance.*

FILITZ We are now faced with the question of who is to take over the direction of Professor Bernhardi's department.

CYPRIAN Say, what's the idea?

BERNHARDI Gentlemen, I may no longer be its Director, but I am a member of the Institute, as much as any of you, and Head of my Department.

ADLER That goes without saying.

WENGER Certainly.

CYPRIAN On that point there can be no discussion at all.

SCHREIMANN It would undoubtedly lead to trouble if the suspended Director of the Institute —

LÖWENSTEIN He is not suspended.

CYPRIAN He has resigned the Directorship.

FILITZ Not entirely voluntarily.

PFLUGFELDER He threw it in your faces!

EBENWALD Order, order, gentlemen!

BERNHARDI *who has now completely lost his composure* No one has the right, of course, to relieve me of the direction of my department, but I will take vacation until this business is over.

CYPRIAN What are you doing?

BERNHARDI — Will take vacation —

EBENWALD It's granted.

BERNHARDI Thank you! And for the duration of my absence I entrust my erstwhile assistants, the Doctors Kurt Pflugfelder and Oskar Bernhardi, with the temporary direction of my department.

EBENWALD I have no objection to that.

BERNHARDI And now, gentlemen, I will begin my vacation and have the honor of taking my leave.

LÖWENSTEIN I likewise.

CYPRIAN *takes his hat.*

BERNHARDI That would suit these gentlemen just fine. I beg of you, stay!

PFLUGFELDER And you stay, above all!

BERNHARDI Here?

ADLER Professor, I would be unhappy if you misinterpreted my actions. It's important to me to express here, in front of everyone, the exceptional respect I feel for you.

BERNHARDI Thank you so much. Who is not with me is against me. Good evening, gentlemen. *Exits.*

PFLUGFELDER *speaks amid growing disturbance which he is often obliged to shout over* And you're letting him go, gentlemen? I ask you one last time, come to your senses. You must not let Bernhardi go. Put aside everything personal. Forgive me, too, if I was too vehement before. Just take a look back, think about how this whole unhappy story began, and you will have to come to your senses. A poor mortal lies deathly ill in the hospital, a young creature is paying a high enough price for her little bit of youth and joy and sin, if you will, with agony and torment and with her very life. In her final hours she becomes euphoric. She feels well, she is happy again, she has no inkling of her impending death. She thinks herself recovered! She dreams that her lover will come to pick her up, lead her out of the halls of misery and suffering and into life and happiness. Perhaps it was the most beautiful dream of her life, her last dream. And out of this dream Bernhardi did not want her awakened into a terrible reality. That is his fault! This is the crime he committed! This and nothing more. He asked the priest to let the poor girl drift off. Asked. You all know it. Even if he had been less courteous, everyone would have to forgive him. What a monstrous mendacity is required in order to see the entire incident other than as a purely humane one. Where is the person whose religious sensibilities would truly have been offended by Bernhardi's behavior? And if there is one, who is to blame for it but those who have taken this incident, maliciously distorted it, and disseminated it far and wide? Who, gentlemen, but those in whose interest it happened to lie that religious sensibilities be offended, in whose interest it lies that there be people who offend religious sensibilities? And if there were no political climbing, parliamentary ploys, human pettiness, in a word, politics, would it ever have been possible to turn this case into an affair? Well, it has happened, gentlemen, because there are climbers, scoundrels, and wretches. But surely we don't want to belong to any of these categories, gentlemen. What blindness drives us, drives you, doctors, human beings, accustomed to stand at deathbeds, us, who have been granted insight into real misery, into the essence behind all appearances, what blindness drives you to be a party to this deplorable fraud, to stage a ludicrous parliamentary parody, with pro and con, with motions and subterfuges, with dirty looks up and down, with insincerities and fancy words — and persistently to avert your glance from the heart of things and out of narrow-minded considerations of the politics of the day to abandon a man who has done nothing beyond what is obviously right! Because I am far from praising him and making him out to be a hero simply because he is a man. And of you, gentlemen, I ask nothing more than that you be equally worthy of this modest title, consider the decisions and resolutions of this meeting today null and void and ask Professor Bernhardi again to assume the position which can have no better, no worthier representative than he. Call him back, gentlemen, I implore you, call him back.

EBENWALD May I ask if Professor Pflugfelder is finished with his little number? It seems so. With that, gentlemen, let us proceed with the agenda.

PFLUGFELDER Good day, gentlemen!

CYPRIAN Good-bye!

LÖWENSTEIN You no longer have a quorum, gentlemen.

SCHREIMANN We will not abandon the Institute.

FILITZ ·We will take responsibility for making our decisions without you.

PFLUGFELDER *opening the door* Ah, this really is fortunate! Doctor Hochroitzpointner, please, just step right in.

LÖWENSTEIN So much for your meeting, Vice-Director!

PFLUGFELDER Well, now the gentlemen are among friends. I wish you a pleasant time!

Cyprian, Pflugfelder, Löwenstein exit.

EBENWALD Do you want anything, Doctor Hochroitzpointner?

HOCHROITZPOINTNER Oh! *He stands at the door.*

EBENWALD Well then, close the door! *The door is closed* We will continue the meeting, gentlemen.

Curtain

FOURTH ACT

Drawing room at Bernhardi's. Doors in the background. Door to the right.

PFLUGFELDER *enters from the right, followed by* LÖWENSTEIN

LÖWENSTEIN *still off stage* Professor Pflugfelder!
PFLUGFELDER Ah, Löwenstein! But you're all out of breath.
LÖWENSTEIN I've been running after you from down the street. *Questioning* So, what's —
PFLUGFELDER Weren't you in court?
LÖWENSTEIN I was called away during the deliberation about the sentence. How long?
PFLUGFELDER Two months.
LÖWENSTEIN Two months, in spite of the priest's testimony? Is it possible?
PFLUGFELDER That testimony! It benefited only the priest himself. Bernhardi didn't derive the least advantage from it.
LÖWENSTEIN But that's — Why the priest?
PFLUGFELDER Didn't you hear the prosecutor's speech?
LÖWENSTEIN Only the beginning. Four times I was called away during the trial today. Other times one can wait days on end before it occurs to a patient —
PFLUGFELDER Well, well, you have nothing to complain about —
LÖWENSTEIN So, what happened with the prosecutor?
PFLUGFELDER Well, the priest's maintaining he felt not a shove but only a light touch on his shoulder provided the prosecutor with the welcome opportunity to praise His Reverence as a paragon of Christian forbearance and mildness and to use the occasion to sing the praises of the entire

priestly profession which could, if need be, live quite well without it, as you know.

LÖWENSTEIN Then Bernhardi was really convicted only on the basis of the testimony of this hysterical Sister Ludmilla and the squeaky clean Mister Hochroitzpointner?! After all, everyone else's testimony did exonerate him completely. I must really apologize to Adler. He behaved splendidly. And Cyprian! Not to mention your son!

CYPRIAN *enters. Greetings.*

PFLUGFELDER Where is Bernhardi?

LÖWENSTEIN Maybe they just kept him there?

CYPRIAN I imagine he'll come with Doctor Goldenthal.

PFLUGFELDER Is that right? He's bringing him, of all people?

CYPRIAN *surprised* I don't suppose we can do without the defense attorney during our consultation today.

PFLUGFELDER We should have done without him from the beginning.

LÖWENSTEIN Very true.

CYPRIAN What is it you have against him? He spoke excellently. Not very dashingly, perhaps —

PFLUGFELDER No, to be sure, one can't say that.

LÖWENSTEIN Goldenthal behaved like a heel, nor was it to be expected otherwise.

CYPRIAN Why not to be expected otherwise?

LÖWENSTEIN A convert! His wife wears a cross this big. His son he gets educated in Kalksburg, at the Jesuit School! Those are quite the people, all right!

CYPRIAN You really do get on a person's nerves with your one-track mind.

LÖWENSTEIN I am no ostrich, any more than I'm a kibbitzer. Doctor Goldenthal is one of those who is continuously afraid someone might, perhaps, still think — With a different lawyer the thing would have turned out differently.

CYPRIAN   I doubt that very much. Maybe with a different defendant.

PFLUGFELDER   What?

CYPRIAN   Well, we don't want to accuse Bernhardi after the fact, certainly not today. But that he didn't act especially intelligently today, not even his most ardent admirers could deny that.

LÖWENSTEIN   Why? I thought he was wonderful. To have kept his composure during this scoundrel Hochroitzpointner's testimony —

CYPRIAN   You call that composure? It was obstinacy.

LÖWENSTEIN   Obstinacy? Why obstinacy?

PFLUGFELDER   *to Cyprian*   He probably wasn't there when Bernhardi demanded that Ebenwald be subpoenaed.

LÖWENSTEIN   Ah!

CYPRIAN   You don't know that? And Minister Flint, too, he wanted to have subpoenaed.

LÖWENSTEIN   Splendid!

CYPRIAN   There was nothing splendid about it. What do Flint and Ebenwald have to do with the case?

LÖWENSTEIN   Come on, now —

CYPRIAN   Absolutely nothing. It looked like out and out sensationalism.

PFLUGFELDER   Well —

CYPRIAN   If we wanted to trace things that far back to their roots, what people would we not have had to summon to court today! It would have been an illustrious company, I tell you.

LÖWENSTEIN   Pity, pity!

KURT *enters*.

PFLUGFELDER   Kurt!

   Goes up to him, embraces him.

LÖWENSTEIN   *to Cyprian*   What moving family scene is this?

CYPRIAN You mean you don't know? Kurt called Hochroitz-pointner a liar in court.

LÖWENSTEIN What —

CYPRIAN And was fined two hundred crowns as punishment.

LÖWENSTEIN Dear Doctor Pflugfelder, may I give you a kiss too?

KURT Thank you very much, Doctor, I consider it given.

LÖWENSTEIN Then let me at least contribute to the two hundred crowns.

PFLUGFELDER We'll take care of it, all right. *To Kurt* But I'll tell you something, Kurt, if you happen to get it into your head to fight a duel with this person —

KURT Let him just try to challenge me. Then I'll bring the matter to a court of honor. And then let's see —

LÖWENSTEIN That'll be the last thing he does.

KURT That's what I'm afraid of too. However, the Hochroitz-pointner affair is not yet settled, even if the Bernhardi affair should be.

CYPRIAN Which we hope it's not.

LÖWENSTEIN What do you have in mind, Doctor Kurt?

DR. GOLDENTHAL *enters. A corpulent man of 45, curly hair tinged with gray and black mutton chops; dignified, somewhat unctuous and nasal.*

GOLDENTHAL Good evening, gentlemen.

CYPRIAN Where is Bernhardi?

GOLDENTHAL I advised the Doctor to leave the courthouse through a side entrance.

LÖWENSTEIN In order to escape the ovations intended for him?

GOLDENTHAL Patience, gentlemen, that too could still come.

CYPRIAN Well —

GOLDENTHAL After all, even if we didn't gain a victory —

LÖWENSTEIN No, we certainly can't claim that.

GOLDENTHAL It was, nevertheless, an honorable defeat.

PFLUGFELDER At least for those who are not going to jail.

GOLDENTHAL *laughs* Might you be referring to the defense attorney, Professor? Now that is one of the few injustices I've never felt a need to fight. *In a changed tone* But now, gentlemen, let's have a serious word together. Maybe it's just as well that the Professor is not here yet. You see, I wanted to ask you most urgently to support me to the best of your abilities during the deliberations that are before us.

CYPRIAN In what way?

GOLDENTHAL Our esteemed Professor Bernhardi is — how shall I put it — a bit obstinate. And unfortunately it showed in the course of the trial today. This notion of subpoenaing the Minister and his stubborn silence afterwards — it did not make a favorable impression! Let's not talk about it any further. But now Professor Bernhardi seems to want to go on playing the injured party and intends from the start to forego all legal remedies against the verdict, and the —

CYPRIAN I could see something like that coming.

LÖWENSTEIN And you want to file for a dismissal of the verdict, Doctor?

GOLDENTHAL Of course.

LÖWENSTEIN It would be hopeless.

PFLUGFELDER I know what we should do now. We should appeal to the public.

GOLDENTHAL Excuse me, Professor, the trial did not take place behind closed doors.

PFLUGFELDER We must talk to the people. That's what I mean. The folly was that we've kept our traps shut up to now. Look at the other side! The clerical papers agitated just as much as they could. They're the ones, in fact, who succeeded in having Bernhardi charged with a felony right off, instead of a misdemeanor, and brought before the jury that way. They didn't wait until the proceedings were over to start writing about the affair, the way our liberal papers obviously found it necessary to do.

LÖWENSTEIN They're simply too high class.

PFLUGFELDER One could call it something else at times too. But things just turned out as they unfortunately do so often in this world. What the crassness and hatred of the enemy could perhaps not have quite accomplished has been taken care of by the laxity and cowardice of our so-called friends.

CYPRIAN You want to speak to the people? To our fellow citizens? The jury today might really have given you a taste of what to expect.

PFLUGFELDER Maybe the proper words weren't found today to move them.

GOLDENTHAL Oh!

PFLUGFELDER Take me for a fool if you like, I believe in a basic sense of justice among those whose minds are free of legal distortions. I believe in the basic healthy common sense of the people.

LÖWENSTEIN Pflugfelder is right! We have to call meetings and explain the Bernhardi affair to the people.

CYPRIAN Meetings for the discussion of the Bernhardi affair might not be permitted.

PFLUGFELDER Other opportunities will present themselves. The State House elections are coming up.

CYPRIAN Are you running, perhaps?

PFLUGFELDER No, but I will speak. And I will not fail to —

CYPRIAN What are you going to speak? You'll be forced to belabor the obvious.

PFLUGFELDER I don't care. If our opponents have the audacity to deny the obvious, then nothing remains for us but to shout it out into the world again and again. The fear that the snobs might take the opportunity to call us phrasemongers must not induce us to abandon the field to the paradoxes and the lies.

LÖWENSTEIN   And it would be most advisable to consider whether Bernhardi shouldn't serve his two months in any event, in the interest of the thing. *Laughter.*

PFLUGFELDER   Certainly, the infamy perpetrated against him would become more evident.

BERNHARDI *and* OSKAR *come in.*

BERNHARDI   *in very high spirits, since he still heard the others laughing* These are fine goings-on here! Count me in. Forgive me for keeping you waiting. *General shaking of hands.*

CYPRIAN   So, did you manage to escape the ovations?

BERNHARDI   Not entirely. As a precaution, a number of — gentlemen were waiting at the side door and gave me a proper reception.

LÖWENSTEIN   Did they unharness your horses?

BERNHARDI   "Down with the Jews!" they yelled. "Down with the Freemasons!"

LÖWENSTEIN   Listen to that!

BERNHARDI   You will join me for dinner, won't you, gentlemen? Will you see if there's enough, Oskar? My housekeeper, you see, has given notice. Her confessor explained to her that she couldn't possibly stay in a house such as this without the greatest danger to her salvation! It will be somewhat frugal, naturally, as befits the table of a convicted criminal. Why, Oskar! I do believe the boy has tears in his eyes. *Softer* Let's not get sentimental.

OSKAR   I'm only furious. *Exits, returns soon.*

ADLER *enters.*

BERNHARDI   Welcome. Doctor Adler. A repentant sinner is more pleasing to my sight than ten righteous men.

ADLER *lightly* I was never a sinner, Professor. Let me emphasize again, this trial struck me as being a necessity from the very beginning, although I could certainly not foresee that Mr. Hochroitzpointner would have more credibility in court than Professor Cyprian and I.

CYPRIAN We can't complain. The priest himself didn't do any better.

GOLDENTHAL Yes indeed, gentlemen, the priest! That was a remarkable, in a certain sense perhaps even an historical moment, when His Reverence testified, and — only in response to my question, of course — expressed his conviction that Professor Bernhardi had not intended any demonstration of hostility against the Catholic church. One can judge how strong certain currents in our population must be if not even the testimony of the priest was able to help our cause.

BERNHARDI Had His Reverence had reason to fear that, he would have testified differently in any case.

GOLDENTHAL Oh, Professor! How can you assume that a servant of the Church would ever knowingly speak an untruth?

PFLUGFELDER Wouldn't be the first time.

ADLER I believe you're doing the priest an injustice, Professor. His words, his very bearing attested to a kind of sympathy for you. This is no ordinary person. Even that time in the sick-room I had that impression.

BERNHARDI Sympathy! I'll believe that only if there's some risk attached to demonstrating it.

GOLDENTHAL I doubt that his testimony today will be of any particular advantage to His Reverence's future career. Be that as it may, let's hope he'll be put in a position to bear witness again; and then, Professor, if justice is done to you, you too will judge more justly.

BERNHARDI I've already told you, Doctor, I decline all legal remedies. The trial today was a farce. I will not subject myself to these people or their like again. Besides, you know as well as I do, Doctor, that it would be completely hopeless.

GOLDENTHAL Excuse me! How the higher courts will act is by no means —

PFLUGFELDER The higher up the worse.

GOLDENTHAL Gentlemen, it will not have escaped you either that in the course of recent months certain changes have begun to be noticeable on the political horizon.

LÖWENSTEIN I notice nothing of the kind. It gets worse all the time.

GOLDENTHAL I'm sorry, I feel a more liberal breeze gradually beginning to blow across our fatherland again — and a second trial could take place under a less overcast sky.

BERNHARDI And what would be the most I could achieve? An acquittal. That is no longer enough for me. If I only get my rights then I'm still far from even with Messrs. Flint, Ebenwald and company.

GOLDENTHAL My esteemed Professor, as I already told you, there are no judicial procedures for the charges you want to bring against these men.

BERNHARDI People will believe me, even without judicial procedures.

GOLDENTHAL But the guilt of these men, in a legal sense, can simply not be established.

BERNHARDI Which is precisely why I'm dispensing with any further legal intervention in the case.

GOLDENTHAL It is my duty, Professor, to warn you against any overly hasty decision. I do so in front of witnesses. I understand that the injustice perpetrated against you makes your blood boil. But the path that you now seem inclined to take is strewn only with new trials —

CYPRIAN And most likely new convictions.

BERNHARDI People will know where the truth lies, exactly as they know it today.

PFLUGFELDER Whatever your intentions, you can count on me.

LÖWENSTEIN On me too. And I think we have to target the entire system.

PFLUGFELDER We have to send Flint to the devil.

GOLDENTHAL But gentlemen!

LÖWENSTEIN Oh, yes, this Flint, in whom you placed such high hopes, and who's now become merely the clericals' handyman. This so-called man of science, under whom the priestlings have grown more insolent than ever. If things continue like this he'll deliver the entire school system to the black brood, this Minister of Religion and Hypocrisy!

GOLDENTHAL Excuse me, it is a well-known fact that unquestionably liberal journalists have equal access to the Ministry of Education. And as to certain measures of the Minister's to which you are obviously alluding, gentlemen, I must say, at the risk of incurring your displeasure, that I do not find them quite so objectionable.

PFLUGFELDER What, you're in favor of obligatory confession for school children? You're for the establishment of a Catholic university, Doctor?

GOLDENTHAL Look, I'm not saying that I would send my sons to be educated there.

LÖWENSTEIN Why not, Doctor? It'll be possible for them to go there straight from Kalksburg with no difficulty whatever.

GOLDENTHAL Kalksburg, gentlemen, is one of the most outstanding schools in Austria. And I am glad for this opportunity to state that even among the clerics, so much maligned in some quarters, there can be found men of intellectual substance and, indeed, as was proven today, courageous and noble human beings. And my principle has always been, even during the most bitter struggle: respect for the convictions of my adversary.

LÖWENSTEIN The convictions of Minister Flint!

GOLDENTHAL He happens to be protecting all convictions. And that is his obligation atop the watchtower upon which providence has placed him. Believe me, gentlemen, there are things one should not stir up — and should not allow to be stirred up.

PFLUGFELDER Why not, if I may ask? The world has made progress altogether only because someone had the courage to stir up things which people whose interest lay elsewhere had maintained for centuries must not be stirred up.

GOLDENTHAL Your ingenious proposition will hardly prove supportable as a general rule and, in any event, it is not applicable to our affair since causing the world to progress was, as he will readily admit, the last thing on our esteemed friend Bernhardi's mind.

LÖWENSTEIN Perhaps one day it will turn out that he has done so anyway.

BERNHARDI Oh my! Where are you drifting off to?!

PFLUGFELDER As things stand, we can only deal with your case from a general standpoint. Your opponents started it. The prosecutor had no qualms either. Or didn't you notice that, Doctor?

GOLDENTHAL I was unable to follow the prosecutor on to that field. It is not my job to get involved in politics but to defend.

PFLUGFELDER If you had at least done that.

BERNHARDI But Pflugfelder, I will not permit —

GOLDENTHAL Oh, let it go, Professor, the thing is beginning to interest me. So, you find that I did not defend my client?

PFLUGFELDER In my less than expert opinion, no. To listen to you, one would really have had to believe the religious feelings of the entire Catholic world, from those of His Holiness the Pope to those of the humblest devotee in the most out-of-the-way village, had been most profoundly offended by Bernhardi's conduct towards the priest. And instead of simply explaining that every physician would have to act as Bernhardi did, and that only a simpleton or a knave could dispute this, you found it necessary to excuse as an act of thoughtlessness what was merely his duty as a doctor. You treated those malicious idiots on the jury, who were determined from the first moment to find Bernhardi guilty, like the finest minds in the country, and the judges, who brought Bernhardi's sentence with them in their briefcases, so to speak, like paragons of sagacity and righteousness. You even handled that scoundrel Hochroitzpointner and Sister Ludmilla with kid gloves and went so far as to concede the good faith of these false witnesses. And you did not act any differently than if you, you, Doctor Goldenthal, yourself believed deep in your soul in the indispensability and power of that sacrament which Bernhardi allegedly offended, and you let it appear that our friend Bernhardi was at bottom very wrong not to believe in it too. Always at first a polite inclining of the head towards your client and then a deep bow to where his enemies stood, to stupidity, slander, hypocrisy. If Bernhardi is satisfied with that, then that's his business. As for me, Doctor Goldenthal, I am unable to muster up the necessary understanding for this kind of defense.

GOLDENTHAL And I, Professor, must rejoice that you have dedicated your great talents to medicine and not to jurisprudence, because with your temperament and your conception of the dignity of the courtroom, you would undoubtedly have succeeded in bringing even the most innocent of clients to prison.

LÖWENSTEIN You're managing that too, Doctor, in spite of your gratifying lack of temperament.

BERNHARDI But this really is enough now. I must ask you — *The door to the dining-room is opened.*

GOLDENTHAL *with a warding-off gesture* My esteemed Professor, happy the man who can call such friends his own. For my part, I will gladly bear the reproach that I am not one of those unscrupulous defense attorneys who for the sake of a rhetorical effect expose their clients to the resentment of their judges. But it goes without saying, Professor, that I have no intention of forcing my advice on you any further, and I leave it to —

CYPRIAN *to Pflugfelder* You see!

BERNHARDI What are you doing, Doctor?

PFLUGFELDER If anyone should be leaving here, then of course it is I. I must also ask you to forgive me, Bernhardi, for letting myself get carried away; I cannot take anything back, of course. Not another word, Bernhardi, I'm superfluous here.

SERVANT *enters, whispers something to Bernhardi.*

BERNHARDI *very perplexed, hesitates a moment, about to turn to Cyprian but does not.*

PFLUGFELDER *has withdrawn in the meantime.*

BERNHARDI Pardon me, gentlemen, a visitor whom I cannot possibly refuse. I hope he will not be too long. Please, start eating. Oskar, please —

CYPRIAN *to Bernhardi* What is it?

BERNHARDI Later, later.

Oskar, Kurt, Löwenstein, Adler, Cyprian, Goldenthal go into the dining room.

BERNHARDI *to the servant* Show him in.

SERVANT *exits.*

BERNHARDI *draws the portière over the dining room door.*

THE PRIEST *enters.*

BERNHARDI *receiving him at the door* Please —

PRIEST Good evening, Professor.

BERNHARDI A condolence visit, Reverend?

PRIEST Not exactly. But I felt an irresistible need to speak to you before the day was over.

BERNHARDI I'm at your disposal, Reverend.

Offers him a chair, both sit.

PRIEST In spite of what was for you the unfavorable outcome of the trial, Professor, it should be clear to you that I do not share in the blame for your conviction.

BERNHARDI If I thanked you for having spoken the truth under oath, Reverend, I'd have to be afraid of insulting you. So —

PRIEST *somewhat out of humor already* I have not come for your thanks, Professor, although I did do more than merely give the answers I was obliged to give as a witness. If you'll be so kind as to remember, I responded without hesitation to one of your attorney's questions by stating that I was convinced you were not motivated by any overt hostility towards the Catholic church in your behavior to me back then, at the door to the sick-room.

BERNHARDI Your Reverence certainly exceeded the limits of your obligations with that, but perhaps you have your reward in the effect your testimony produced.

PRIEST Whether this effect may be characterized as being to my advantage everywhere outside the courtroom as well, Professor, is something we needn't discuss. But you may well imagine, Professor, that I have not come to recapitulate in private my testimony in court. What induces me to call on you today, at this late hour, is the fact that I have a — still more sweeping admission to make to you.

BERNHARDI A still more sweeping admission?

PRIEST Yes. In court I expressed my conviction that you did not act with hostile intent against me or against — that which I represent. But now I see myself obliged to admit to you further, Professor, that in this particular instance — understand me well, Professor — in the particular instance in question here, you acted absolutely correctly in your capacity as physician, that within the bounds of your duty, exactly as I within mine, you could not have acted otherwise.

BERNHARDI Have I understood you correctly? You're admitting to me that I acted absolutely — that I could not have acted otherwise?

PRIEST That as a physician you could not have acted otherwise.

BERNHARDI *after a pause* If this is your opinion, Reverend, then I must certainly say that a better opportunity, perhaps the only appropriate one for this admission presented itself a few hours ago.

PRIEST I needn't assure you that it was not a lack of courage that sealed my lips. Would I be here otherwise, Professor?

BERNHARDI What, then —

PRIEST That is what I want to tell you, Professor. What allowed me to remain silent in court was the insight, striking me with the power of divine inspiration, that I could, with one more word, inflict immeasurable harm on something truly sacred, indeed, to me the most sacred of all things.

BERNHARDI I cannot imagine that for a man as courageous as you are, Reverend, there can be anything more sacred than the truth.

PRIEST What? Nothing more sacred, Professor, than the trifling truth which I could perchance have pleaded to the end in this individual case? Surely you yourself don't mean that. Had I admitted in public not only your good intentions, in which I already went further than some well-wishers will forgive me for, but, beyond that, also have recognized your right to turn me away from the bed of a dying woman, a Christian, a sinner, then the enemies of our holy church would have exploited such a statement beyond all measure, for which I would then have been responsible. Because we do not have only honorable enemies, Professor, as I'm sure you are aware. And the trifling truth I would have spoken would thereby, in a higher sense, have turned into a lie. And what would have been the result? I would have stood before those to whom I must justify my behavior and whom I must obey, and before my God himself, not as an all too indulgent individual, no, but as an apostate, as a deserter. That is why I did not speak.

BERNHARDI And why are you doing so now, Reverend?

PRIEST Because at the moment that inspiration came over me I swore an oath to make a confession to you in person, as the only one to whom I might owe it, one which the public would have misunderstood and misinterpreted.

BERNHARDI For that I thank you, Reverend. And let us hope that you will never be in a position of having to testify in public in an affair where more is at stake than — my trifling fate. After all, it could happen that you will then also perceive as divine inspiration what strike me as being your highly personal scruples, and that a still higher truth would come to harm than the one you believe you must represent and protect.

PRIEST I can recognize no higher truth than my church, Professor. And my church's highest law is conformity and obedience. For if I am expelled from the community from whose work such infinite blessings radiate over the world, then for me, unlike for independent professional men such as you, Professor, for me the possibility of any meaningful work and with it my entire reason for living would be eliminated.

BERNHARDI It seems to me there have been priests whose reason for living began only when they freed themselves from their community and, without consideration of trouble or danger proclaimed what they held to be right and true.

PRIEST If I were one of those, Professor —

BERNHARDI Well?

PRIEST — then I imagine God would have let me say in court today what you may hear, only now, within these four walls.

BERNHARDI So it was God who sealed your lips there? And now God sends you to me so you can admit to me in private what you were forbidden to say in court? One must say, he arranges things quite comfortably for you, your God!

PRIEST *getting up* Excuse me, Professor, I have nothing to add to my admission, which you, oddly enough, seem to interpret as a confession of a wrong done to you. It was not part of my oath to get into a discussion with you on things about which we can hardly understand each other.

BERNHARDI And so you slam the door in my face, Reverend? At any rate, I don't recognize this as proving you to be on the inside and me on the outside. Anyway, nothing remains for me now, Reverend, but to regret that you took the trouble to come here in vain.

PRIEST *not without irony* In vain?

BERNHARDI That I was not able after all to absolve you as completely as you may, perhaps, have expected after so unusual a step.

PRIEST Absolution? I doubt I was concerned about that, Professor. Perhaps about reassurance. And this has come to me, in far greater measure than I even dared hope. Because now, Professor, I am beginning to see this whole affair in a new light. It is gradually becoming clear to me that I was mistaken about the real reason for my coming here, for my having been sent here.

BERNHARDI Oh!

PRIEST I had no confession to make to you as I believed at first, but to free myself of a doubt. A doubt, Professor, of which I was not yet aware as such when I entered this room. But now it is resolved, everything is clear, and what I admitted to you earlier, Professor, I'm very sorry, I have to take it back again.

BERNHARDI You're taking it back? That's a bit difficult now that I've accepted it.

PRIEST It is no longer valid. Because now I know, Professor, you were not in the right when you turned me away from the bed of that dying woman.

BERNHARDI Ah!

PRIEST Not you! Others in the same circumstances might have
been. But you are not one of these. I know that now. It is a
matter of self-deception at best if you think that what made
you deny me entry into that sick-room was a physician's
caring or human compassion. This compassion, this caring,
they were only pretexts: not fully conscious ones perhaps, but
still nothing more than pretexts.

BERNHARDI Pretexts? Suddenly you no longer know what you
knew and admitted to me only a few minutes ago, Reverend,
that there was an obligation imposed on me — as on you!?

PRIEST And I will continue to admit it to you. What I'm
disputing is that it was only out of this sense of responsibility
that you denied me entry to the death-room. The real reason
for your attitude towards me lay not in your sense of
responsibility, nor in the noble impulse of the moment, as
you perhaps imagine and as even I was close to believing, but
much deeper, in the roots of your very being. Yes, indeed,
Professor, the real reason was — how shall I put it — an
antipathy towards me, an uncontrollable antipathy — or
rather a hostility —

BERNHARDI Hostility?

PRIEST — against that which this garment here represents for
you and those like you. Oh, you've given me more than
enough evidence in the course of this conversation that it's
so. And now I know also that even back then, just like today,
your entire bearing, your every word, really did express
hostility against me, that insurmountable, profound hostility
which men of your sort cannot help feeling against people
like me.

BERNHARDI Hostility! You keep repeating it. And what if it
were! Everything I've been up against the past few weeks, all
the agitation against me, which you yourself perceive to be
mendacious and undeserved, could it not in retrospect justify
what you call hostility, if I really did feel something like that
before? And I will not deny that in the course of these past

few weeks, in spite of an innate, almost annoying tendency towards righteousness, I have felt an inkling of that hostility well up within me, not so much against you personally, Reverend, as against the crowd that has collected around you. But this I can swear to, Reverend, when I barred your entry into that sick-room, at that moment there was not a trace of this hostility in me. I faced you there in my capacity as physician with so pure a heart as ever some member of your profession could have while he performed a church ritual at the altar. With no less pure a heart than you faced me with — you who had come to bring my patient the last consolations of religion. You knew that when you came into my room before. You confessed it to me. You should not suddenly reject this perception again — because you feel what I also feel, and have never felt more strongly, perhaps, than at this moment, that we are separated by something — the existence of which we could not deceive ourselves about, even under friendlier circumstances.

PRIEST   And you never felt it more strongly than at this moment?

BERNHARDI   Yes, at this moment, when I am, probably, standing before — one of the freest men of your profession. But for that which separates us, and probably must separate us for all time, Reverend — for that "hostility" seems too poor and small a word. It is something of a higher nature, I think, and — a more hopeless one.

PRIEST   You might be right there, Professor. Hopeless. Just this time, just between you and me it turns out that way. I've had opportunities in the past to carry on similar conversations, touching upon certain not unobjectionable boundaries, with men from your circles, with — scholars, with enlightened men *somewhat ironic* but never did all communication seem to lie so beyond the realm of possibility as here. On the other hand, maybe on the evening of this particular day I should have avoided following your conversation to those boundaries.

BERNHARDI I hope you will show me enough respect, Reverend, not to attribute my manner of looking at the world to, say, a bad mood caused by my personal experiences of today.

PRIEST I'm far from that, Professor. When an abyss opens so unbridgeably, so deep between two men like you and me, both of whom may be without — *smiling* hostility, then I suppose there must be a deeper cause. And I see the cause in this, that while communication may be possible between faith and doubt, it is not between humility and — you will not take the word the wrong way, if you'll recall some of your earlier statements — between humility and arrogance.

BERNHARDI Arrogance?! And you, Reverend, who can find no milder word for what you suspect to be at the foundation of my soul, you think yourself free of hostility against — men of my sort?

PRIEST *wants to be somewhat more vehement at first, then, after briefly recollecting himself, with a barely perceptible smile* I know I am free of it. I, Professor, am commanded by my religion also to love those who hate me.

BERNHARDI *strongly* And I am commanded by mine — or by that which has settled into my heart in its stead — also to understand where I am not understood.

PRIEST I do not doubt your good will. But the understanding has its limits, Professor. Where the human intellect rules — I am sure you've experienced it often enough yourself — there is delusion and error. What does not deceive, what cannot deceive a person like me is — *hesitates* I prefer to choose a word at once which not even you will find objectionable, Professor, and that is — the inner feeling.

BERNHARDI Let's call it that, Reverend. This inner feeling, even though it may flow into my soul from different sources, I try to trust in it too, you know. What else remains for us to do in the end? And if it's not as easy for — one of us as for men of your calling, God, who created you so humble and me — so arrogant, this incomprehensible God will surely have his reasons for it.

PRIEST *looks at Bernhardi a long time; then, with a sudden resolve, extends his hand to him.*

BERNHARDI *hesitating, with a very slight smile* Across the abyss, Reverend?

PRIEST Let us not look down — for one moment!

BERNHARDI *shakes his hand.*

PRIEST Farewell, Professor!

He exits.

Bernhardi remains alone, seems undecided for a while, with a furrowed brow which becomes smooth again; makes a gesture as if he were shaking something off, then he pushes the portière aside and opens the door. The others are visible sitting at the table, some are already standing about and smoking.

CYPRIAN Finally!

ADLER We're having our cigars already.

CYPRIAN *coming out of the room, up to Bernhardi* What was it? A patient this late — today?

BERNHARDI That is difficult to answer.

OSKAR *coming out of the room* Here's a couple of telegrams that came for you, father.

BERNHARDI *opens one* Ah, that's nice.

CYPRIAN May I ask?

BERNHARDI A former patient who assures me of his sympathy. A poor devil who spent a few weeks with us in the Elisabethinum.

GOLDENTHAL May I see? Florian Ebeseder?

LÖWENSTEIN Ebeseder? Florian? But that sounds like a Christian.

PFLUGFELDER *touching his shoulder* It happens!

BERNHARDI *opening another telegram* Oh God! *To Cyprian* Here, take a look.

ADLER Read it aloud, read it aloud!

CYPRIAN *reads* "We assure the manly fighter for freedom and enlightenment of our most heartfelt veneration and sympathy and beg him to believe that he will always find us at his side in the battle against the forces of darkness. Doctor Reiss, Walter König —"

BERNHARDI Names I don't know at all.

GOLDENTHAL This is a most gratifying manifesto. We may assume it will not be the only one.

BERNHARDI And one can do nothing against that?

GOLDENTHAL *laughing* What? That is all we need, for us to —

OSKAR Father, won't you have your dinner now?

SERVANT *brings a calling card.*

BERNHARDI What now?

OSKAR *reads* The Directorate of the Brigittenau Association of Freethinkers.

BERNHARDI The freethinkers from Brigittenau? I am not at home. Please tell the gentlemen that.

GOLDENTHAL But why?

BERNHARDI I'm already in prison. I've been executed.
  Goes into the dining room, likewise the others except Goldenthal and Löwenstein.

GOLDENTHAL *to the servant, whom he manages to catch at the door* Tell the gentlemen, the Professor is exhausted now, but it will be his — when are the Professor's visiting hours?

SERVANT From two o'clock on.

GOLDENTHAL Fine, it will be the Professor's pleasure to receive the gentlemen tomorrow at a quarter to two.

SERVANT *exits.*

LÖWENSTEIN A pleasure? Are you convinced of that?

GOLDENTHAL Leave it to me to protect my client's interests, won't you?

LÖWENSTEIN *shrugs his shoulders and goes into the dining room.*

SERVANT *enters with a calling card.*

GOLDENTHAL *turning around* What's the matter? Let me see. Oh!

SERVANT The gentleman refuses to be put off.

GOLDENTHAL Just bring the gentleman in here.

SERVANT *exits.*

GOLDENTHAL *clears his throat, prepares himself.*

KULKA *enters.*

KULKA Oh, Doctor Goldenthal, if I'm not mistaken?

GOLDENTHAL That's my name. Since we know each other, Doctor Kulka, you will have to make do with me for today. The Professor is somewhat tired, as you may well imagine —

KULKA Tired? Hmm. Then I suppose I'll have to — another time — I couldn't answer to my editor —

GOLDENTHAL But I have just told you, Doctor —

KULKA Yes, of course, I heard you. I understand too, but what good does that do me? As far as my editor is concerned it'll still be my fault if I can't speak to the Professor in person.

GOLDENTHAL Perhaps I'm in a position to speak with you.

KULKA *hesitating* If you would be so kind — Perhaps I may ask, Doctor, whether it's true that Professor Bernhardi does not intend to file an appeal?

GOLDENTHAL We have merely chosen to take some time to reflect on the form it will take.

KULKA *has taken out a notebook.*

GOLDENTHAL *influenced by that, in an oratorical tone* Because even if it is far from our intention to raise the least doubt about the legal knowledge and the wisdom of Austrian judges, nor yet to feel mistrustful of the healthy common sense of the Viennese citizens on the jury, still, we cannot close our minds to the suspicion that the partisan position of a certain faction among the print media, one I do not wish here to characterize more closely, seemed designed to prepare the ground for a miscarriage of justice and —

BERNHARDI *enters.*

KULKA Oh, Professor.

BERNHARDI What's this?

GOLDENTHAL I took the liberty, Professor, since you did not wish to be disturbed — and I believe in a manner entirely after your own mind —

BERNHARDI With whom do I have the pleasure?

KULKA Kulka, from the "Latest News." My Chief, who has the honor of knowing you personally, sends his regards and —

GOLDENTHAL There have been rumors spread which had best be checked immediately.

KULKA That is to say, it's been reported that the Professor will dispense with —

GOLDENTHAL I have already explained to the gentleman that we have merely reserved some time for reflection.

BERNHARDI That's right. *Löwenstein, Cyprian, Adler, Kurt, Oskar gradually come in from the dining room.*

KULKA I am very grateful for this explanation. But now, Professor, I still have a special request from my Chief to convey to you. In the course of the proceedings today, you demanded the subpoenaing of the Minister of Education. It is evident from this that there are weightier issues involved in this matter that did not come up in the course of the trial, or were not permitted to come up. Now my Chief would feel especially honored, Professor, to put the pages of our paper at your disposal —

BERNHARDI *warding him off* Thank you, thank you.

KULKA It is surely not unknown to you, Professor, that our paper, even if it did welcome His Excellency at the beginning of his administration with the greatest confidence, has recently found it necessary to oppose energetically certain surprising anti-progressive, indeed, downright reactionary measures of the Minister's, in doing which we always preserved that moderate tone which has at all times seemed to us a prerequisite for any positive effect in the political arena. And thus it would be most welcome to us in our struggle for progress and freedom to have at our side a man like you, whose passion, moderated by good taste, assures us of an ally.

BERNHARDI Excuse me, I am not your ally.

KULKA But we are yours, Professor.

BERNHARDI That's how it appears to you today. My case is a purely personal one.

LÖWENSTEIN But —

KULKA Some personal cases just happen to carry the seed of the political in them. Yours —

BERNHARDI That is a coincidence for which I'm not responsible. I belong to no party and do not wish to be claimed as a member by any.

KULKA The Professor will not be able to avoid —

BERNHARDI I will not do anything to that end. Whoever intercedes for me does it at his own risk. *Always lightly, and now with his characteristic ironic smile* Just as I was accused of having offended the Catholic religion today, it could happen to me in the near future to be suspected of enmity towards another one, one closer to you —

KULKA I am without denomination, Professor. We all are, at least inwardly. Our position, the position of our paper, as is generally known, is that of absolute freedom of conscience. What does Friedrich say? Everyone should find bliss after his fashion.

BERNHARDI Well, then, I will ask you to deal with me in accordance with that principle. Thank your Chief for his kind invitation, but it would simply be a misuse of his trust, a kind of false reporting, if I took him up on it.

KULKA Is that really your last word, Professor?

BERNHARDI They are rarely different from my first ones.

KULKA My Chief will regret it endlessly. I really don't know - But please, Professor, in case you should still decide to make public your feelings towards His Excellency, may we at least depend on it that no other paper —

BERNHARDI You may depend on it that whatever I do, I have no intention of placing myself under the protection of some newspaper. My best regards to your Chief.

KULKA I thank you, Professor. My pleasure, gentlemen.

Exits. Short, awkward pause.

CYPRIAN That wasn't exactly necessary, now.

GOLDENTHAL Really, Professor, I must say too —

BERNHARDI Come, gentlemen, do you still not understand that I want absolutely nothing to do with people who want to turn this case of mine into a political affair.

LÖWENSTEIN But it is one, you know.

GOLDENTHAL Certainly, as things have turned out, we are at the center of a political battle. And actually, we should welcome it —

BERNHARDI I beg of you, dear Doctor, don't welcome anything! I will not wage any political war. The ludicrous battle-cry that will rise from a number of sides will not seduce me into playing a role which does not fit me, for which I do not feel at all suitable, precisely because it would be a role. And as far as time for reflection is concerned, Doctor, I am asking you herewith to consider it elapsed.

GOLDENTHAL I don't understand —

BERNHARDI I wish to begin serving my sentence. In fact, as soon as possible. Preferably tomorrow.

CYPRIAN But —

BERNHARDI I want to have this business over with. That's the only thing that concerns me now. These past few months have been a total loss for my work, my profession. Nothing but conferences and hearings. And what came of it? The thing was unpleasant enough already as a legal case; and now it's supposed to become a political issue? From that I'm going to hide, in jail if need be. My business is to make people well, or at least to persuade them that I can. That is what I want the opportunity to do again as soon as I can.

LÖWENSTEIN And your revenge?

BERNHARDI Who's talking about revenge?

LÖWENSTEIN Well, Flint, Ebenwald. You simply want to let them go like that?

BERNHARDI It shall not be revenge, merely a settling of accounts. We will come to that too. But it will not suddenly become the purpose of my life to fight with these people. I intend to settle that along the way. But have no fear. They'll not get off scot-free.

CYPRIAN Whether you want to carry on the matter politically, legally, or entirely privately, I maintain that it was not necessary for you to show this Mr. Kulka the door, as it were.

GOLDENTHAL I too wish to stress once more that the friendship of the paper which Mr. Kulka represents —

BERNHARDI *interrupting him* Esteemed Doctor, one must take one's enemies how and where one finds them; my friends I can choose — fortunately.

Curtain

FIFTH ACT

An office in the Ministry, furnished accordingly, not entirely lacking comfort.

COUNCILOR WINKLER, *around 45 but younger appearing, slim, with a fresh face, small mustache, short blond hair flecked with gray, sparkling blue eyes. He is alone, busy with documents. He stands up and files the documents in a cabinet. The telephone rings.*

WINKLER *goes back to the table, picks up the phone* Imperial and Royal Ministry of Education and Religion. No. Councilor Winkler. Oh, Professor Ebenwald. He's not here yet. In half an hour, perhaps. I'm sure His Excellency will not be off to Parliament before one thirty. Well, I'm not in any position to give out information on that, unfortunately, not over the phone, at any rate. It'll be my pleasure. Good-bye, Professor. *Hangs up; continues with his earlier work.*

SERVANT *enters, brings the mail and a calling card.*

WINKLER Doctor Kulka?

SERVANT But wishes to speak to His Excellency in person.

WINKLER Then he'll have to come back later.

SERVANT There were two gentlemen from newspapers here earlier also. They're coming back too.

WINKLER Look, you needn't announce these newspapermen to me at all. They all want to speak to His Excellency in person.

SERVANT *exits.*

The telephone rings again.

WINKLER Imperial and Royal Ministry of Education and Religion. Councilor Winkler, yes. Ah, as if I didn't know that voice. Good morning, dear lady. This evening? Yes, if

I can, gladly. I have nothing to say to the elections. No. Because I don't like it that beautiful women are nowadays taking up politics too. Not one of them understands politics. You still have at least twenty years to go before you reach that point, dear lady. Well, good-bye, dear lady. Best regards to your husband. *Hangs up.*

SERVANT *enters with a calling card.*

WINKLER Another one? Ah, Doctor Feuermann. Well, show him in. *Servant exits.*

DOCTOR FEUERMANN *enters, bows deeply.*

WINKLER Good morning, Doctor. To what do we owe the pleasure?

FEUERMANN I've come on a very serious matter, Councilor Winkler.

WINKLER Oh, Doctor, not another misfortune right after the good judgment of the honest citizens of Oberhollabrunn —

FEUERMANN To be sure, Sir, I was acquitted. But what good does it do me? Not a single patient shows his face any more. If I were to stay on as District Doctor in Oberhollabrunn I should simply starve. Hence I am taking the liberty of requesting a transfer and — *the telephone rings.*

WINKLER Excuse me, Doctor. *Into the phone* Yes. Councilor Winkler. Oh, yes, Councilor. How's that? What? *Amazed* Go on! Seriously? Sister Ludmilla? That would be a remarkable coincidence. Well, because he's getting out today, you know. Of course Professor Bernhardi. Today, yes. You're coming over yourself? Yes. Well, I'll be. Of course I won't say anything to His Excellency for now if you wish. Good-bye! *Hangs up. Very agitated at first, then to Feuermann* So, please.

FEUERMANN And I wanted particularly to ask for your support, Councilor, who have always —

FLINT *enters.*

FLINT Good day, Councilor. *Notices Feuermann* Ah —

FEUERMANN   *bowing deeply*   Excellency, my name is Feuermann.

FLINT Oh, of course. I have already — from the "Monday Chronicle"?

WINKLER *softly* As it happens, not a journalist, Excellency. Doctor Feuermann from Oberhollabrunn.

FLINT Oh, of course — Doctor Feuermann.

WINKLER *as above* Who was charged with so-called malpractice and acquitted.

FLINT Oh, I remember. Professor Filitz delivered a brilliant expert opinion. Ten votes to two.

FEUERMANN Nine against —

WINKLER *motions for him to stop.*

FLINT I congratulate you, my dear Doctor Feuermann.

FEUERMANN I am most touched, Excellency, by Your Excellency's interest in my trifling affair —

FLINT For me there are no trifling affairs. There mustn't be any for men in our position. Everything is of equal importance in a higher sense. *He casts a quick but approval-seeking glance at Winkler* And it will afford you a certain satisfaction, perhaps, to learn that in no small part as a result of your "trifling" affair, a thorough reform of the medical curriculum is being taken into consideration. I hope it will be possible to carry it out by decree. In general, if one didn't always have to ask Parliament first — *glance at Winkler* how easy it would be to govern.

WINKLER Faster at any rate, and that's the main thing, after all.

FEUERMANN I've taken the liberty, Excellency —

WINKLER I assume you've cited everything in your petition, Doctor.

FEUERMANN I would only like to add —

WINKLER That's probably in there too —

FEUERMANN Yes.

WINKLER So, just let me have it, Doctor, it'll be taken care of as quickly as possible. Good-bye, Doctor.

FLINT *who has in the meantime received several newspapers from the servant* Good day, Doctor. *Shakes hands with him. Feuermann exits.*

FLINT *looking at a newspaper* What does he actually want?

WINKLER Request for a transfer, Excellency. The poor devil is naturally being boycotted in Oberhollabrunn, in spite of being acquitted.

FLINT Well, yes, you'd probably not let him treat you either.

WINKLER Certainly not if I were having a child.

FLINT *throwing the paper down angrily* What else is new?

WINKLER Professor Ebenwald phoned. He'll stop in sometime this morning.

FLINT Again? He was here only the day before yesterday.

WINKLER They urgently need money at the Elisabethinum. The debts are getting beyond them.

FLINT But the Board rescinded its resignation after Bernhardi's removal.

WINKLER Yes, but it turns out Bernhardi was the only one to stir the Board up a bit. Since then they're all asleep. Even I.

FLINT They have to get a subvention. I promised it to Bernhardi back when he was still there.

WINKLER We have a huge proposed budget this time, we won't be able to squeeze out more than three thousand. The Minister of Finance is already very angry with us. I'm not even sure yet whether we'll get the money for the new building of the Physiological Institute. And this is —

FLINT If we don't get this through the budget committee, as well as a few other things, then I'll ask for a separate subsidy in Parliament.

WINKLER Oh!

FLINT They won't refuse me. The Liberals and the Social Democrats can't do it, they would be cutting off their own noses if they suddenly demanded austerity of the government in the building of scientific institutes. And as far as the Christian-Social gentlemen are concerned, I imagine I have the right to expect that they will not cause me any trouble. Don't you think so?

WINKLER The gentlemen in question have every reason, at the very least, to be grateful to Your Excellency.

FLINT Not a palpable hit, dear Winkler. In public life it's not a matter of gratitude but of accurate bookkeeping. Wait and see what the final statement looks like. Come to think of it, I must congratulate you on yesterday's State Legislature elections. Ten new Social Democratic seats. That was not to be expected.

WINKLER Excellency, I will not be in a position to accept congratulations until after the parliamentary elections.

FLINT Those may turn out differently. The margins of victory yesterday weren't particularly overwhelming. So don't celebrate your victory too soon, my esteemed Mister Anarchist.

WINKLER Excellency is promoting me rather quickly. Just now I was distinguished with the title of Social Democrat.

FLINT Not much difference.

WINKLER Oh, by the way, I mustn't neglect to offer my congratulations on your speech yesterday.

FLINT Speech? Please, those few improvised words. But they had an effect.

WINKLER As all and sundry are confirming. *Indicating the newspapers.*

FLINT In any case, dear Councilor, it bears witness to a praiseworthy objectivity on your part that you too are congratulating me. I was downright afraid of you, you know.

WINKLER Too flattering, Excellency.

FLINT Because it seemed unlikely to me from the first that you, dear Councilor, should be in favor of an increase in the hours of religious instruction.

WINKLER And you yourself, Excellency?

FLINT My dear Councilor, what my personal position is with regard to this and other questions, that's a separate chapter. Simply to blurt out one's views is the manner of political dilettantes. The deep sound of conviction has a hollow ring. What really has an effect, in politics too, is counterpoint.

WINKLER Until someone comes along with a new melody.

FLINT Not bad. But to get back from our metaphors to reality, do you really believe, then, dear Councilor, that the people are mature enough today, or will ever be mature enough, to exist without religion?

WINKLER What I understand by religion, Excellency, can be better learned at any other time than during the so-called religion lesson.

FLINT Well now, are you an anarchist, my dear Councilor, or aren't you?

WINKLER You know, Excellency, it seems as a bureaucrat one has only one alternative — to be an anarchist or an idiot.

FLINT *laughing* Oh, I'm sure you'll concede there are a few intermediate steps. But believe me, dear Councilor, anarchy is an unfruitful state of mind. I also passed through a stage like that once. I got over it. Now my world view can be expressed in two words, my dear Councilor: Work, Service! All the rest fades into the background in the face of this one compelling demand. And since, as you know, I have all sorts of plans for which I cannot do without the cooperation of Parliament, I am obliged to make concessions, as people call them. Anarchists, too, make concessions, dear Councilor, otherwise they couldn't become councilors. *More seriously* But you're mistaken if you think it's always an easy thing to make concessions. Or do you believe, dear Councilor, that it was not a sacrifice for me to throw my old friend Bernhardi into the jaws of these people? And yet, it was necessary. The connections will become clear one day. Everything has been preserved. And should the time ever come when I shake certain people off my coat-tails, well, I don't want to say anything more, but people will understand one day that I am not a Minister of Education and Catholicism, as one reporter is pleased to call me today in a so-called lead article.

WINKLER Ah!

FLINT Quite after your own heart, what? And it's not even his at that. The phrase comes from the worthy Pflugfelder, who introduced it recently during one of those highly superfluous election rallies, where he found it necessary to roll out the Bernhardi affair. On the whole, dear Councilor, I find that our government's representatives have failed to show the necessary energy where some of these rallies are concerned.

WINKLER But Excellency, the rally at which Pflugfelder spoke was broken up. One really can't ask for more.

FLINT But when? Not until he attacked the Archbishop for transferring the priest who testified so much to Bernhardi's advantage to somewhere on the Polish border.

WINKLER Yes, archbishops naturally enjoy greater protection from the government than its cabinet ministers.

FLINT This whole Bernhardi affair! It seems the people don't want to let it rest. That was an absolutely perfidious article recently in the "Work," your favorite journal, Councilor.

WINKLER It wasn't badly written. But I don't have a favorite journal. I am against all newspapers.

FLINT How do you think I feel? And even the liberal papers who have held back so far are starting now to make Bernhardi out to be a kind of martyr, a political victim of clerical intrigues, a kind of medical Dreyfus. Have you read the article today in the "Latest News"? A regular festive greeting addressed to Bernhardi on the occasion of his release from prison. It is really strong.

WINKLER Bernhardi had nothing to do with it, at any rate.

FLINT Not quite. He obviously feels comfortable in his role. Of course, since you were kind enough to bring him the message, you know that it was suggested to him as early as the third week of his detention that he address a petition for clemency to His Majesty, one which would not have been turned down.

WINKLER Your Excellency does know that I tried to persuade him. But honestly, I did very much like his not wanting to hear anything about clemency.

FLINT Well, it would be regrettable if he were to let himself be rushed along by his friends into something where he'd always come off second best. Because I am in no way disposed to stand idly by while certain intrigues continue — and the Minister of Justice, with whom I discussed the matter yesterday, agrees with me entirely. We have before us an adjudicated case and are prepared, if need be, to proceed without pity. And I would be sorry for Bernhardi's sake if that were to become necessary; because as unwisely as he has behaved up to now, and as much trouble as he has already caused me, in here — *pointing to his heart* there is still a certain sympathy for him. It seems one never gets rid of that sort of thing entirely.

WINKLER Ah, yes, youthful friendships..

FLINT Of course that's it. But a man in my position should be entirely free of such sentimentality. When all is said and done, what does it have to do with this whole affair that we were both Rappenweiler's assistants twenty-five years ago? That we strolled together in the hospital garden and confided our plans for the future to each other? In our position, we should have no memories, if possible, no heart; we should be able to step over corpses — yes, my dear Councilor.

SERVANT *enters, brings a calling card.*

WINKLER Professor Ebenwald.

FLINT Show him in.

SERVANT *exits.*

FLINT   How much did you say we could ask for the
Elisabethinum?

WINKLER   Three thousand.

EBENWALD *enters, bows.*

FLINT   Good morning, my dear Professor. Or Director, rather.

EBENWALD   Not yet, Excellency, acting only. It is by no
means impossible for Professor Bernhardi to be reelected in
the next few days. He is only suspended, you know.

FLINT   The reelection wouldn't count for much; as things stand
at present, Bernhardi is neither Professor nor Doctor.

EBENWALD   But there's no doubt that the legal consequences
of his conviction will soon be rescinded now. Thanks to the
efforts of some friends and a certain press, a reversal in the
general mood appears to be in the offing. Your Excellency
probably already knows that he was just now escorted home
from prison in triumph.

FLINT   What?

EBENWALD   Yes, my students just told me.

FLINT   In triumph, what does that mean?

EBENWALD   Well, a number of students is supposed to have
greeted him at the prison gate with cheers.

FLINT   All we need now is a torchlight procession.

WINKLER   Perhaps, if Your Excellency desires that instructions
be given to that end —

EBENWALD   If I may be allowed a comment, I think it very
likely that these demonstrations have something to do with the
results of yesterday's elections.

FLINT   You think so? It would not be impossible. Yes, yes, you
see, my dear Councilor, one shouldn't underestimate that. By
which I do not mean to say that I attribute any special
significance to these demonstrations. Zionists, probably.

EBENWALD   They've already got a certain degree of power in
the country too.

FLINT Well. *Changing the subject* You've come about this subvention business, my dear Professor?

EBENWALD That's right, Excellency.

FLINT We'll be able to make only a fraction of the anticipated amount available to you, unfortunately. On the other hand, I can inform you that the nationalization of your Institute will receive serious consideration.

EBENWALD Your Excellency surely knows as well as I do how long a road it is, unfortunately, from considerations to decisions.

FLINT Very true, my dear Professor. But you mustn't forget that we here are occupied with not only the Elisabethinum and not only with the medical faculty, but with the entire enormous area of Education and Cath — and Religion.

EBENWALD And we members of the Elisabethinum dare simply hope that Your Excellency, coming from our profession yourself, besides being a shining light of our faculty as a classroom teacher, will bestow special assistance upon that branch of medical instruction so badly neglected under your predecessor.

FLINT *to Winkler* This man knows how to exploit my weak point. Dear Professor, I have not forgotten that I am a doctor and a teacher. That is to say, one can stop being anything, but a doctor — never. And let me tell you something, my dear Professor, but don't repeat it to anyone or it'll be used against me in Parliament, I sometimes feel a kind of homesickness for the laboratory and for the ward. It's quieter and more agreeable work, I can assure you. And if one accomplishes something, the others notice. An occupation like ours, I mean that of politicians, the results of which sometimes become apparent only to a later generation —

SERVANT *brings another calling card.*

WINKLER Professor Tugendvetter.

FLINT Him I leave to you, dear Councilor. Please, Professor — *Flint and Ebenwald exit.*

TUGENDVETTER *enters.*

TUGENDVETTER Good morning, Councilor. I won't keep you long. Merrily flows the task along by merry talk accompanied — right?* Well, I'm taking the liberty once again to inquire how things stand with my little business.

WINKLER It's well on its way, Professor.

TUGENDVETTER I don't have to tell you, Councilor, that the title is of little consequence to me personally. But you know how women are.

WINKLER How should I know that, Professor?

TUGENDVETTER Oh, yes. I am solitary but not alone — right?** Well, between you and me, my wife is mad for that title, Councilor. She can hardly wait for it any longer. And if it could be managed that the appointment be made prior to the first of June — that's my wife's birthday, you see. I would like to present her with my title as a gift.

WINKLER A practical and inexpensive gift, in any case.

TUGENDVETTER So, anything you could do to speed my request along, Councilor —

WINKLER *in forced official language* Concerning the bestowal of titles, the Ministry of Education is unfortunately not in a position to take into consideration the private relationships, specifically the family circumstances of the professors involved, insofar as such bestowal did not happen to be assured by means of special determinations.

SERVANT *brings a calling card.*

WINKLER *amazed* Ah.

---

* *Merrily flows the task along by merry talk accompanied*: cited from Schiller's poem, "Die Glocke."

** *I am solitary but not alone*: cited from *Preciosa*, an 1821 opera by Carl Maria von Weber.

SERVANT The gentleman wishes to speak with His Excellency in person.

WINKLER I'm sure there is nothing to hinder that, but it would be a particular pleasure for me to receive the Professor in my office first.

SERVANT *exits.*

TUGENDVETTER I'm probably intruding.

WINKLER It's a close acquaintance of yours.

BERNHARDI *enters.*

TUGENDVETTER *somewhat astonished.*

BERNHARDI Oh, you're not alone, Councilor.

TUGENDVETTER Bernhardi!

WINKLER *shaking his hand very warmly* I am very glad to see you again, Professor.

BERNHARDI I, too, am very glad.

TUGENDVETTER Hello, Bernhardi. *Extends his hand to him.*

BERNHARDI *takes it coolly* His Excellency not available?

WINKLER He won't be long. Won't you sit down, Professor?

TUGENDVETTER You — you look terrific. I — I — say, you know, I had completely forgotten. Since when are you actually —

WINKLER *to Bernhardi* I have to congratulate you on the ovations you were given this morning.

TUGENDVETTER Ova —

BERNHARDI Ah, you've been informed here already. But ovations, that really is somewhat of an exaggeration.

WINKLER There's even talk of a torchlight procession that's supposed to take place outside your window tonight — of a serenade by the Brigittenau Freethinkers Association.

TUGENDVETTER You know, my dear Bernhardi, I had completely forgotten that your sentence runs out today. It's amazing, actually, how quickly two months pass.

BERNHARDI Especially out under an open sky.

TUGENDVETTER But you really look absolutely splendid. Doesn't he, Councilor? If he had been on the Riviera he couldn't look any better. Absolutely rested.

WINKLER Perhaps you'll decide to commit some small blasphemy, Professor, then I could guarantee you an inexpensive vacation like that.

TUGENDVETTER *laughing* Thank you, thank you.

BERNHARDI It really didn't go badly for me, by the way. An angel watched over me: the bad conscience of the people who brought me there.

TUGENDVETTER I'm glad to have this opportunity to tell you that my sympathies in this case were firmly on your side.

BERNHARDI Do you have the opportunity, finally? I'm glad.

TUGENDVETTER I hope you never doubted that I —

BERNHARDI Wouldn't it be possible to announce me to His Excellency? I mean, it's a fairly urgent matter.

WINKLER I'm sure His Excellency will appear right away.

TUGENDVETTER Do you know what I heard recently? That you intend to write a history of the entire affair.

BERNHARDI So, is that what they're saying?

WINKLER That could turn out to be an interesting book. You've had an opportunity to get to know people.

BERNHARDI Most of them, my dear Councilor, I already knew beforehand. And the fact that people behave shabbily towards a person they dislike or because they derive a certain advantage from their attitude can hardly be surprising in the end. Still, one type has always remained a mystery to me —

TUGENDVETTER Namely?

BERNHARDI The individuals of disinterested meanness. You know, the ones who behave meanly without gaining the least advantage from it, only for the joy of the thing, so to speak.

FLINT *and* EBENWALD *enter.*

FLINT *quickly in control* Oh, Bernhardi!

EBENWALD *also immediately in control* Good morning, Professor.

BERNHARDI Good day. The Professor is here on behalf of the Elisabethinum, I suppose?

EBENWALD That's right.

FLINT It has to do with the subvention.

BERNHARDI I always thought the interests of my work would be in good hands with you — for the duration of my absence.

EBENWALD I thank you for the kind acknowledgment, Professor.

FLINT *to Bernhardi* You want to speak with me, Bernhardi?

BERNHARDI I won't take up much of your time.

WINKLER *to Ebenwald and Tugendvetter* Perhaps I could ask the gentlemen. *Exits with both of them.*

FLINT *with quick determination* I am glad for the opportunity to convey to you my best wishes on your release from custody. It was impossible for me, unfortunately, in my official capacity, to let you know in an appropriate manner how painfully the outcome of your trial surprised me; it will please me all the more, now that the affair is settled, if I can be of service to you in some way.

BERNHARDI You are really very kind, dear Flint. In fact, I have come to ask a favor of you.

FLINT I'm listening.

BERNHARDI You see, the thing is this: Prince Konstantin is very ill and has sent for me.

FLINT So? But I don't know —

BERNHARDI Sent for me as his physician. I am to take over his treatment again.

FLINT Well, fine, what keeps you from it?

BERNHARDI What keeps me? I don't want to be guilty of another offense.

FLINT Of an offense?

BERNHARDI You know. It would amount to quackery if I took over Prince Konstantin's treatment again. Since I let myself be carried away so far as to obstruct religion, and was convicted for it, I lost my license and with it my right to practice medicine. Hence I am taking the liberty of delivering in person my request for the rescinding of the legal consequences of my conviction. I am coming to you, my old friend, who, as has already been shown in other cases, is in a position to influence somewhat the decisions of the Minister of Justice, and I am also asking, should my request be granted, for all possible speed in order that the Prince not have to wait long.

FLINT I see. I see. You've come here to make fun of me.

BERNHARDI But how? I'm only observing procedure. I have absolutely no desire to go to jail again, as well as it went for me, relatively speaking. Thus, if you'll be so kind — *hands him the petition.*

FLINT Granted. I will assume all responsibility. There is no reason why you can't respond to the Prince's summons immediately. I give you my word that no consequences of a criminal nature will result for you. Will that do for you?

BERNHARDI It might do this time, I suppose, since, after all, keeping your word in this instance should not be connected to unpleasantness of any kind for you.

FLINT Bernhardi!

BERNHARDI Excellency?

FLINT *immediately in control* Well, don't I know you, my dear friend? Didn't I know right away that you haven't come on account of Prince Konstantin? Just as well. Let's talk about the matter you allude to. I couldn't have spared you from it anyway. So, you accuse me of breaking my word.

BERNHARDI That's right, my dear Flint.

FLINT And do you know what reply I make to that? That I never broke my word. Because I had never given you any other than to intercede for you. And that I could not do better than by seeking and effecting the clarification of your case through the judicial process. Furthermore, even if I had done what you call "breaking one's word," it would be foolish of you to reproach me for that since you were lost, even if I had kept my word. There was already a private complaint pending against you as well, and your trial could no longer be prevented. Finally, do try to grasp that there is something more important in public life than to keep one's word or what you designate as such. And that is, to keep one's goal in view, not to let one's work be imperiled. I never felt this more profoundly than in that remarkable instant when I, on the point of taking your side, felt the ill will, the mistrust, the bitterness of Parliament rushing ever closer to me, and when I succeeded, with a fortunate turn, in calming the looming storm, smoothing the surging waves, and becoming master of the situation.

BERNHARDI A turn, that's true.

FLINT My dearest Bernhardi, my only choice, as I recognized in a flash at that instant, was either to plunge into an abyss with you, that is, to commit a kind of crime against myself, my mission, perhaps even against the state, which needs my services, or to abandon a person who was lost anyway; that is, to continue to be in a position to build new scientific institutes, to reform the curriculum of the various faculties in a manner corresponding with the modern spirit, to further public health, and to carry out or at least to prepare reforms in the most diverse areas of our intellectual life, which, as you yourself will admit to me later on, might not have been too dearly paid for with two months of a not especially onerous jail term. I mean, I hope you won't believe that your martyrdom makes any particularly strong impression on me. Of course, had you taken all the unpleasantness upon yourself for some great cause, for an idea, for your fatherland, for your faith, unpleasantness long since counterbalanced by all sorts of small triumphs, then I would be able to respect you. But I see in your entire conduct — I can say this to you as an old friend, I hope — nothing but a tragicomedy of obstinacy, and I will, moreover, go so far as to question whether you would have carried it through with the same persistence if we were still burning people at the stake here in Austria.

BERNHARDI *looks at him a while, then begins to applaud.*

FLINT What's this?

BERNHARDI I thought you'd miss it.

FLINT And you can find no response to me beyond this mediocre joke.

BERNHARDI You know the proper reply to what you said as well as I do; I even think — I can say this to you as an old friend, I hope — you could find more suitable words than I could. So, what sense would it make to answer you here, in private?

FLINT I see. So. Well, you mustn't think that your intentions are unknown to the Ministry. Only, I can't understand what could induce you under these circumstances to distinguish me with the honor of your personal visit? On account of Prince Konstantin —

BERNHARDI Maybe I was a little too thorough, my dear friend. Understandably, it had to interest me to know what you could come up with by way of explanation for your behavior towards me. And this conversation between the Excellency and the ex-convict would make for a rather effective final chapter for a certain book, if it were worth the effort to write it.

FLINT Oh, I hope you won't let yourself be held back. After all, it could serve as your campaign speech at the same time.

BERNHARDI Campaign speech?

FLINT Oh, it's surely only a question of days or hours before they offer you a spot on the ticket.

BERNHARDI My dear Flint, I intend in the future to go on leaving politics entirely to you.

FLINT Politics! Politics! If you would all finally leave me in peace with that. To hell with politics. I accepted the portfolio simply because I know there is no one else in Austria today who can do what must finally be done. But even if I have been ordained to usher in a new era, as far as my life is concerned, these few years — or months as Minister will be nothing more than an episode. I have always known this and feel it more strongly with each passing day. I am a physician, a teacher, I long for patients, for students.

WINKLER *enters*.

WINKLER I'm very sorry for interrupting, Excellency, but I've just received an extremely important message from the Justice Ministry, and since it has to do with the Professor's affair besides —
BERNHARDI With mine?
WINKLER That's right. To wit, Sister Ludmilla, the chief witness in your case, has entered an affidavit in which she accuses herself of perjury during your trial.
BERNHARDI Herself —
FLINT Say, what is —
WINKLER Councilor Bermann from the Justice Ministry will be here very shortly to give a full report in person. But there can be no further doubt as to the facts. The Sister's affidavit has been filed.
FLINT Has been filed?
WINKLER And you, Professor, will of course request at once that your case be reopened.
BERNHARDI Reopened?
WINKLER Naturally.
BERNHARDI I wouldn't dream of it.
FLINT Ah!
BERNHARDI What for? Should I go through the entire farce yet again? Now in a different light? All reasonable people know I was imprisoned unjustly, and the two months no one can give me back in any event.

FLINT The two months! Always these two months! As if it were a matter of that. There are higher values in question here. You have no sense of justice, Bernhardi.

BERNHARDI Obviously.

FLINT Do you know any further details yet, Councilor?

WINKLER Not very many. The strangest part of the thing, as Councilor Bermann told me on the phone, is that according to Sister Ludmilla's affidavit, she first admitted to her perjury during confession, and the father confessor himself urged her to make up for her grave sin insofar as it lies in her power to do so.

FLINT The father confessor?

WINKLER Evidently he had no idea what it's about.

FLINT Why? How do you know that?

BERNHARDI I'm supposed to go to trial again? I'm liable to provide expert evidence that Sister Ludmilla is severely hysterical and not accountable for her actions.

FLINT That would be just like you.

BERNHARDI What good will it do me if this person is put in jail this late in the day?

WINKLER But it could happen to someone else too at the same time. We have here a certain Mister Hochroitzpointner who might fare badly, all the more since fate threatens to catch up with this gentleman from another side as well.

BERNHARDI And I suppose fate is named Kurt Pflugfelder in this case?

WINKLER I believe so.

FLINT You are remarkably well informed, Councilor.

WINKLER My duty, Excellency.

BERNHARDI This pitiful wretch is really not worth that great an expenditure of time. That our good Kurt, who truly has better things to do as well —

FLINT *who has been pacing back and forth* During confession. That will startle certain people, I imagine. It may turn out that Catholic customs can sometimes be accompanied by fairly beneficial consequences for non-believers as well.

BERNHARDI I waive the beneficial consequences. I want to be left in peace!

WINKLER It is not to be assumed, Professor, that the further development of the case will depend on you alone. It will follow its own course now, even without you.

BERNHARDI It will have no alternative.

FLINT I do want to point out to you, Bernhardi, that this matter does not involve your convenience exclusively. And it would make a curious impression if now, when you've been shown the proper way to attain your rights, you entered upon one perhaps less worthy of you, and became involved with all sorts of people, reporters and —

BERNHARDI I'm not entering upon any more ways at all. I've had enough. For me this case is closed.

FLINT My, my.

BERNHARDI Absolutely closed.

FLINT So suddenly? And it was even said that you wanted to write a pamphlet about the case or even a book. Isn't that so, Councilor, people were saying —

BERNHARDI I realize that it's no longer necessary. And if it comes to a second trial, my testimony from the first is on the record; I have nothing to add to it. I will forego the subpoenaing of the Education Minister.

FLINT I see. But you'll hardly be able to do anything about it if I myself should deem it appropriate to appear in court. People will understand; even you, Bernhardi, will have to understand eventually, that my goal from the start was nothing more than to clarify the situation. The first trial was a necessity, for how else could we arrive at the second, which will clear everything up completely. And maybe it's not a bad idea, my dear Bernhardi, not to use up one's ammunition all too soon.

Indicates his breast pocket.

BERNHARDI What is that?

FLINT A letter, my friend. A certain letter which might still serve in the struggle that lies before us. Your letter!

BERNHARDI Ah, my letter. I was already thinking it might be your article.

FLINT What article?

BERNHARDI Why, that famous one from your Assistant years: "Houses of God — Houses of Healing."

FLINT Oh, that one —

WINKLER *a questioning gesture.*

FLINT Yes, my dear Councilor, one from my — revolutionary period. If you're interested I'll be glad to look for it some time and —

BERNHARDI It exists?

FLINT *placing his hand on his forehead* My, the tricks one's memory plays. Why, I never wrote it. But who knows, maybe I'll be in a position shortly to speak it.

SERVANT *enters* Councilor Bermann wishes to speak to His Excellency in person.

FLINT Ah! *To Bernhardi* Perhaps you'll be kind enough to wait a little while longer?

BERNHARDI Well, but Prince Konstantin —

FLINT Has waited two months for you. Another half hour will not make much difference to him. Keep him here for me, dearest Councilor. We may need to consult about a joint action. So, Bernhardi, I can ask this small favor of you, I trust. *Exits.*

WINKLER The Professor has been summoned to Prince Konstantin? Today? That's just like him!

BERNHARDI I'm going there only to ask him to dispense with my services for the near future. It's my intention to get away from what appears to be developing now.

WINKLER I'm only afraid you'll then have to stay away longer than might be agreeable to your numerous patients; because now the story is just beginning, Professor, and it can last a long time!

BERNHARDI Well, what shall I do?

WINKLER One gets accustomed to it. In time one even gets to be proud of it.

BERNHARDI Proud? Me? You have no idea, Councilor, how ridiculous I appear to myself, actually. Beginning this morning — the reception at the prison entrance! and the article in the "Latest News" Have you read it? I was truly ashamed. And with this dull awareness of becoming ridiculous all sorts of plans turned to nothing.

WINKLER Plans? Ah, you mean — your book.

BERNHARDI Not exactly. As far as the book is concerned something similar already happened earlier in the proceedings. When I set about to write it, in the contemplative seclusion of my cell, I was still thoroughly enraged, but in the course of my work the feeling went up in smoke. My indictment against Flint and his associates gradually became — I can't rightly say myself, how — perhaps by my remembering a very specific experience, something like a philosophical treatise.

WINKLER With which your publisher will be less happy.

BERNHARDI The problem was no longer Austrian politics or politics altogether, but it suddenly had to do with general ethical concerns, with responsibility and revelation, and in the final analysis, with the question of free will.

WINKLER Oh yes, it always comes down to that if one gets to the bottom of things. But it's better to slam on the brakes early enough, otherwise it can happen to a person one fine day that he begins to understand and to forgive everything. And if one may no longer love and hate, what's left of life's charm then?

BERNHARDI One simply keeps on loving and hating, my dear Councilor! But, in any event, you can imagine there wasn't much room left in my book for His Excellency Minister

Flint. And then I decided, if he is not going to get to read what I have against him, then he shall at least hear it.

WINKLER So it's that to which we owe the pleasure of your visit?

BERNHARDI Yes, it was my intention to tell him to his face — well, you can figure out more or less what. It was still my intention this morning, as I awoke in prison for the last time. But then came the applause and the article, and the letters I found at home; and then I sought only to confront my old friend again as quickly as possible, in order to still have at my disposal at least the seriousness necessary for calling him to account. But as I finally stood face to face with him, the last residue of ill will was also extinguished. If only you could have heard him! I could not possibly be angry with him. I almost believe I never was.

WINKLER The Minister has always liked you too. I assure you!

BERNHARDI And now this business with Sister Ludmilla on top of everything else — and the prospective appeal; so, you can understand, Councilor, that, in order to be myself again at all and to regain my self-respect, I have to get away from all the noise which is now rising all around me merely because the people are gradually figuring out that I was right.

WINKLER But Professor, what are you thinking of? No one has yet become popular by being right. Only when being right suits some political party can that happen. And besides, Professor, it's only a fancy of yours that you were right.

BERNHARDI What, Councilor? A fancy, that I — Have I understood you correctly?

WINKLER I believe so.

BERNHARDI You find, Councilor, that — You'll have to be kind enough to explain that to me. In your view, I should have let His Reverence —

WINKLER Indeed you should have, my esteemed Professor! Because you were most likely not born to be a reformer.

BERNHARDI Reformer? But please —

WINKLER No more than I was. Probably because we don't feel inwardly prepared to follow our conviction through to its logical conclusion and potentially even to risk our lives for it. And therefore it is the best, indeed, the only decent thing for individuals like us not to get mixed up in this sort of business to begin with.

BERNHARDI But —

WINKLER Nothing comes of it. What would you have accomplished in the end, my dear Professor, if you had spared that poor person on her deathbed a final moment of fright? That strikes me exactly as if someone wanted to solve the social question by making a present of a villa to some poor devil.

BERNHARDI You're forgetting only one thing, my dear Councilor, like most other people — I did not have the least intention of solving any question. I merely did what I took to be right in a very specific instance.

WINKLER That precisely was your mistake. If one were always to do the right thing, or rather, if one simply began one morning, without any further thought, to do the right thing and simply continued without interruption to do the right thing all day long, he would most certainly wind up in jail before supper.

BERNHARDI And shall I tell you something, Councilor? In my position you would have done exactly the same thing.

WINKLER Possibly. Then I would have been — I'm sure you'll forgive me, Professor — just as unreasonable an ass as you were.

Curtain

COMEDY OF WORDS

Three One-Act Plays

THE HOUR OF RECOGNITION

CHARACTERS

DR. KARL ECKOLD, *physician*
KLARA, *his wife*
PROFESSOR DR. RUDOLF ORMIN
SERVANT
MAID

The action takes place in Dr. Eckold's apartment in Vienna.

Dining room in Dr. Eckold's apartment. Doors at the rear leading to the anteroom, one on the left to the waiting room, and one on the right to the remaining private rooms. The furnishings are comfortable, of an old-fashioned appearance.

DR. KARL ECKOLD, *45 years old, dark brown beard, in early stages of baldness, uses a pince-nez to read, and* KLARA, *his wife, 40, still attractive, are sitting at the table having dessert.*

SERVANT *brings a calling card* The lady asks to be seen at once, if possible.

ECKOLD *calmly, with the card in his hand* It is common knowledge that my office hours begin at three. It's barely two-thirty. The lady should be so kind as to wait patiently. Is anyone else there?

SERVANT Three people were there before her.

ECKOLD I can only see them in order, of course.

SERVANT *exits.*

MAID *brings the coffee.*

KLARA *pours.*

ECKOLD I see you laid three settings, Anna. You seem to have forgotten that Miss Bettine — or rather, Doctor Bettine Wörmann is having lunch in Salzburg today, or in Zurich, or God knows where.

KLARA The setting was for Ormin, just in case.

ECKOLD Oh, of course. Did he phone to say he wasn't coming?

KLARA No, he hadn't said for sure he'd come. But I'm sure he'll still come to say good-bye.

ECKOLD He'll have all sorts of things to do before such a long trip. You'll have me called, then, won't you? I would like to say good-bye to him too. *He has gotten up, goes towards the right, and half turns around* You are staying home, aren't you?

KLARA I have nothing planned. Why do you ask? Is there something you want to talk to me about?

ECKOLD Nothing special. There's no rush at all. Well — *He looks at his watch and makes for the door on the right.*

SERVANT *enters with a telegram and a newspaper.*

ECKOLD *goes towards him.*

SERVANT *places the newspaper on the table.*

ECKOLD *opens the telegram* From Bettine.

KLARA *going up to him* Already?

ECKOLD From Bettine and Hugo, naturally.

KLARA *next to him, reads along.*

ECKOLD From Innsbruck.

KLARA Right! So they drove straight from their wedding dinner to the train yesterday evening.

ECKOLD Quite sensible.

KLARA *reading* "Tomorrow Zurich. For day after we ask news Lucerne, Palace Hotel."

ECKOLD *reads* "Thousand regards."

KLARA Exactly the route we took twenty-two years ago. Only we weren't in such a hurry to get to Innsbruck.

ECKOLD *without changing his expression* Modern tempo. We didn't exactly stop off at the Hotel Palace in Lucerne either.

KLARA That didn't even exist back then.

ECKOLD Even if —

KLARA It was very nice — even without the Palace.

ECKOLD Still, Bettine made out better than you.

KLARA Now — *Touches his arm lightly.*

ECKOLD *moves away from her, to the table; he remains standing while opening the newspaper* By which I do not intend in any way to reproach myself for anything. But a paternal million like that is simply not to be sneezed at; especially when everything else comes together as beautifully as it does in our son-in-law. *Glancing at the paper* Incidentally, here's something about Ormin. *Reads* "The medical team of the Austrian Red Cross, under the direction of the Royal and Imperial University Professor Rudolf Ormin, will leave Vienna today on the 8:20 express for Trieste, where it will board the Austrian Lloyd Line's steamship 'Amphitrite' sailing for Japan tomorrow at noon, thence to depart for the theater of war." *He hands her the paper and observes her as she reads.* Needn't be too bad. *He sits down.*

KLARA *still standing* But you went through something like that once too.

ECKOLD You mean Bosnia? You can't very well compare the two.

KLARA It was a kind of war, wasn't it?

ECKOLD Not only "a kind" — a very real one. You might have gathered that from those pages in my diary, I imagine. I did give them to you to read at the time. You do remember, don't you?

KLARA *smiling* Certainly I remember.

ECKOLD They fired down at us from the rocks. Cared damned little about the red cross. In fact, they obviously aimed specifically at the medical corps. *In a different tone* But one has to go thorough that sort of thing in a position of leadership — like Ormin's now. I was a very young doctor at the time, just graduated. And today I would probably not be good at it any more. It requires greater flexibility, greater idealism, to a certain extent, greater youth.

KLARA Ormin is two years older than you. And what's more, I've heard it said there is something not quite right with his heart.

ECKOLD Oh, it's not the years that do it, not even one's health. What keeps one young is success, recognition, fame.

KLARA If you had gone into an academic career —

ECKOLD Well, of course, it's not like there's such an awful difference in our talents, at any rate. It was more the result of other things, certainly. I know that perfectly well. Above all, Ormin had that inner facility. That was it. The inner drive, so to speak. What's more, one can't deny him a certain superficiality. One has to be born with that.

KLARA And he never had to chase after a practice.

ECKOLD I never did that either. And by the way, when we were both young doctors, he wasn't much better off materially than I was. Not at all, to give the truth its due. He too had to worry and to struggle.

KLARA But only for himself.

ECKOLD His worries first started in earnest after he married. Only he always took them lightly. That's the important thing. Always. I'm convinced that if he were to die today or tomorrow, Melanie would not be left particularly well off.

KLARA She must have an allowance, I imagine, since they're not legally divorced.

ECKOLD An allowance! Around two thousand crowns! She'd get really far on that, our good Melanie. She probably spent that much on gloves and hats alone. Earlier on, at least.

KLARA People accused her of much more than she deserved, most likely. They're always so severe with the wives of great men.

ECKOLD Great? let's say — famous. Well, that's one unpleasantness you've been spared, thank God, yes. Well — *He is about to exit right.*

PROFESSOR ORMIN *enters. Lean, with a sharp featured face, clean-shaven, around 50.*

ORMIN Good day. I hope you didn't wait to have lunch. *He kisses Klara's hand, extends his own to Eckold.*

KLARA That we couldn't do, I'm afraid.

ORMIN Naturally, I've already —

KLARA But a cup of coffee?

ORMIN If I might.

KLARA *rings, gives instructions to the maid who enters at once.*

ECKOLD I'm glad to see you before you leave. So, tonight on the Amphitrite?

ORMIN Yes.

ECKOLD Here it is in the paper, too. I hope you'll have a good passage. Especially now, in June. When are you supposed to get there, to the spot?

ORMIN In four weeks. It'll probably take considerably longer for us to arrive at the actual war zone.

ECKOLD Who knows, maybe it'll be all over before you get there.

ORMIN Over? But it's barely begun. And to all appearances, the thing will drag itself out a bit.

MAID *brings coffee.*

KLARA *pours.*

MAID *exits.*

ECKOLD You're taking one of your assistants along?

ORMIN Yes, Marenzeller. Kleinert will take my place at the clinic here. *Drinks coffee* By the way, do you know who is shipping out from Trieste at the same time we are? Likewise on the Amphitrite? Our good old Flöding.

ECKOLD Flöding? Well, yes, I suppose he too is getting old with the years, but good? I doubt he could manage it just like that.

KLARA In what capacity is Flöding going to Japan?

ECKOLD Surely as a correspondent?

ORMIN Yes. For the "Rhenish Messenger," from what he writes me.

KLARA You keep in touch with him?

ORMIN Not with any regularity, exactly. But since we were together for a few weeks last summer — quite by chance, after many years — but I did tell you about it —

KLARA We hear nothing at all from him any more, you know. If you hadn't brought us his greetings from Helgoland —

ECKOLD What should we hear from him? After all, it's been

ten years since he left Vienna.

ORMIN *to Eckold* He speaks of you as if you had been the closest of friends.

ECKOLD Friends? I doubt whether I've ever had a friend. *To Ormin* You, maybe?

ORMIN I did, some. You're probably too exacting in your demands.

ECKOLD What good is it? I've seldom had one met.

ORMIN *in a light, joking way to Klara* What's bothering him? *Recalling* Oh, yes. The little daughter! By God, I miss her too. Have you had any news from her yet? No, that's not possible so soon, I imagine.

KLARA It is. A telegram just came.

ECKOLD From Innsbruck.

KLARA They'll be in Zurich tomorrow, in Lucerne the day after.

ORMIN Well — and in four weeks you'll have her back here again.

KLARA Unfortunately not. They're moving into their apartment in Berlin right after they return from the honeymoon.

ORMIN Is that so? Do they need Wörmann so urgently in Berlin?

ECKOLD Since his predecessor was called to Breslau as Senior Lecturer —

ORMIN That's right! By the way, he's going to make a name for himself, your son-in-law! An Assistant at the Physiological Institute at twenty-eight, and most deservedly so, one must say —

KLARA Why couldn't it have been here?

ORMIN It's not that far, from Berlin to Vienna.

KLARA *to Ormin* Just think, the day before yesterday she was still sitting here. For seventeen years she sat on that spot. And now — No rational reflection is of any use now. It is such a deep rupture!

ORMIN I wouldn't have thought you'd take it that hard. After all, every father and mother must be prepared for something of the kind.

KLARA What use is preparation?

ECKOLD Truly, one had best never have had children.

KLARA *almost frightened* How can you say that?

ECKOLD *impenetrably* I'm simply saying it.

ORMIN Well — *Pause* What I still wanted to tell you, for the sake of order, is that included among the Red Cross nurses who are going to Japan with my team is Mrs. Melanie Ormin.

KLARA Ah!

ECKOLD Your wife?!

ORMIN My — former wife, yes.

ECKOLD You'll see, you'll be coming back remarried in the end.

ORMIN I don't think that very likely.

KLARA Give Melanie my best regards.

ORMIN You remember her in such a friendly way?

KLARA I always liked her. You know that.

ECKOLD Please deliver my compliments as well. And don't forget to say hello to Flöding for me. You can also tell him that it's particularly mean to let me hear absolutely nothing from him, if we were once as "good friends" as he claims to have been with me.

ORMIN You ask for more than you give. You yourself just denied him.

KLARA For all that, he was very fond of him.

ECKOLD Fond? He interested me. He was an amusing wretch. Malicious and sentimental.

ORMIN Not a rare combination among aesthetes who were otherwise somewhat poorly provided for by nature.

ECKOLD Poorly provided — because he limped a little? He made up for it by having such beautiful blue eyes.

ORMIN That isn't the most serious contradiction in his nature. I find it worse that he possesses such a poetic soul and no poetic talent. That ruins one's character, as it seems.

KLARA I know some pretty verses of his.

ORMIN There is nothing objectionable in this up to a certain age. But he's still writing them. Last summer, along the beach on the North Sea, he even read me some.

KLARA Well?

ORMIN There was a strong surf; I really have no opinion.

SERVANT *enters with a calling card.*

ECKOLD *takes it* You'll excuse me, Ormin. I'm afraid I have to — my golden practice, you know. But perhaps I'll still find you here?

ORMIN I hardly think so. I have all sorts of things to take care of before I go.

ECKOLD You'll keep my wife company for another fifteen minutes, won't you? And you two will have me called, maybe, before you leave? Surely we don't want to — without any pomp at all. So, see you later! *Exits right.*

KLARA *interjecting quickly* I find it very nice that Melanie is going with you.

ORMIN Not with me, she's simply going along as part of the team.

KLARA But she probably wouldn't have considered it otherwise.

ORMIN One can't say. Just think how many things she's tried in her life and, in part, accomplished too, since she left me.

KLARA Wasn't she living in Vienna most recently?

ORMIN Not for a long time now. She came back again only three months ago — from Madeira, where she managed a small hotel.

KLARA I thought she lived in America.

ORMIN That's longer ago. Do you know that she played in the theater there? English. I just found out about it recently myself. Not from her. She's even said to have had some talent.

KLARA A remarkable person. Perhaps you'll get to be happy

with her again after all!

ORMIN But —

KLARA Fifteen years ago you were probably not ready to be a husband.

ORMIN I was. Actually, I was always ready for that. I only needed to find the right woman. *Quite simply* But her I met a few years too late.

KLARA *smiles* You would have run away from the right one just as you did from your Melanie.

ORMIN Why do you say that? I didn't run away from Melanie. That's a misconception of yours. We only began at a certain time, Melanie as well as I, each for himself, to undertake our little journeys. From a distance that can easily be seen as running away. I don't believe, by the way, that it was my fault. I myself, even if you doubt it, was born for fidelity, for domestic life at the very least. Especially me. Much more so than Karl, for example.

KLARA More so than Karl — You?!

ORMIN Of course. Most assuredly, there is in him, deeply hidden, mind you, something of a totally undomestic, indeed, of an adventurer's nature.

KLARA *smiling* In Karl?

ORMIN Yes, in your husband, the General Practitioner Doctor Eckold, consultation hours from three to four.

KLARA *shaking her head* I suppose you think yourself a great judge of people?

ORMIN One has to bear the burden. It's not always pleasant, I assure you. But to speak seriously: we have both lived contrary to our natures, Karl just as much as I. For my part, I actually yearned for peace my whole life long, for inner peace. Had I had it, most likely more would have become of me.

KLARA You really could be satisfied, I think.

ORMIN Satisfied? Oh, you're thinking of the so-called career. I'm called Doctor, Professor even . . . As if it were a matter of that! But I would probably have brought it somewhat further under more peaceful circumstances.

KLARA   Under peaceful —?

ORMIN   Well, let's say, in the peacefulness of a home, even if it may sound a bit insipid. But that was not granted me.

KLARA   There was probably a reason why it wasn't granted you.

ORMIN   A reason? I doubt that, since I know very well where, under different circumstances, I could have found that peace. *In a warmer but entirely simple tone*   We both know it, Klara.

KLARA   *softly shaking her head*   What could you be think- ing of?

ORMIN   One might be permitted to remember again, I imagine, before saying farewell.

KLARA   *smiling*   But not to speak of it.

ORMIN   *seriously, but not heavily*   When one feels that perhaps he has never used the right words to say it, and that he might not have another occasion so soon —

KLARA   *smiles, without looking at him*   I hope you have no evil premonitions.

ORMIN   Premonitions? I've never suffered from those, which naturally doesn't exclude my weighing the probabilities against each other.

KLARA   But I do have premonitions. And I foresee — I know: nothing will happen to you.

ORMIN   I'm not excessively uneasy either. And no one is forcing me to travel to war and pestilence zones. In the end, one is exposed to the certain, inscrutable decrees of fate everywhere, — *smiles* more so with every passing year, as it were.

KLARA   You are still so young.

ORMIN   I? Look here, one can say that of Karl more readily than of me.

KLARA   Yes, one can say it of him too.

ORMIN   He has kept himself more youthful than I have. Actually, he still looks the same to me as he did as a student. And things worked out better for him too.

KLARA *smiling* In spite of his adventurer's nature?

ORMIN *remaining serious* Perhaps even in his profession as well.

KLARA   Surely you won't envy him that?

ORMIN   Why not? Is mine perchance on a higher plane? I assure you, at times there is something downright eerie about being summoned to some strange house and introduced first of all — not to some human being, but to a sick stomach. At least Eckold gets to know his patients.

KLARA   I wonder if that's especially —

ORMIN *interrupts her* Yes, the life of a general practitioner does have its very own attraction. Especially if one has a certain measure of general human kindness at his disposal.

KLARA   Do you consider Karl a kind man?

ORMIN   Hmm, you're asking me a difficult question there. Kind — kind I suppose he is. We all are, more or less, you know. But kindly. . . ? I don't rightly know. Do you understand what I'm saying? Kindliness, that's something very noble and rare, you know. One could even commit crimes out of kindness — or sins.

KLARA   I doubt that could ever happen to good people.

ORMIN   Quite right. Good people at best never manage to get beyond petty meannesses.

KLARA *smiling* That — that is something Flöding might have said.

ORMIN   You think so? Then I would rather take it back.

KLARA *somewhat embarrassed* It seems our old friend did not succeed in gaining your good will.

ORMIN   We were together every day during the summer. And on vacation people give themselves away even more than usual.

KLARA   I wonder whether he didn't make himself out to be

different than he is for you. That's part of his nature. If you saw the real him, then he must have changed very much.

ORMIN One doesn't change, Klara. One dissembles; one tells lies to others, occasionally to himself as well, but in the depths of one's being one does always remain who he was.

KLARA If only we knew exactly where these depths are hidden.

ORMIN On that score I dare say we're agreed. There, where our desires sleep, or feign sleep.

KLARA In the end the only thing that counts is how we've acted and lived, not what we desired or longed for.

ORMIN Quite right, Klara. All the more reason for us not to fancy we know a human being as long as his features appear blurred behind the mist of so-called experiences.

KLARA *smiling* And your glance penetrates these mists?

ORMIN *seriously* At times. And so, for example, the fortuitous circumstance of your wandering through life as the carefully faithful housewife of my old friend Karl Eckold has never been able to keep me from recognizing that deep within you there slumbers the soul of a great lover.

KLARA *paling* A great one yet? *Smiling* You flatter. I love Karl, yes. I have always loved him. But beyond that there is nothing out of the ordinary in it.

ORMIN *seriously* You know very well I didn't mean it that way.

KLARA *equally serious* I never wished for a different lot in life. Never. I can say of myself that I have made the hardworking and anxiety-filled life of a person who was dear to me above all others as beautiful as it lay within my power to do. It wasn't always easy, but at least I knew what I had been put on earth for.

ORMIN Yes, I can well believe that — that Karl needed you.

KLARA As I did him.

ORMIN Really, Klara? You have always been convinced that Karl Eckold, and only he, signified the meaning and purpose of your life?

KLARA *sharply* He and Bettine. Yes. The meaning and purpose.

ORMIN Forgive me!

KLARA What is there for me to forgive?

ORMIN Perhaps I didn't quite succeed in maintaining the tone today as I did a hundred other times, when I *he stands up* was able to say in conclusion: until tomorrow — or the day after, dear lady!

KLARA *smiling* Until — six months from today!

ORMIN *as lightly as possible* Let's hope so. Well, now, — *he is about to take his leave; responds to a movement on her part* Oh, please, it would be better if you didn't have Karl called. We've already said good-bye. And — for all my good feelings towards him — the last impression I take from this house — *He interrupts himself; simply* Good-bye, Klara!

KLARA Good-bye!

They are together at the door; he holds her hand in his.

KLARA Ormin!

ORMIN Klara!

KLARA Evidently you feel you've missed something — through some fault of your own.

ORMIN *vaguely* Missed? Who hasn't?

KLARA I do want to set you at ease in this regard before you go, at least where I'm concerned. So, dear friend, believe me, you haven't the slightest reason to reproach yourself for anything.

ORMIN I really don't understand —

KLARA Even if you had been more impetuous or skillful back then, ten years ago, I mean, than you were, you still would not have succeeded in including me in your collection.

ORMIN Hmm — but I really don't know, Klara, why you're trying, with your choice of words —

KLARA *interrupting him* Oh, I would have certainly been one of the rarest specimens, I have no doubt of that. But it was not to be. It could not be. You see, I was in love with you.

ORMIN *after a short pause* Oh . . . oh, what a simpleton I was.

KLARA *smiling faintly* You do yourself an injustice. It really didn't depend on you. I repeat. Every effort would have been in vain. Had I loved you less then I could have been yours — maybe. But you would have been — more than my lover. You would have become my destiny. That is why it couldn't be. And not only my destiny.

ORMIN What would it have mattered? For us it would have been happiness. How many human beings are granted something like that? Happiness! We would have experienced it.

KLARA For six months, maybe a year. And even during this short period we would not have had the pure enjoyment of it.

ORMIN It could have become pure. It would have become pure in time.

KLARA Never.

ORMIN Bettine?

KLARA Not only on her account.

ORMIN Him? What could he — mean to you, back then?

KLARA What he was for me — what he remained for me, remained to this day. Never did I realize so very clearly that I belong here — belong to him — than at that time.

ORMIN Just then?

KLARA I never realized it so very clearly. *Pause.*

ORMIN Forgive me, but if I remember correctly — it seems to me that it was precisely at that time that we're talking about now that your relationship with Karl left a good deal to be desired.

KLARA *looks at him in surprise.*

ORMIN Oh, it wasn't difficult to notice. There is probably no more transparent material than what marriages are made of. The individual can disguise himself if need be, but for human relationships there are no masks.

KLARA *after a short hesitation* We were estranged at the time, I don't deny it. But in spite of that, indeed, because of it — *she interrupts herself, continues more ardently* You wouldn't understand! You never figured out what a marriage means, what a marriage can mean. You don't know what a mutual existence of many years — and ours was truly mutual for many years — what ties it creates, stronger than any which mere passion between man and woman is able to create. Whatever pulls or gnaws at them, the ties don't tear. The couple simply belong together. And they never feel it more deeply —

ORMIN Than when they would prefer to part.

KLARA You have no idea how true that is, what you're saying. In the midst of distrust and torment they still belong together, exactly like before — and perhaps afterwards — in devotion and tenderness — even more solidly, further beyond recovery! I could never have left him. Never been permitted to leave him. At that time less than ever. Do you understand now, *with a slight smile* that all your efforts would have been in vain, and that you really have nothing to reproach yourself with?

ORMIN Whether I understand it or not is probably no longer the point. But that you're telling me about it today of all days.

KLARA *without looking at him* I had to sometime or other, I suppose.

ORMIN *quite lightly* You do seem to have some slight doubt that I will be allowed, in a year or two, be it here within these four walls or somewhere else, to sit across from you like today and —

KLARA *quickly* You mustn't carry a false picture of me away with you.

ORMIN *lightly* To eternity.

KLARA To a distant place.

ORMIN   And does it give you great satisfaction that while abroad I will keep the picture of a saint inside me instead of that of a woman?

KLARA   I am not a saint. The word describes me much less than you might suspect.

ORMIN   Let's not take words to be all too serious and important.

KLARA   Take them to be only as serious and important as you wish. I am as little a saint as I ever was a great lover. I am a woman like hundreds and thousands of others, believe me. No worse, perhaps, but most certainly no better than a thousand others.

ORMIN   Really, that sounds like — *closer to her* Is there another secret, Klara?

KLARA   No other for you, Ormin, at this hour.

ORMIN   No other for me?

KLARA   None.

ORMIN   Do I understand you correctly, Klara?

KLARA   I believe that you do understand me correctly.

ORMIN   But it will remain a secret? *Pause.*

KLARA   A name — is it that important?

ORMIN   I won't ask. *Pause.*

KLARA   Life is full of strange coincidences, Ormin. Tomorrow at this time you'll probably be walking up and down the deck of the Amphitrite in his company.

ORMIN   In his — What are you saying? But that's —

KLARA   Him. *Pause.*

ORMIN   And in his case there was no question of any danger of his becoming your destiny?

KLARA   Why do you ask? *Indicating her surroundings with a glance* You have the answer right here.

ORMIN   Which you couldn't foresee at the time.

KLARA   Perhaps I could.

ORMIN   You will never convince me that you got yourself involved in an affair of this kind in a calculated way. There must be some sort of explanation why he, of all people —

KLARA *smiling* And one must most likely be a man, and a little vain, to seek an explanation for such a far from uncommon case, if he himself —

ORMIN Wasn't the happy man.

KLARA The happy one?

ORMIN You loved him.

KLARA I don't deny it.

ORMIN More than me.

KLARA *smiling involuntarily* Less than you.

ORMIN And still he could have become your destiny. Yes, even he! It didn't lie in your power, after all. If he had clung to you, if he hadn't released you again, if he had insisted on — his rights.

KLARA Rights? He asked nothing more than I was ready to give. He hadn't been spoiled by life like some others.

ORMIN *softly, to himself* Like some others!

KLARA He had been really lonely since his youth. He hadn't even known the peace of a family home.

ORMIN *smiling* And so, to be sure, you could also be a bit of a sister and mother.

KLARA His lover is what I was, and his beloved.

ORMIN *still simply* And in his dull existence, the first ray of sunshine! The great, the only happiness of a man's life.

KLARA I was that, I suppose.

ORMIN Or had every reason, at least, to lull yourself into thinking you were.

KLARA For him I was. And perhaps more than happiness. After all, I don't know what life has made of him. It didn't afford him all he might have hoped for, all he might have demanded, perhaps. But I know what he was then. You didn't know him. No one knew him. Who made the effort to peer into that defiant, lonely soul? I did. That is why I was, of all people, the first to mean anything to him. And at the time I meant the world to him — and without having to destroy another life.

ORMIN   And besides — which does have to be taken into account, it was almost an adventure.

KLARA   Adventure?

ORMIN   An affair! At a time when you, for various reasons, had grown ripe for something of the sort.

KLARA   *shaking her head* I probably should have foreseen it.

ORMIN   *questioning expression.*

KLARA   That my features will become blurred for you now. Yes, for you too. It's the way you said before — about the others: behind the clouds of experiences my picture will grow indistinct to your sight. *After a light sigh* I shouldn't have told you, Ormin.

ORMIN   Surely you don't regret it, Klara? Because I am so very grateful to you. It was wonderful and good that you — that both of us, at this hour — finally told the truth.

KLARA   Can we be quite sure of that?

ORMIN   Klara!

KLARA   Well, yes. If it hadn't been in words.

ORMIN   The words we will forget. They don't matter. They're only —

ECKOLD *enters from the right.*

ECKOLD   Well, you're still here, I see.

KLARA   I was about to have you called.

ORMIN   *ready to leave* Dear friend —

ECKOLD   I thank you for being so patient.

ORMIN   Meanwhile it's gotten to be high time I left.

ECKOLD   Nor do I want to detain you any longer. So, once again, bon voyage! *They shake hands* By the way, I don't want to hide from you on your departure that I envy you a little.

ORMIN   Really? Well, come along. Leave your practice for a few months and come with us.

ECKOLD What am I to do with you? Surgery is not my field.

ORMIN That won't present any obstacle. We can offer you plague as well. But that doesn't seem to tempt you especially either, does it?

ECKOLD It wouldn't work out, even if it did tempt me. I've never managed to get beyond the longing stage.

ORMIN Isn't he being a little unjust to his fate?

KLARA I tell him sometimes.

ECKOLD Well — *Pause* So, do well, cure as many people as possible, and see to it that you yourself come back in one piece.

ORMIN Let's hope so. Well, good-bye. Think of me some- times. Good-bye, Klara. *Shakes hands with both of them and exits. Klara and Eckold remain silent for a moment.*

ECKOLD *looks at his watch, rings.*

SERVANT *enters.*

ECKOLD Has anyone else come in the meantime?

SERVANT No, Doctor.

ECKOLD The carriage pulled up yet?

SERVANT *to the window* Not yet. *Exits.*

KLARA It's only four-thirty. *She has gone slowly to the window.*

ECKOLD *sits down, picks up the newspaper.*

KLARA *turns to him* You wanted to say something to me?

ECKOLD It can wait till tomorrow too.

KLARA About Bettine, isn't it? About paying out her grandfather's bequest? Are there any difficulties with that? You did go to see the notary today.

ECKOLD Yes. That too. The business with the inheritance is going quite smoothly, of course. In a couple of weeks it'll be all wound up. Besides, that trifling sum is of no concern to Bettine now. Yes — but — actually I wanted — tell me, I suppose you miss her a great deal?

KLARA And you?!

ECKOLD Of course. But I, I have my profession when all is said and done. You, I think, will find it more difficult getting used to Bettine's not being here any more.

KLARA I was prepared for it.

ECKOLD Even so. Your entire existence, at least in the course of the last few years, was totally filled with Bettine. You're going to feel a terrible emptiness.

KLARA *smiling faintly* I imagine there's a number of other things — or not?

ECKOLD *staring straight ahead* All the same, if you happened to feel like moving to Berlin — for my part, I would not refuse my consent.

KLARA *looks at him in surprise.*

ECKOLD I'd have nothing against it, nothing at all, all the more so since now that Bettine is not here any more, there no longer exists any really compelling reason for us to continue living in the same house.

KLARA I don't understand you.

ECKOLD Is it all that difficult?

KLARA *ever more surprised* You want — you think — I should move to Berlin?

ECKOLD It's a suggestion. We'll still have to discuss the details. But all things considered, I believe —

KLARA What does this mean? What sudden idea is this?

ECKOLD Sudden? It only seems that way to you. It's only that I've not mentioned it until now. It would've been premature. I like to speak of things only when they've become relevant. But I can assure you, it's a very old idea of mine that after Bettine's marriage we could — we could break up our common household.

KLARA Our common —

ECKOLD Yes, a very old idea, a cherished idea. I could even tell you how old, almost to the day I could tell you. It's been ten years. It was ten years this past May — to the day. Do you understand me? *He stands opposite her; they look in each other's eyes. Pause.*

KLARA And for ten years you kept quiet.

ECKOLD Yes, I did that. But I make no claim of any sort to your admiration. It was much easier than you think. One merely needs to know exactly what he wants. And I knew. To interrupt the outwardly calm course of our existence, to cause such a radical reordering of our lives, while our daughter was still living in the parental home, that would have been most impractical, immoral even. And it would be just as immoral if we continued to live together now that Bettine is no longer at home.

KLARA You managed to keep this to yourself for ten years?

ECKOLD But I knew this day had to come. And to a certain extent, I lived in anticipation of it.

KLARA Of this day, for ten years? I don't believe it. I don't credit any person with such self-control, least of all you.

ECKOLD You have always underestimated me, I know that. Both of you did. *Pause.*

KLARA Why didn't you send me away at the time?

ECKOLD By the same token I could ask, why didn't you leave at the time?

KLARA I could answer that question. Because I believed my home to be here. Because my home was here, always, in spite of everything.

ECKOLD There is something to be said for that view, especially its extraordinary convenience.

KLARA It was your view as well.

ECKOLD Oh —

KLARA Yes it was. Otherwise you would have thrown me out. It would have been your right according to general opinion. What kept you from it — at the time — was, simply, nothing but the perception that our relationship had not been essentially changed.

ECKOLD Ah!

KLARA That by that time hardly anything could have been

changed between us any more through any action on my part.

ECKOLD I don't quite understand.

KLARA We had been distant from each other — at the time. That was the essential point. And what happened then, in addition, that was hardly of any great consequence in relation to the estrangement that had taken place between us.

ECKOLD Estrangement? What period are you speaking of? What do you call estrangement?

KLARA You really don't remember? Is it possible that this of all things, which led to everything else, should have slipped your mind?

ECKOLD Ah, now I see, all right. You're referring to the gloomiest period of my life, the time of my most difficult worries and struggles, the time when I finally had to give up my academic and scientific dreams and when it was determined once and for all that I was destined and condemned, not exactly through a lack of personal ability on my part, to remain nameless in my field, instead of achieving what simply fell into some other people's laps. I'll admit to you quite candidly, I was in a thoroughly foul frame of mind at the time. But I could picture a woman who stands at her husband's side during such a difficult period, comforts him, seeks to offer him compensation at home for all the pettiness he has to fight against out in the world. But you try or, at any rate, tried to make my gloom out to be some sort of fault, and the so-called estrangement was nothing more to you than a welcome pretext for — *with scorn* finding your happiness outside the house.

KLARA You are unjust. I honestly did my best at the time to help you get over all your disappointments and bad experiences. I probably lacked the strength for it. Perhaps I wearied too quickly. But it never occurred to me to blame you for your unfortunate temperament, as you claim. That this estrangement developed was probably nobody's fault, yours as little as mine. It may well be that human relationships are subject to their own illnesses, just like people. Surely you must have felt that as I did. And therefore you also knew that the deed itself — the betrayal, as people are accustomed to calling it, no longer meant much. Otherwise you would not have put up with it as you did.

ECKOLD   You think? Well, I guess I have to explain how I could — put up with it. I was prepared. I saw the fated event coming. One always does, you know. Some people close their eyes. I did not. And then I was clever enough to anticipate you. Do you understand what I'm saying? You'll have to give my vanity credit for that much, I'm afraid. I did not wait until *scornfully* your destiny and mine had been fulfilled. I saw it coming on, it was not to be stopped, and so I simply anticipated you. It's astonishing that you didn't even suspect anything! How little you must have cared about me. And I made no secret of it whatever. Especially he, your — lover, knew all about it. Is it possible that he didn't even give you a hint? That would be strange. Maybe you've forgotten? Well, it's all the same. In any event, it was fairly easy to bear — the destiny — especially since I had my definite plans for the future.

KLARA   *calmly* It would have been nobler to turn me out.

ECKOLD   And nobler of you, in any case, to leave at the appropriate time. These things never are very noble, you know. But it would not have been smart if we had separated at the time, regardless of where the idea of such a separation originated.

KLARA   And today, today, all of a sudden it's supposed to have become smart?

ECKOLD   Today, in fact, it's the only possibility.

KLARA   You don't believe that yourself.

ECKOLD   Why not? Would my decision appear more reasonable to you if I rolled my eyes, raised my hand against you, and raged like a madman? That's how it would have happened ten years ago, I imagine, had I been a fool. Surely you can't ask that of me today.

KLARA   There are no witnesses, Karl. You will no more take me to be presumptuous than I would take you to be —

ECKOLD   What?

KLARA   A comedian who doesn't want to have his scene spoiled. So, let it suffice. You wanted your triumph; you have it. Be satisfied with it. As you may well imagine, I'll be with Bettine often, as often as possible. That's what I want myself. But why all the rest? Why sever today a union in which nothing, or next to nothing remains which would justify any long-delayed punishment and revenge? What I have been to you these past few years — and you to me — that we can go on being to each other. Surely you haven't been putting on an act all these years! That would exceed all human strength. Inwardly you had forgiven me long before, even if you didn't admit it to yourself maybe. Oh, earlier already, much earlier — long before we became nothing more to each other than good friends.

ECKOLD   Good friends? That too is a word. Naturally, people have a lot to talk over with one another when they live under one roof and are connected by various common interests, not to mention by a child. If you want to call a connection of that sort friendship, there's nothing to keep you from it. For my part, it never hindered me from keeping my existence separate from yours in the depths of my soul and from living for the hour that has now finally arrived.

KLARA   But then you've been living for it only since we became truly nothing more to each other than housemates. Because at one time it was different.

ECKOLD   It was never different.

KLARA   It was different! Do try to remember! After the dark period of estrangement, of lies, if you will, there did come another — a better one — the time when we found each other again!

ECKOLD   We two — each other again?!

KLARA We both knew what we had suffered, even without telling each other. And much was made good again. Everything! Yes, try to remember. We were happy again, happy like before, happier than we had ever been. That is something you cannot wish away now. Just think of our trip — soon after. Of the wonderful days we spent together in Rome, in Naples. Surely you weren't acting a comedy for me then! Have everything else your own way, for all I care. But that time, when we came back to each other from our affairs and realized anew what we meant to each other, that was no lie and no self-deception. Just think back. It's difficult to speak of it today, of course. But I know it, and you know it too, I was never so entirely yours, never, not even during our earliest years together so very much your lover as then, when we found each other again.

ECKOLD That — that is simply a mistake.

KLARA It can't be.

ECKOLD It is! You were neither my wife nor my lover back then, any more than you became my friend later on. You could never become any of those for me again.

KLARA Karl!

ECKOLD Yes, I remember. It certainly had its charms too, that time; but you weren't my lover. At best —

KLARA *passionately* Don't say anything you can never make good again.

ECKOLD Who's got anything to make good here? You became for me merely what you could still be under the circumstances —

KLARA Karl! If that is true —

ECKOLD It is true.

KLARA Then you were obligated to tell me, before taking me again. You had the right, maybe, to turn me out, perhaps even to kill me in the end. But to keep secret from me the punishment you chose to inflict on me, that right you did not have. You've deceived me far worse and in a manner a thousand times more cowardly than I did you. You have degraded me far more deeply than any human being has the right to degrade another!

ECKOLD *triumphant* Do you feel that? Yes? Do you realize it? Oh, that makes me feel good. And it was worth the effort to wait ten years for this hour if you really feel your degradation today as deeply as I felt mine back then.

KLARA I did not degrade you.

ECKOLD Yes, you did! Degraded, mocked, and covered me with shame! If it hadn't been him, I almost believe I could have forgotten, could have forgiven you; and my anger would have long since been dissipated, my hatred extinguished in time. But that it was he of all people to whom you gave yourself, who had everything fall in his lap from childhood on, everything which was denied to me, no matter how desperately I toiled for it, that it was he, who always thought himself the better man just because nature had endowed him with an easier temperament — that filled my heart with bitterness against you. But it also gave me the patience to let my hatred swell within me without bursting my heart.

KLARA He? What fell in his lap? Who in the world is so happy that he may be described in such terms?

ECKOLD Do you want to hear his precious name again? The name of Ormin, of the magnificent, Ormin the superior, Ormin the darling of the gods —

KLARA *as if numb* Ormin?! But this is really. . . ! Ormin?! And — and if all this weren't true?

ECKOLD What's this all of a sudden?

KLARA Where is your evidence? Where is it?

ECKOLD It's a bit late for that idea. You would have betrayed yourself ten times, a hundred times this past hour, had that still been necessary. But could the two of you really imagine that everything would be taken care of, and all precautions exhausted by his registering in your love-nest under an assumed name? To be sure, the investigation was made a bit more difficult through the ingenious alias Ernst Mayer, but it did lead to the goal, if only in the nick of time. Had you ended you relationship on the tenth of May, instead of on the day after, then I really would have no evidence in hand. Because by the following day — it seems you didn't feel entirely secure after all — Mr. Ernst Mayer had departed, left town, destination unknown — and your romance was at an end. I'm well informed, aren't I? And how splendidly everything turned out for us all. Had I seen you disappear into that house on the following day also —

KLARA Well?

ECKOLD It would still have been possible for your lover's hour to have come to a bad end. Because there is something of the fool in all of us — in the Ormins as well as in the Eckolds. But this way I was given time to think it over, which I did, and I decided to remain silent until today.

KLARA And to him, even today —

ECKOLD What do I care about him?! That sentimental dandy, who now, in his declining days, because his skills are beginning to fail him, including in surgery as I've been told, is traveling across the ocean to face the dangers of pestilence and war in order that he might, by way of a melodramatic finale, be reunited with his worthy spouse?

KLARA You will not insult him.

ECKOLD Why not? Wasn't his entire life one big insult to me?

KLARA If you felt it to be so, then you would have had to, at least once, today, told him to his face.

ECKOLD Must men speak seriously and in detail about such things? What women meant to me, meant to me from a certain moment on, the others exactly the same as you, I never kept that a secret from him. Likewise, he's always known that I see through him all the way into the farthest corner of his tastefully furnished soul.

KLARA There is nothing in him to be seen through! He never acted a part as you did. He has always been genuine.

ECKOLD Is the magic still working, even today? I'm beginning to feel sorry for you.

KLARA There is no reason for that. I have been happy. As happy as ever a woman can be on earth. I am still happy today that I was his once, and neither you nor anyone else can take that from me! It just turned out to be him and no one else. I can't help you there. And I loved him beyond words. Beyond words! Do you understand me? Like nobody else in the world! Oh, that I spent good times in this house too, and that I was not connected to any human being over the course of many years as intimately as I was with you, that I will never forget — and you too — later on, soon, when you've calmed down a bit, you too will remember it all again. But what was everything life granted me, what was domestic harmony, a mother's happiness — compared to the short period of bliss when I was his — his — when I — was Ormin's lover!

ECKOLD You have seen him today for the last time. Do you know that? He will not return. Did he tell you?

KLARA He knows?

ECKOLD It hasn't been kept from him as far as I know. Perhaps now you'll understand also why I preferred to forego having a discussion with him.

KLARA I understand. Oh, I understand everything. And I understand everything so well that I — am going to leave your house this very evening.

ECKOLD We're agreed. But why leave today? You can have as much time as you wish.

KLARA I will go today. It'll still have been ten years too late. *Pause.*

ECKOLD *shrugs* You know that I'm of a different opinion. I am by no means ungrateful for those first years of our marriage either, which. . . . But, today was the day to speak of all the rest. Cruel words are unavoidable in such cases. *Looks out the window* I don't think it out of the question for us to talk quietly later on as well. You have nothing more to say to me? Well — until — until this evening. Obviously, it is necessary for us to discuss certain formal points. Now I have to go. I have to . . . *he hesitates, then* Good-bye.

KLARA *remains silent.*

ECKOLD *exits.*

KLARA *remains alone a while, entirely still and rigid; then, as if awakening, she goes into the room on the left and returns wearing a hat and coat. Hesitates. Then she sits down at the small desk to the right, takes a piece of paper and prepares to write. Stops* What for? To no one. Words lie. *She stands up.* Bettine? She doesn't need me any more. *She rings.*

MAID *enters* Madame?

KLARA I'll be home a little later today. Don't wait dinner for me. *She exits.*

MAID *looks after her somewhat surprised.*

Curtain

THE BIG SCENE

CHARACTERS

KONRAD HERBOT, *actor*
SOPHIE, *his wife*
EDGAR GLEY
DOCTOR FALK, *theater director*
VILMA FLAMM
A STAGE MANAGER
A HOTEL BELLHOP
A WAITER

The action takes place in a hotel room in Berlin.

Fashionable hotel room; a door in the background leading to the corridor, another, covered with a portière, to the left a door, leading into the adjacent room. Front left a fireplace with a burning log fire, a small table and chairs. In the center, towards the right, a desk with a telephone on it. A divan up against the desk. At the rear right, an alcove concealed by a curtain. To the right, a fairly large window overlooking a theater. Armoires on either side of the door in the background. It is late afternoon at the end of autumn. The stage is empty for a few minutes. A knock at the door. Pause. A second knock.

The BELLHOP *enters through the door in the back with some letters at the same time that* SOPHIE *enters from the left.*

SOPHIE Letters?

BELLHOP *who was on the point of placing the letters on the desk, goes up to her.*

SOPHIE Any for me? *She takes the letters, looks through them quickly, places three of them on the desk, keeps the fourth in her hand.* Right! From him!

BELLHOP *exits.*

SOPHIE *goes towards the window with the letter, which she has opened hastily, reads it through, smiles, shakes her head, continues reading. There is a knock at the door* Come in!

BELLHOP *enters with a calling card which he hands to Sophie.*

SOPHIE Vilma Flamm? Never heard of her.

BELLHOP The lady says she was told to come.

SOPHIE Told to come? I see. Tell her my husband is not at home.

BELLHOP *exits.*

SOPHIE *continues to read her letter; she seems moved* No — the things he gets in his head. He can't seriously believe — *A knock at the door.* What is it now? Come in!

VILMA FLAMM *enters. She is 22, dressed in a modern way,*

but in neither a very elegant nor an excessively striking manner, except for her very large hat. Her hair-do, black, is pre-Raphaelite. Lively eyes. When she sees Sophie she becomes somewhat confused Excuse me —

SOPHIE Miss Flamm?

VILMA That's right. You see, I was told to come here —

SOPHIE The bellhop probably didn't deliver my message, did he? Mr. Herbot is not at home.

VILMA I'm so very sorry; the thing is, I thought there must be a mistake since I was directed to come here today at five. In fact, I was even afraid I was late. Will Mr. Herbot be coming back soon?

SOPHIE *very cool* I don't know. Perhaps you'll try another time. Or wait down in the lobby.

VILMA Wait! That is not my strong suit, waiting. And especially — you must be Mr. Herbot's secretary?

SOPHIE No, I am his wife.

VILMA *involuntarily* Ah!

SOPHIE *smiling* That seems to astonish you somewhat, Miss.

VILMA Not at all. I only thought — I mean, it is said — Herr Herbot is divorced.

SOPHIE *cool* A mistake.

VILMA Fortunately.

SOPHIE *who had already half turned away, turns back to her* Very kind of you. *In a friendlier tone* Perhaps you'd like to leave a message for my husband?

VILMA If Madam would be so kind — although — it's more of a personal matter. That is, I was expecting to audition for Mr. Herbot.

SOPHIE Audition?

VILMA I'm studying to be an actress, you see. For the past six months I've been studying with Mrs. Fuchs. But I've recently begun to doubt whether her method is the right one for me. My family is dead set against it. My father is a merchant. He owns a notions store. Flamm and Sons. The sons are my brothers. But I explained all this in detail in a letter to Mr. Herbot, a whole week ago; and in response Mr. Herbot had the great kindness of asking me to come here today at five. Could he have forgotten, perhaps?

SOPHIE It's possible, since it was a whole week ago. *A knock at the door.*

VILMA *quickly* Come in! Oh! I beg your pardon —

SOPHIE *smiles involuntarily.*

BELLHOP *enters with a calling card.*

SOPHIE But of course, ask him to come in.

DIRECTOR FALK *a short, slim man; clean shaven, with clever eyes, horn-rimmed pince-nez which he removes from time to time; he is wearing an overcoat, carrying a walking stick and several manuscripts* And he doesn't have to be asked twice, he's here already.

SOPHIE *delighted, offering her hand* Good evening, dear friend. *To Vilma, who has remained standing and is beaming at the Director* You'll excuse me, Miss, perhaps you had best write again —

VILMA I will take the liberty to do so. But if Madame would perhaps be so kind as to introduce me to the Director —

FALK *turns away after throwing her a scathing glance.*

SOPHIE *somewhat taken aback* I've forgotten your name, Miss.

VILMA Then perhaps you will allow me — my name is Vilma Flamm, actress, beginning actress. You see in me, Mr. Falk, one of your most ardent admirers; I hardly ever attend a theater other than yours, and I take this opportunity —

FALK *sharply* I do not, Miss. *Turns away.*

VILMA I had no intention — but it seemed to me as an absolute sign of fate —

FALK You have obviously misunderstood this sign. I discuss matters regarding the theater only in my office between two and three in the afternoon by prior appointment.

VILMA Then I'll be so bold, tomorrow at two —

FALK Don't be in too great a hurry, Miss. We have no openings. You're young, try the provinces. Germany has a wealth of excellent —

VILMA *studiously joining in* Theaters.

FALK Train connections, I was going to say. Good evening, Miss.

VILMA In any event, I will always remember this moment.

FALK That I cannot prevent you from doing, Miss.

VILMA Good evening, Madam, good evening, Director Falk. *She exits.*

FALK *still holding his walking stick* Why do you allow something like that in the door, Sophie? May I? *He lays his hat, walking stick and overcoat on the divan, keeps the rolled up manuscripts in his hand.*

SOPHIE I couldn't help it. All of a sudden she was standing there. Herbot had asked her to come. In order to audition her.

FALK Why not? He does have his pedagogic attacks sometimes.

SOPHIE *bitter* I wonder if I shouldn't pack up my few things and get out again.

FALK Oh, sure, that would really be worth the effort. On account of this fledgling actress, who appears to be of no concern whatever to either you or me, or for that matter, even to him. You see, he wasn't even at home.

SOPHIE He wrote to her a week ago, when he still considered himself divorced.

FALK That he never did.

SOPHIE And if I hadn't arrived yesterday —

FALK *interrupting* But you did. And that, my dear Sophie, is what we want to hold fast to for the time being. Because it's in order to offer his most humble welcome and congratulations on this, your return, that the undersigned takes the liberty of waiting upon you.

SOPHIE I gladly accept your welcome, but whether or not there is any cause for congratulations —

FALK I should think so. For numerous congratulations even. Your husband I already congratulated during rehearsal today, and myself I find in a state of uninterrupted self-congratulations on the occasion of winning back my top actor.

SOPHIE I didn't notice you had ever lost him.

FALK Well —

SOPHIE I did keep track of the repertoire. From the first of September until today, the thirtieth of October, he played six times a week, and during this time he created two new parts, one classical and one modern; and I hear they were both triumphs.

FALK Triumphs? Hmm. Well, with me he did not triumph. I even booed him, very softly, of course, more or less to myself, since, as you know, loud expressions of disapproval are forbidden in my theater. The people liked him, naturally. My God, by the time the audience or, for that matter, the critics finally notice that one of their favorites is starting to lose it — a dozen new geniuses can go to ruin in the meantime. Recently, in *Tasso*, he got stuck no less than seven times. The good people most likely took them to be seven fresh nuances. And what's more, he's fallen into hollow declamation again, as he was doing back when I got him from your Burgtheater.

SOPHIE Don't abuse the Burgtheater; it is still better than — most others.

FALK Yes, I know, that's a fixed idea of you Viennese. On the other hand, it is my own, dearest Frau Sophie, that it would have been Herbot's ruin —

SOPHIE If he had stayed —

FALK No, not at all. I mean, if you two hadn't reconciled. And therefore, as a promoter of German art in general and as Director of the playhouse in particular, I was especially obligated to bring you to your senses.

SOPHIE Oh!

FALK And to lead you back to his arms again.

SOPHIE So, it was the theater director who wrote me such heart-rending letters.

FALK Let's leave aside whether they were heart-rending or not. At all events, I'm pleased to see they've accomplished their purpose, and flatter myself that not only my theater but also Herbot personally, and you as well, Frau Sophie, will benefit from it. For that I will gladly forego all expressions of gratitude.

SOPHIE They would be premature at the very least.

FALK Now that I can't agree with. I make no claims, as I said, but it is good, for you as well, that you two are together again. You simply belong to each other. Yes. Beyond that, you may both do or have done whatever you like.

SOPHIE Both?!

FALK It was a figure of speech, Frau Sophie, at least where you're concerned. But as for him — I'm not saying this for the first time, you know — him you simply must take as he is. Geniuses are simply troublesome, for directors just as much as for wives.

SOPHIE Except that for the director the trouble pays better.

FALK Don't say that Frau Sophie. It pays you as well. It must be a wonderful feeling for you to know that a splendid fellow like that is absolutely dependent on you, and more so with every passing year; that he can neither live nor do a decent job of acting without you. Look, if there is such a thing as irrefutable proof of love, here it is. And since you, likewise, can't live without him —

SOPHIE That remains to be seen.

FALK Well, all the same, you're here. The rest will work out, if it hasn't yet. But now, let me have a look at you, kind Frau Sophie. Your solitude has agreed with you quite well — if it was solitude.

SOPHIE Say, Doctor, what are you thinking?

FALK No one would've held it against you, truly. He least of all. And revenge is sweet, I've been told.

SOPHIE A thirst for revenge, that's not part of my nature.

FALK Well, yes, high class it isn't, of course, if only because revenge, at least in a case such as this, is seldom undertaken for its own sake alone. For the avenger a good part of the sweetness does fall by the wayside, a fact not foreseen in the proverb. But why are you laughing, Frau Sophie?

SOPHIE I'm thinking how clever that is, what you just said, and how ruthlessly you'd still cross it out if one of your playwrights had thought of it.

FALK Properly so. Sagacity on stage is useless. But, to continue our unedited dialogue, I must observe that Madam has gotten somewhat slimmer and yet looks somewhat pale.

SOPHIE Don't go talking yourself into anything, Doctor. I look terrific. And things went splendidly for me too. Solitude is not such a bad thing — and healthy, healthy! Just think, to stroll alone along the seashore for hours at a time, or to read some nice book or to lie in a boat and look at the blue sky and — not to have to listen to any lies, any lies the whole day.

FALK Well, Frau Sophie, you're exaggerating a bit, probably. Lies! There are no lies in the world. There are only people who let themselves be cheated. And you never belonged among them. On the other hand, there are certain human relationships which are built on lies. Something else to be edited out, isn't it? But that Herbot loves you and has always loved you, that does remain an irrefutable truth, one not to be edited out, in spite of everything that's happened.

SOPHIE And that will happen.

FALK Nothing more will happen. You shouldn't let this tragedy of the departing actress affect you this much. Herbot could not have known a week ago that you would finally have a change of heart. So maybe he wanted to lay in provisions for the winter.

SOPHIE And you can come up with an excuse even for that! Don't you know that all this time he wrote to me almost every day, in spite of my hardly ever sending him a few cool lines in return. And what letters!

FALK Even more beautiful than mine?

SOPHIE One would really have believed, indeed, been obliged to believe that he had no other thought, no other longing than for me!

FALK It's true, too. Shall I tell you how often this spoiled child — I trust you won't make any use of this — whined like a baby on your account? And not only in my quiet cell. Only recently, in the restaurant — he had been apparently quite cheerful a moment earlier — suddenly he had his head down on the table and began to howl like a pampered dog.

SOPHIE And in your apartment like a baby. A fine distinction.

FALK Well then, let's say, like a pampered child.

SOPHIE But in the restaurant you first had champagne, at any rate.

FALK I won't deny it.

SOPHIE So, he drank too!

FALK Only when the pain overpowered him!

SOPHIE But he enjoyed the taste anyway, didn't he?

FALK Yes, life takes its course, as one of my authors maintained not very profoundly but exceedingly accurately. And in this spirit, let us all surrender to our destinies — and today, after *Hamlet*, conclusion at 11:45, empty a bottle of Sekt to the couple's happy reunion and to German art! And I guarantee you, tonight Herbot will not cry. But really, what's keeping him?

SOPHIE He's taking his afternoon walk, an old habit of his, or he's deceiving me with some tragedienne, or banker's wife, or shopgirl.

FALK Oh, please — deceiving you! Before *Hamlet*! What an idea!

SOPHIE *laughing against her will* By the way, what are you swinging back and forth there all the time?

FALK Oh, this, this is a new play. Very interesting part. I want him to take a look at it. I can rely on his judgment now, since it has fortunately *with a bow* come back again.

SOPHIE You are too kind.

FALK By the way, when did you arrive, dear Frau Sophie? a name which translated into our beloved German means, not without justice, Frau Wisdom.

SOPHIE Last night. Oh, you needn't make your confounded face. The hotel was full. I got the room next door here only this noon.

FALK Let's have a serious word now. Isn't it a noble stroke on his part that he left your beautiful apartment closed up, and made a sacred vow not to set foot in it again other than arm in arm with you?

SOPHIE Oh, yes, there are vows that he keeps. In any case, it's more convenient here in the hotel, directly across from the theater, — to audition and to teach as well —

FALK That really is enough now. One either makes up or one does not make up. You can't start with the suspicions again right away. You see, I didn't come here for the sole purpose of congratulating you on your return, but also to extract a promise from you.

SOPHIE A promise?

FALK That you will never again make such trouble for me.

SOPHIE Trouble? Me?

FALK That you will never leave him again. One really does not want to be left vulnerable to explosions of certain primal forces in the middle of the season. This time you gave him the slip on August fourteenth; it took him until the first of September before he could play again. But what am I going to do if something like that happens to me just when there's a hit running? I can't take that risk. So, you must promise me —

SOPHIE Shouldn't we draw up a contract while we're at it?

FALK Contract? — Please! I want you to give me your word out of conviction, out of insight, out of your understanding of the situation. I know he'll never do it again. He's learned something from the experience this time. But all the same, I'm obligated as manager of an entertainment establishment with a ban on smoking to anticipate all eventualities. So, even if such a trifle takes place again —

SOPHIE Doctor! You are really astonishing me now! Trifle! Have I been talking to the wall all this time? Or must I assume that in this lying world even so decent, so noble a human being as you loses his ability to distinguish between frivolity and — infamy?

FALK But — but!

SOPHIE That you think it possible I would come back yet again —

FALK I don't mean you should come back, I mean you should never again leave in the first place. After all, you yourself have already proven it's possible for you not to take certain things tragically. And I really don't understand why just this time —

SOPHIE You really don't understand? You, who were so to speak a witness to the entire business?

FALK I was a witness to that other business too, three years ago. But I don't see any difference. Unfaithfulness is still unfaithfulness. I really don't know why just this time —

SOPHIE There are differences, dear friend. That time, three years ago, it was only a matter for Herbot and me to settle with each other. There weren't any other destinies involved.

FALK All the same, there was surely a third person involved back then as well. That's the nature of these affairs.

SOPHIE A starlet like that, who had already had all sorts of affairs and who had no responsibilities for either herself or anyone else. And then, when a man plays the same dangerous role with such a creature a hundred times in a row — it's practically preordained. I had seen it coming on opening night, when it turned out to be such a huge success. The only question was after which performance destiny would be fulfilled.

FALK It was after the ninth. But by the twenty-fifth it was over.

SOPHIE You do keep precise books, Doctor.

FALK Well, yes, one does play a bit of the father, after all. And let me assure you, if it hadn't been over soon, I would have replaced her. Entirely for your sake, Frau Sophie. Because his unfaithfulness wasn't quite as indifferent to you at the time as you want to make out today either.

SOPHIE Indifferent? No. But I understood it. I said to myself, how would you fare if you had to play opposite a person like Herbot every night. There happens not to be another like him, unfortunately. I can well imagine, it comes over a person like some ecstasy, like madness, like a dream, — until one wakes up again. I did not have this insight at once, of course. At first I wanted to kill them.

FALK Both of them?

SOPHIE *completely serious* Him first of all.

FALK Then I would have had to cancel the play. And it would never have recovered.

SOPHIE *laughing involuntarily* Oh please, Doctor, others played the role after Herbot.

FALK Later, much later. By then it was possible. But leading men may under no circumstances be murdered prior to the fiftieth performance. Yes, indeed, here one can first see what casting problems threaten without one's suspecting it. In any case, dear Sophie, I have every reason to thank you retroactively for having thought better of it. Exactly like this time.

SOPHIE Whether it was better this time too, that is still an open question.

FALK As certainly as then. I know perfectly well that it was only after that crisis back then that you first became such a truly happy couple. Famously happy! At least until August of this year. And now you will become one again.

SOPHIE Famously happy!

FALK That's right, Frau Sophie!

SOPHIE I don't believe it. Even if I am here again, happiness it can never again become.

FALK But!

SOPHIE Consider who the chosen one was this time. A young girl, an innocent young girl, engaged to be married! And the fiancé an excellent, truly distinguished human being who is madly in love with the girl, and with whom Herbot was downright friendly. Does one have the right to meddle in people's lives this way?

FALK In a higher sense I suppose not, but one could also ask whether any meddling into other people's lives has really taken place here. The young man knows nothing, the wedding's in a week.

SOPHIE That may be the worst part of it.

FALK I think you've seen too much Ibsen in my theater, Sophie. Fortunately, Herbot dislikes Ibsen and views the matter as substantially less harmful, no different than that other business with the little actress, even if this time it did involve a young girl from a good family, indeed, an engaged one, which need not, of course, always imply an enhancement of the experience. He has never concerned himself with pangs of conscience. His is a far too primal or, to be plain about it, too healthy a nature.

SOPHIE Healthy nature! One could call it something else too.

FALK And to be honest with you, I really wouldn't have thought you'd be all that upset about it either. At first, there at the lake, just when the thing was developing, I absolutely did not have that impression. You even seemed rather pleased and didn't notice, or didn't want to notice anything. I was a little surprised, even; or to be still more honest, let me qualify that: I would have almost been surprised.

SOPHIE That sounds a bit obscure, Doctor.

FALK Well, I'm trying to say that I would have been surprised that you allowed things to continue in their course if at precisely the critical time I hadn't found you occupied yourself, spiritually and in other ways.

SOPHIE *smiling* My, the things you notice, dear Doctor.

FALK It didn't require any particular sharpsightedness on my part. With which observation I cannot, as an old and experienced dramaturge, help shifting a part of the tragic blame over to you.

SOPHIE *very serious* Perhaps you're right. Perhaps I'm not entirely blameless. Otherwise I might not have come back!

FALK And I wonder — a rhetorical question from the immoral moral theorist — whether you wouldn't feel much better today if you — if you had also — how shall I put it — become entirely guilty.

SOPHIE Possibly. I had similar thoughts myself in my solitude.

FALK You had similar thoughts, and still it remained solitude?

SOPHIE You still doubt me?

FALK Wouldn't dream of it.

SOPHIE All the same, I have to think you don't have a very accurate picture of the business you alluded to before. And since I feel you're my friend — *She hesitates.*

FALK You have no better one.

SOPHIE That's why I want you to be quite clear about all this. As clear as I am myself. Here's a letter I received an hour ago. From him!

FALK From him? From the young man with the hunting hat? My chess partner?

SOPHIE He's the one you were speaking of, isn't he? Or do you suspect me with still another person? It's a letter from the young man with whom I struck you as being so inwardly and, I suppose, outwardly occupied, that I allowed matters between my husband and Daisy to proceed as they did. Do

•

you want to read it?

FALK Typewritten? No, handwritten, — then you'll have to be good enough to excuse me, Frau Sophie. Read it to me yourself, won't you, with your dark, resonant voice.

SOPHIE Only a few places that will explain everything. Wait. *Turns some pages and reads* "I hear you are still in Brioni, dear lady, and still alone. Since you left the shores of the Attersee a few days before me and have not, to my knowledge, set foot in Vienna, it follows that you have not seen your husband in more than two months." *She breaks off* The letter was forwarded to me here. *Continues reading* "It is no more my intention to intrude into secrets, dear lady, than to attempt to intrude into a freely chosen seclusion. Whatever may have happened, or whatever you intend to do, must not concern me, at least not more than you wish to allow. But if I may recall to your memory today an hour, a wonderful hour on the shore of the lake just before sunset" — *lowers the letter* a wonderful hour, during which my husband was sailing far out on the lake with Daisy and her fiancé.

FALK I don't imagine the "wonderful" in the letter refers to that. I assume our friend means something between the two of you —

SOPHIE It was the hour in which he spoke to me of his feelings for the first and only time. No, not spoke of them, allowed them to be guessed in his quiet, bashful, moving way. He kissed my hand, that was all.

FALK That can be a great deal.

SOPHIE Still, you'll have to admit, the measure of my transgression was quite small.

FALK And that is all the more praiseworthy since it truly did involve a particularly nice young man. I have seldom become friendly with a person as quickly. His entire being gave off such a pleasant woodsy fragrance. Such totally unliterary persons are a true godsend. I'm sure he's never written a play in his life.

SOPHIE   Yes, there's something to be said for them, these individuals who are not geniuses, but simply honest people.

FALK   Well, honest, that's just another word. The wonderful hour along the shore of the lake — I think it depended only on you — and all the honesty —

SOPHIE   Oh, you don't know him well. Even at that moment he had — how shall I put it — highly honorable intentions, exactly as now, which, by the way, is evident from this letter as well. I want to read you the conclusion. Listen. *She turns some pages.*

FALK   You're leaving a lot out.

SOPHIE   *reads*   "The same . . . I am the same man I was this summer. If you need a friend, call me or, better still, come yourself."

FALK   Are you coming yourself?

SOPHIE   Just listen some more. *She reads*   "My life belongs to you. I am completely alone and free in all respects. If you are *too*, Sophie, but only then, when you are as free as I am led to suppose" —

FALK   *brusquely*   He's got it wrong, completely wrong. Have you written to tell him that yet?

SOPHIE   His letter arrived an hour ago.

FALK   "Come yourself!" Not bad. The young man seems to have this fixed idea of inviting everyone to his hunting lodge in Klein-Reifling.

SOPHIE   Everyone?

FALK   Yes. You see, he's invited me too, this summer. During a wonderful hour. "If you really want to get away from the bustle of the theater for a few days sometime," he said, "then come visit me in Klein-Reifling. A splendid region, we can play chess every evening, you needn't shoot any deer." Most likely he didn't ask that of you either, Frau Sophie.

SOPHIE   *letting the letter sink down*   Ah, how foolish we can be. Why are people like us so created that we can become totally enslaved by another person, — one who doesn't even understand it.

FALK   Doesn't understand? A lack of understanding is something Herbot could accuse you of also to a certain extent! Has he actually been as bad — at least in the way you ascribe to him? I mean, does he care about the lives of others? What are other people to him altogether? To him, who is accustomed always to playing the leading part? Extras in single scenes, who never exit to applause and who die off-stage without a sound. Surely one cannot wrong such people when one is the hero. — What's the matter?

SOPHIE   He — he's coming. I hear his footsteps and my heart beats like a young girl's. This is crazy.

FALK   On the contrary, it's very nice.

KONRAD HERBOT *enters; forty-five, dark curly hair, a little speckled with gray already, black eyes; he is somewhat loud and in high spirits at first. Wearing a hat and coat.*

HERBOT   Good evening, folks! *Slaps Falk on the shoulder* Well, what do you say, old boy, here we are back home again, so to speak, even if it's only a hotel room for the time being. *Strokes Sophie's cheek* Good evening, darling. *To Falk* She looks great, doesn't she? It is nice that she's here again.

FALK   I'll say.

HERBOT   We've been back together for a few hours and right away it's as if it had never been otherwise. The two months gone and forgotten! Incredible!

SOPHIE   One really can tell I've been away. You're talking like a Berliner again.

HERBOT   Oh, right. *Taking his coat off* She can't stand that, you see. *In an exaggerated Viennese dialect* Don't worry, I'll be good again, *Schatzerl*!

FALK   Well, I'll leave you two alone now, you newlyweds.

SOPHIE   Won't you have a cup of tea with us?

FALK I'm afraid I can't.

SOPHIE *rings.*

HERBOT Why are you going again?

FALK I've been here for an hour already. Where were you wandering around all this time?

HERBOT *looking at his watch* Damn, five-thirty already. Oh, there's something tremendously charming in walking about the streets when you know there's someone waiting for you at home.

FALK Except that for the one waiting the thing is usually less charming. Well, then, I'll see you in the theater! *To Sophie* I've had the usual seat in the box reserved for you, Frau Sophie. By the way, it's sold out.

HERBOT Big deal!

FALK Good-bye!

HERBOT I'm always telling you, you pay me too small a salary. Addio! Will you be inside too?

FALK On the assumption that you will finally give a decent performance again today.

HERBOT You scoundrel! By the way, couldn't we, in celebration of the day, go to Kannenberg's together afterwards for a bottle of Sekt —

SOPHIE Konrad!

HERBOT What's the matter? Oh, right! *In the Viennese dialect* So then we'll go for a spritzer afterwards and for a small goulash, ok?

FALK That will be for Frau Sophie to decide.

WAITER *enters, takes Sophie's order, and exits again.*

HERBOT *noticing the manuscript* What's that?

FALK The play I spoke to you about this morning.

HERBOT Another one?! Well, thank God Sophie's here. Yes, it's all over with vacation now, Sophie. There's another half dozen lying there. Say, Falk, I tried again to take a glance into one or the other. They really are pure trash.

FALK Will you listen to that! *To Sophie* The foremost names in Germany.

HERBOT Look, I want to tell you something quite candidly, Falk. Every play has struck me as absolute nonsense when I read it. And mostly I've been right, too. Of course, with this or that one, when one sees it on stage —

FALK And Konrad Herbot plays the leading part —

HERBOT To be sure, that's not a disadvantage, usually. But cross your heart, surely you feel yourself at times that all this theater stuff is nonsense somehow, don't you? Backdrop and wings and the curtain goes up and down and the white prompter's box in front with that fellow inside —

FALK Well, him you can just leave alone.

HERBOT But the craziest part, that's we ourselves, we actors, who are in part quite reasonable people in real life. We strike a pose up there and declaim some memorized stuff as if we took it quite seriously and enter and exit; and they sit down below and gape, and clap their hands. Unbelievable. That they should fall for something like that. Do you know what I think sometimes? All this dramatic art is actually only an invention of the box-office.

FALK A broadminded notion or perhaps a profound one too.

HERBOT Well, yes. If the discovery got out among the people, that would spoil business for you. I'll keep it to myself for the time being. But I wouldn't want to guarantee that I won't write a pamphlet on the subject sometime, or one of those Christmas supplements — they're always after me for one of those, you know.

FALK But wait a little while longer, until you no longer draw as an actor. Next year, or the year after.

HERBOT Yes, that would suit him, then he could save some real money! Well, so long! Oh, yes, the other thing I still wanted to say, if there's another racket outside my dressing room today like the day before yesterday during *Tasso*, I'll make such a row that —

FALK And if you stink up your dressing room with smoke

again, then I'll make use of my right to give you notice and fire you on the spot.

HERBOT But that's what I'm waiting for. I could lead a sensible life then. Lie on green lawns, look at the blue sky, or cross the fields, the meadows, a hunting rifle at —

FALK Hunting rifle?

HERBOT Well, yes, it wouldn't be so bad. A crying shame that I have to play-act instead.

FALK Has my chess-playing friend in the green hat invited you too, by any chance?

HERBOT Herr von Bolschan? Of course he has.

FALK This seems to be an obsession of his.

HERBOT A charming fellow. Just ask Sophie. She likes him very much too. Yes, my darling, one has eyes in his head.

FALK You're not getting any vacation from me. You have no business in Klein-Reifling. Well, I'll see you later. I'm inviting myself into your box, Frau Sophie. *Exits.*

HERBOT A sweetheart of a man. But he took me to the cleaners with the last contract. Well, he'll have to shell out some more, all right. Or I'll go to America. They do only pay starvation wages here. Well, Sophie — *pulling her to him abruptly* so we're really together again. I can't believe it yet. But now tell me, did you seriously intend to abandon me for good?

SOPHIE You can see I'm back again. So let's not talk about it any more. Let's forget it.

HERBOT Forget! Sure, if one could just like that. I don't imagine you have any idea what a terrible time I had here. I wasn't at all myself. I walked around as in a dream, a bad dream. And I acted like a pig too. Not always, but often enough.

SOPHIE Yes, that's what Falk says too.

HERBOT What? The impudence! I played more than well enough for him. For the entire lot of them altogether! Too well, in fact! Falk's only saying that so he can beat me down.

You first have to get to know the man. He'll hang himself for a hundred marks. But they're all like that. I know he's spreading the rumor that I'm losing it. But nobody believes him. They have eyes and ears, after all — fortunately! The audiences — I have them! Still, and for a long time to come. And especially now, now that you're here again. If you hadn't come back — yes, then, of course. Without you I'm lost, that's for sure. I would have left the stage. Or gone into vaudeville. One can travel around in the world more in vaudeville too, and they also pay much better. *The waiter comes in with tea and baked goods and begins to arrange them on the small table.* By the way, know what? I'm taking vacation in February and we're going to the Riviera together. I won't have any contradiction here. I dare say I've earned it, by God. It's something I've wanted to do since I was a boy. And today I'm forty-three. Almost twenty-seven years in the theater. Twenty-seven. "As a sixteen-year old boy he ran away" — you know — *Waiter exits.*

SOPHIE *while pouring tea* Yes, only to this day I've been unable to discover from whom you actually ran away. Your parents were quite in agreement with your going on stage.

HERBOT Why, of course. By the time I was fourteen I was already acting at home. "The late Royal Bavarian Court Actor Story it was, who saw in the young disciple of Thespis" — *he notices the card* Who is Vilma Flamm?

SOPHIE Vilma Flamm is a young lady.

HERBOT What sort of young lady?

SOPHIE A young artiste whom you asked to come here.

HERBOT Asked to come here?

SOPHIE Yes. You wanted to see if she has any talent. She wrote you a week ago.

HERBOT Oh, yes. Silly goose. I hope you showed her the door.

SOPHIE That I did. But all the same, you asked her to come.

HERBOT Possibly. You know, sometimes I answer and

sometimes I don't. Anyone else show up?

SOPHIE Not today.

HERBOT Well then, just throw them all out. You have full authority. I do not assess talent, I do not teach, I do not give autographs. By the way, she could also have been a phony. I'll be damned if I can recall the name Vilma Flamm. *They are now sitting at the table.*

SOPHIE You seem to have a bad memory altogether.

HERBOT One should have a memory for that sort of thing too! That's all I need. Just think of everything I have to cram into my skull. The glorious words of our greatest authors' masterly figures and all the modern garbage; naturally, there's no room for other memories.

SOPHIE For none at all?

HERBOT Anyhow, that's entirely under my control. I remember and I forget as it suits me. And I assure you, Sophie — because I know what you're thinking — if I — if I were to run into a certain young woman on the street, I would not recognize her any more. I have absolutely no idea any more what she looks like. If I tried to call her picture to mind it would be in vain. She is a shadow, a ghost, someone's great-grandmother.

SOPHIE *bursting out* How could you ever have done that?

HERBOT Yes, how could I ever have done that!

SOPHIE Her fiancé was your friend.

HERBOT No — friend — I wouldn't go that far. But still, it was a mean trick. And I was prepared to pay for it.

SOPHIE You were — For what were you prepared?

HERBOT On the morning I came home from her arms — I beg your pardon — and found you no longer there — only your few words of farewell, those horrible — when I was forced to believe I had lost you, lost you forever, do you know what my first impulse was? To go up to him, to tell him, I am a wretch, I have betrayed my wife, I have seduced your fiancée, — well, and so on. For hours I wandered along the lake in the early morning light, fought a terrible battle with myself, until I finally realized that I mustn't do it. If only on account of Daisy's family. But I tell you, Sophie, they were difficult days, those last five days in the country, at our villa, and the most difficult part was this having to lie, this constant having to lie.

SOPHIE You think so?

HERBOT Well, yes; after all, I had to find a plausible reason for your sudden departure. And so I invented a tale about a broken water pipe in our apartment in Berlin. Oh, I invented details, details — entire letters from you, humorous turns. You have no idea! Yes, that's how I had to go on living, a broken water pipe on my lips and death in my heart. Yes, my dear child, it wasn't easy to get through the days as if nothing had happened; bathing, having breakfast, sailing —

SOPHIE As if nothing had happened. The days and the nights —

HERBOT Sophie, I swear to you, from the day you left me, I swear it, it was also over between —

SOPHIE Don't swear. No more oaths relating to things in the past, Konrad. The past is buried. For all time.

HERBOT Long since buried.

SOPHIE But the future, Konrad, that belongs to us, — if only you want it.

HERBOT If I want it?! And how I want it, my little Sophie!

SOPHIE And I beg of you, Konrad, be truthful! It's the only thing I implore of you. I can understand everything, you see, forgive everything, only this one thing I implore you, don't put on any act. Not for me. It isn't necessary. And everything you've been saying now, that wasn't you, either. Here and there a glimmer of you shone through your mask, but it wasn't you, not the real you. Because you exist so deep within yourself, so deep. And I do feel that what you are is something good, something one could believe in. You need only believe in it yourself. Deep down in your soul, Konrad,

I can feel it, you are a child, truly a child. So —

HERBOT A child. There may be something to that. I feel it
myself at times, — a child. How do you know that? Yes, that
in itself explains a lot to me. I want to tell you something,
Sophie. When I think of myself, or dream of myself, I never
actually see myself as a fairly grown-up, already somewhat
gray-haired gentleman then, but, rather, as a small boy who
is being led by the hand by someone, — by his father or his
tutor. And yet I never had a tutor. Actually, it surprises me
sometimes — you mustn't tell anyone — that people talk to
me as to an entirely reasonable, fully grown up human being.
That's when I feel like saying to them, do leave me in peace,
I don't understand anything about all these things, I don't
belong in your company at all. Yes, Sophie, that was an
extraordinarily fine observation. A child — yes. *A knock at
the door* Who the hell is that? Come in!

BELLHOP *enters with a card.*

HERBOT *without reading it* I'm not at home. *Reads it, starts*
What?

SOPHIE Who is it? *Takes the card from his hand* Edgar Gley
— Edgar —

HERBOT *to the bellhop* You heard me, I'm not at home. I'm
performing tonight.

SOPHIE You have to see him, Herbot.

HERBOT I have to? I don't see it that way.

SOPHIE *to the bellhop* Wait.

HERBOT Where is this gentleman?

BELLHOP In the lobby.

SOPHIE *softly, to Herbot* You won't be able to avoid this
conversation. So, the sooner the better.

HERBOT *to the bellhop* Ask him to come up.

BELLHOP *exits.*

SOPHIE *anxious but controlled and serious* Konrad —

HERBOT Well, what can it amount to? A total lack of

consideration, by the way, — before *Hamlet*. *Paces up and down.*

SOPHIE You haven't heard anything more from him?

HERBOT If I tell you, it's been two months — it is completely out of the question for him to know anything. It needn't have anything to do with her, you know.

SOPHIE Konrad! How does he happen to come here — to Berlin? She lives in Vienna — he is in Villach, with the government, and now, suddenly, he's here.

HERBOT Vacation, most likely! Berlin *is* a very interesting city after all.

SOPHIE The two of you must have been careless, I know it. You climbed through the window at night. Someone saw you.

HERBOT Not he, otherwise he'd have been here before today.

SOPHIE Just don't do anything silly now. This last time you may — you must lie.

HERBOT Thank you for the kind permission! Here you can depend on me. But now please go down to the lobby, all right? If you were to stay next door here you would — And I want to remain uninhibited. If I knew you were listening it would make me unsure of myself. So —

SOPHIE *anxiously* Konrad!

HERBOT Easy, my child. Calm down. *He strokes her hair. As he wants to pull her towards himself she fends him off gently and goes into the adjoining room. Herbot stands still for a moment, then picks up the manuscript, turns a few pages, and lights a cigarette. He grows impatient, stands up, goes up to the door on the right and listens. There is a knock at the door. He tip-toes back into the room, and picks up the manuscript. There is a second knock.*

HERBOT Come in!

EDGAR *enters* Good evening.

HERBOT Good evening, Herr Gley, I'm glad to see you in my — in my hotel, that is.

EDGAR I don't want to keep you long, Herr Herbot.

HERBOT Oh! — Although I am performing tonight.

EDGAR I know.

HERBOT I'm sure I can still spare a quarter of an hour. Won't you sit down. My wife will be very sorry —

EDGAR *somewhat taken aback* Your wife is here?

HERBOT Yes, of course. Where else should she be? She was away for a couple of weeks, oh — but you know. Our apartment was in a terrible state, perhaps you still remember, I did tell you about it — a broken water pipe. But tomorrow or the day after it'll be in perfect condition again. It was completely flooded. A mess, I tell you! And damage of at least ten thousand marks. That means guest appearances again. And I have the loss of a number of irreplaceable manuscripts to mourn besides. I collect old manuscripts, you see. Are you interested in that, Herr Gley? *Edgar wants to speak but is not yet able to do so; Herbot, noticing this, continues* But here I am, always talking about my affairs. How is your fiancée? You're coming from Vienna, I imagine, aren't you?

EDGAR No, straight from Villach. I have a question to put to you, Herr Herbot. Answer with a simple yes or no. Were you Daisy's lover?

HERBOT *stands up* Was I —?! Herr Gley, I don't know what to say. What foul slanderer —

EDGAR It's clear to me that you have to say that. But it's just as clear that nothing is proven by it. *Herbot wants to speak but he continues* Not even your word of honor would prove the slightest thing.

HERBOT One has nothing else besides one's measly word of honor, unfortunately. There are people who would be satisfied with Konrad Herbot's word of honor.

EDGAR In a case such as this as well? I'm afraid I'm in no position —

HERBOT What, then —? Won't you at least tell me from what source? Won't you show me the anonymous letter? It will soon become apparent, you know —

EDGAR Let's stop this, Herr Herbot. I ask you again: were you Daisy's lover?

HERBOT Well, since you don't seem willing to tell me anything about this monstrous — no, about the grounds for your suspicion, and thus make it impossible for me to def — to respond in a relevant manner, I suggest, Herr Gley, that we leave the young lady out of it entirely. Say to me, simply, that you don't like my nose; I will be as offended by that as ever you might desire, and I'll see you in one of those little woods everybody loves!

EDGAR I am far from doubting your courage, and I assume that mine is beyond question for you as well. Let's not play a scene with grandiose words here, Herr Herbot; let us, if possible — and it is possible for me — speak to each other like two men — no, beyond any vanity and even beyond any question of honor in the ordinary sense — like two human beings. I'm asking you for the last time, Herr Herbot, let go the manner you've adopted up to now, the correctness of which is certainly beyond objection. Understand, at last, that there is a human being standing before you, Herr Herbot, who asks nothing other than the truth, the truth, whatever it may be — understand me, Herr Herbot — and who feels strong enough to bear it, no matter what it is! Do understand me Herr Herbot — finally! I haven't come here as either fool or avenger, to one who was a rascal or who is being wrongly suspected. One human being to another. If it did happen, Herr Herbot, then maybe it was not a rascally trick. If it did not happen, then maybe it wasn't far from it. But whatever did take place, it would not be negated in any way by our facing each other with pistols and one of us — *Herbot wants to speak* Not yet. Now you would still lie, perhaps. Hear me out a while longer. I am capable of understanding many things. I have lived through all sorts of things myself. I know what the rapture, what the fragrance of a summer night can make of us, know how many things we are able to put behind us, even our own destinies, like dreams told to us by another person, and I know that I would be capable of enduring everything except doubt, forgive everything except a lie, especially when it's made so easy for a person to tell the truth as it is for you in this instance. I hope you're beginning to understand me, Herr Herbot! Or maybe now you're afraid that I want to lure you into a trap? I have put myself entirely in your hands, Herr Herbot, I would be standing here like — like the most pitiful of comedians if now, after a frank admission on your part which I had insidiously elicited, I suddenly wanted to play the injured bridegroom again. You could then refuse me every satisfaction, you could spit in my face, because, whatever you've done, I would then be the greater wretch of us two. Can you still be hesitant now, Herr Herbot? Never, I feel, has a human being stood face to face with another as I with you. Were you Daisy's lover, Herr Herbot? You are silent? Now you must speak. You must tell the truth before it's too late. That's right, before it is too late, Herr Herbot. Because if I were to learn the truth later on — there are such coincidences, Herr Herbot, there are women's confessions, belated confessions — then I will not fight a duel with you, then I will crush you like —

HERBOT Quiet! No more. I — I'm at your disposal. That's right, at your disposal. There is no other way out of this, neither for you nor for me.

EDGAR So you were Daisy's —

HERBOT I was not. And still it looks like one of us must leave this world —

EDGAR The truth! The truth! Herr Herbot!

HERBOT What are words?! Oh, if anyone had predicted to me — I'm sorry, I can't any more. *He goes to the window, appears shaken; unnoticed by Edgar, he looks at his watch; remains standing at the window.*

EDGAR Will you finally say something, Herr Herbot?!

HERBOT *turning to him again* Man alive, how simply you still
see the world! Yes and no! Truth and lie! Faithfulness and
unfaithfulness! If it were only that simple, young fr — Herr
Gley. But it happens not to be that simple. By God, it would
be the most convenient matter in the world if I were one of
those who ease their conscience by not having to say more
than what was asked of them. And it would be the easiest
thing in the world for me, in fact, if someone other than you
had come, you of all people, Edgar Gley, whom I am getting
to know only today; if another man were standing here, one
of the dozens of human beings whose spiritual destiny I didn't
care about, whom I could dismiss back into the everyday life
whence he came. To him I could say, swear, nothing
happened. Because from the point of view of the honest
burgher nothing did happen. But to you, even if you'll call
me inhuman, perhaps, to you I cannot make such an answer.
Because it would be the most cowardly of all lies; it would be
one of those which one could swear to as truth in court. But
there would be still another possibility, also easy, but in a
different way, devilishly easy, so to speak. And that would be
to give you an answer: it happened, Edgar Gley! Daisy was
my lover. . . . And then to take you at your word, send you
back out into the world, and exult that the way is clear for
me to flatter myself anew like the old fool I am, with the
hope that perhaps now that he, the young man, the beloved,
the fiancé has been gotten out of the way, the impossible will
come to pass in the end, the maddest wishes will be granted.
And who knows if I wouldn't be capable of this deviltry if I
weren't too clever! If I didn't foresee that the dream couldn't
last, that it would have to end in disillusionment, in
repentance, in curses. So, Edgar Gley, I loved your fiancée,
I worshipped her. I wanted to separate from my wife. I loved
Daisy, like a schoolboy I loved her. And did not keep it a
secret from her. Poems I wrote her, old Herbot wrote poems,
promenaded in front of her windows every night, sneaked

around the garden, like Romeo, threw his tender little letters through the window — *stops suddenly as if something had occurred to him* Ah, now I understand everything. Someone saw me! Someone saw me in the garden one night or maybe in the boat across from the house. But who can that have been? You've received anonymous letters, just admit it.

EDGAR That's all the same, really. Go on.

HERBOT What else do you want to know?

EDGAR You declared your love to Daisy — and she listened to you calmly?

HERBOT Listened — that I cannot deny.

EDGAR Read your letters? *Herbot smiles* And answered them? Say something.

HERBOT Won't you spare me that, Herr Gley?

EDGAR I'm sorry.

HERBOT *with the obvious intention that the untruth of the following statement be noticeable* I have nothing in writing in my possession —

EDGAR Herr Herbot — A lie is still a lie. If you have led me astray with some incidental matter then everything else will also —

HERBOT Don't insist! Let's stop here.

EDGAR Impossible.

HERBOT Well, then there's nothing left for me to do; do as you please, Herr Gley, I am entirely at your —

EDGAR You've gone too far to stop now. I promise you, no human being will learn anything of the content of this conversation. Not even — not even my fiancée. Don't torment me any longer. You have my word of honor.

HERBOT *after a dramatic pause, reaches into his pocket and takes out a letter* This is a letter from Daisy to me. *In response to an involuntary movement on Edgar's part* Don't. Let me read it to you myself. Of course, you can verify afterwards whether I've left out a single syllable. But it has to be heard in the proper tone, otherwise one might misunderstand it. *He reads* "Konrad Herbot — I beg of you, go away from here."

EDGAR When was this letter written?

HERBOT *shows him the date* On the twenty-seventh of August, in the morning. "Don't bring unhappiness to people who have done you no harm. Don't forget, Konrad Herbot, what you already meant to me long before I knew you. Let that be enough for you. When I see you again on stage in one of your magnificent — " Ah, let's skip that. "Never before has a man like you had such an —" This is a bit awkward. Miss Daisy merely meant that never had a person of whom so much is written in the papers declared his love to her before. And so on and so forth. But now listen carefully. *Reads* "Do keep in mind, you have a charming wife who adores you, and I am engaged to a young man who is very fond of me and whom I love as well. Yes, Konrad Herbot, I love him, and I will never love any other but him. Believe me. But you, Konrad Herbot, you are dangerous, I can't put it any other way. Sometimes I feel as if I hated you. I can only ask you, go away from here. I beg of you."

EDGAR *takes the letter* From the twenty-seventh. And you left —

HERBOT A few hours later. Naturally. *Pause.*

EDGAR And if you had stayed there —?

HERBOT Herr Gley, I might just as well have stayed. I only learned of my "dangerousness" through this letter. Up to that time — you yourself had occasion to observe how Miss Daisy acted towards me, usually.

EDGAR But you told me yourself just now it was your intention —

HERBOT To tear you out of Daisy's heart. Yes. I don't deny it, I was a fool. This letter here brought me to my senses. "I will never love any other but him."

EDGAR She wavered. This letter shows that she wavered

between you and me, and that it depended only on you —

HERBOT *interrupts him* I too would believe that, if I were still a fool today as I was for maybe half an hour. She's always belonged to you alone. But fame — have you any idea, my young friend, the effect that has on a young girl's heart? We never know, we poor folk in the limelight, whether this enthusiasm is meant for us or for the aura of immortality that surrounds us. How often have I envied those happy people who need never doubt that they're loved for their own sake. If I hadn't been Konrad Herbot, but some ordinary gentleman, a landowner from Klein-Reifling, for example, I would have struck your fiancée as ridiculous, nothing more. But that it was Konrad Herbot who almost lost his wits over her, that touched her a little. That she may have been Konrad Herbot's last love moved her, and certainly there was a moment when she came close to taking this emotional agitation to be love. She is not the first. But if anyone was guilty, if one can speak of guilt in such matters altogether, it was I, I alone. It would never have gone so far, not even as far as this letter, if I could have kept my feelings hidden. But I could no longer control myself. Like fate it came over me.

EDGAR You said before you wanted to leave your wife. She left before you — and I wonder —

HERBOT *quickly interrupting* Not because of the broken water pipe, Herr Gley, you can satisfy yourself on that score anytime. She left because I could not keep my emotional state a secret from her. I have no secrets from her. She's a wonderful woman. As soon as I had fled from Daisy after receiving this letter I let her know. I asked her to come to me, to stand by me, to rescue me from my despair. But she felt it unworthy to live with me as long as my heart belonged to another. She did not want to come back until I could write her in good conscience that even the last spark had been extinguished in me. This I was able to write her three days ago. She's been here again since yesterday, and tomorrow old

Herbot will have his home again. *Pause.*

EDGAR Why didn't she tell me anything of all this?

HERBOT Have you really no idea, Herr Gley, how close she was to doing so, how often the confession was on the tip of her tongue? I — I saw it. And I wanted her to speak to you then. Because you couldn't have taken it, you would have been too proud, you would've gone off, and I — I would have stayed there. Let's thank God it turned out otherwise. It would've been a terrible awakening for all of us.

EDGAR Why did she remain silent?

HERBOT Shall I tell you? Because she sensed, with her infinitely fine instincts, that what she would have taken to be a truthful confession would still have been only a lie. She never loved me, Herr Gley, that must finally be clear to you. Never. And I would go so far as to maintain that you, Herr Gley, may enter marriage with a more beautiful sense of security than many another young man who has nothing, as the saying goes, with which to reproach his bride. Miss Daisy has her adventure behind her. And the day will come when she will tell you about it on her own. She will tell you about it even before she goes to the altar with you. And if you'll allow me one request, wait for that moment. Don't bring it up yourself. *Since Edgar remains silent* But that's foolish; of course, you won't be able to remain silent that long. Naturally, you'll tell her everything, you'll tell her that I read you this letter too —

EDGAR *quickly glances through it once more and throws it into the fireplace* Never, as surely as it's being consumed in these flames. Of this letter, never. Nor of this visit.

HERBOT Don't promise too much, Herr Gley.

EDGAR *looks at him* I do not promise more than I am sure to keep. Good-bye, Herr Herbot.

HERBOT Have you any other question for me, Herr Gley?

EDGAR *looks at him a long time* None. *Quickly extends his hand to him.*

HERBOT *almost genuinely* Be good to her, Herr Gley. I beg
of you, — be good.

EDGAR *exits.*

HERBOT *comes back from the door, serious at first, then a
satisfied but not all too conceited smile crosses his lips. He
looks at his watch. Gestures: there is still time. He rings. The
bellhop enters* Will you ask my wife to come up? She's in
the lobby. *The bellhop exits.*

SOPHIE *has entered from the left.*

HERBOT *turns around, sees her* Oh! You were —

SOPHIE Yes. The entire time —

HERBOT But you did promise me. . . . But I understand.
Maybe it's better this way. I hope you're reassured.

SOPHIE Yes.

HERBOT It wasn't easy, you know. I can admit that to you
now. I had a bit of stage fright at the beginning, in spite of
not being entirely unprepared. I was quite weak at first too.

SOPHIE Well, it went —

HERBOT But then it didn't turn out badly, did it? You
probably pictured it differently, right? You thought I would
simply deny everything. But only dummies deny. Sensible
people —

SOPHIE — lie.

HERBOT Lie? No, Sophie, it wasn't all a lie, there were a
number of things that were true too. That precisely was the
delicious part, how they were mixed together, the true and
the false. That's how it became so absolutely plausible. Well,
thank God, one can breathe freely again now.

SOPHIE You think so? Have you forgotten?

HERBOT What?

SOPHIE If he discovers the truth sometime in the future, then
he'll want to, he will — and he will discover it. It's merely
been postponed.

HERBOT What are you talking about? He will never discover
it. It is absolutely out of the question.

SOPHIE Out of the question? Surely he'll talk to her. You can't deceive yourself on that score. And, of course, contradictions will crop up.

HERBOT Contradictions? But why?

SOPHIE That business with the letter, first of all. What was the purpose of that forged letter anyway?

HERBOT Forged? It was genuine.

SOPHIE The letter was genuine?

HERBOT Of course it's genuine. Daisy really did write it to me. Not on the twenty-seventh of August, to be sure, but on the second. It was no big deal to insert the seven.

SOPHIE I don't understand —

HERBOT But sweetheart, it really is quite simple. Naturally, we had to take into consideration the possibility of some gossip. It was obvious that an anonymous letter or something of the sort could turn up. And so Daisy and I figured out exactly how we would behave in the event. That a bare denial would not help, that was evident. In fact, we could have gotten ourselves into a pretty mess that way.

SOPHIE I see. Very good. Now I'm beginning to understand —

HERBOT And the letter — I read it beautifully, didn't I? the letter, which in reality, of course, first brought the thing to a head, it seemed absolutely made to order to serve us as — how shall I put it — an alibi.

SOPHIE Extraordinary.

HERBOT The other letters no longer exist. Other kinds of evidence either. And that she — Daisy, that is — will surely play her part famously as well, on that score, I dare say one can rest easy.

SOPHIE Let's hope so. But not as well as you, by any means.

HERBOT Maybe better. A girl like that — Women altogether — it's innate with them, you know. By the way, didn't you find him splendid too?

SOPHIE He?

HERBOT Edgar Gley. Of course, he had it easier. But — shall

I tell you something, Sophie? There were moments when I
was so swept along — it wouldn't have taken much for me to
have believed the whole story myself.

SOPHIE What story?

HERBOT Well, you did hear it. Towards the end I felt as if the
girl and I — as if really nothing happened. The power of
genius, one might say.

FALK *enters, wearing hat and coat* Say, look here, have you
gone crazy? A quarter to seven? What's going on?

HERBOT Come on, what do you think, I need an hour to
change into Hamlet?

FALK Paragraph seven: Actors with parts in the evening's play
are to be in the theater an hour before the beginning of the
performance. Besides, the Crown Prince is coming tonight.

HERBOT What? With spouse?

FALK And suite.

HERBOT Well, what do you say, Sophie? Here I am, drawing
high society into his dive too, which he had chased off in
disgust with his modern nonsense. Haven't you hurried to
raise the prices in time? Well, let's you and I have a serious
word about the new contract before the day is out, over our
champagne. Especially concerning vacation. In February
we're going to the Riviera, you see. Right, Sophie?

FALK Will you finally —

HERBOT So, Sophie, get yourself ready fast. Tonight I'm
going to play exclusively for you again. His Majesty himself
could be present then, for all I care, or the Lord.

FALK In any case, you would not find it unusual if the Lord
were to see your Hamlet before anything else in Berlin.

HERBOT No. If he were ever to come to Berlin he'd have
someone get him tickets for Reinhardt's theater. Don't you
think so?

FALK It would be in the papers, at any rate.

HERBOT *quickly strokes Sophie's cheeks, kisses her forehead*
Addio! Arrivederci! *Takes his hat and coat and exits.*

FALK   He is in some high spirits. You somewhat less, Frau
   Sophie. You're standing there like a statue. What happened?
   A scene? Is it starting over again?

SOPHIE   *motionless*   No. It is not starting, it is ending.
   Conclusively.

FALK   *after a short pause*   Well, you'll still be wanting to get
   ready for the theater too. See you later!

SOPHIE   I'm not going to the theater. I'm leaving.

FALK   What?

SOPHIE   Tonight, in an hour, in half an hour. It's over.

FALK   Say, what's —

SOPHIE   That I cannot tell you in brief.

FALK   Well, without wanting to appear obtrusive, I can live
   without the scene with the ghost, with that of Hamlet's father,
   I mean. So, if you haven't suddenly stopped seeing me as a
   friend —

SOPHIE   Why should I — *After a short pause*   Edgar Gley was
   here.

FALK   Oh!

SOPHIE   He wanted an explanation. My husband gave it to him.
   I was in the next room the entire time. I heard everything.

FALK   Well then?

SOPHIE   I never suspected a person could lie like that.

FALK   What did you think? But you must be glad.

SOPHIE   It was an entirely preconcerted scheme, between him
   and the young lady. They were prepared for it. And my
   husband told the poor young man a fairy-tale here, as if he
   had almost gone mad over Daisy and she had not listened to
   him. And all the time he climbed through her window night
   after night.

FALK   Well, he couldn't tell Herr Gley that, probably. And it's
   still always better to lie skillfully in such cases than not at all.

SOPHIE   You ought to have heard it. And he — he senses
   nothing of all this, he's even happy about it. Oh, if you had
   heard you would understand that I can't spend another day,

another hour with this person —

FALK Yes, but where will you go?

SOPHIE What do I know. Away, away!

FALK Might you not know, after all?

SOPHIE What?

FALK Where you're thinking of running to. Or suspect you —

SOPHIE If that were it, do you think I'd need to make excuses
to myself? I'm not drawn to anyone! I want to go away, and
I want to be alone, for the rest of my life, alone.

FALK That will not be possible. You are to return here again
in two weeks. Longer vacation than that I will not give you.
Our contract —

SOPHIE You can joke about it? Do you really not understand?
It is over for good. There is nothing left, nothing, only
disgust, no, a horror, an immense horror. How can I go back
to him? One can go back to a person even if he sinned, if he
committed a crime, if he injured someone deeply, fatally.
One can go back to someone who repents, as well as to one
who does not. But he does have to recognize what he has
done. Herbot doesn't recognize it. He understands nothing
about me and nothing about himself and nothing about anyone
else. Love, deceit, murder, in reality none of these carry any
greater weight for him than if it appeared in one of his parts.
We speak different languages, and there is no longer any
communication possible between us. If I were to throw
myself out the window in despair, for him it would signal the
end of an act. Down comes the curtain — and he goes to
drink his champagne. A human being — him? A harlequin
gone mad, who, if the opportunity arises, is also prepared to
play a human being; — but not a human being — no — *She
sinks down on the divan, hands covering her face. Pause.*

FALK Pity, pity.

SOPHIE Not a pity any longer either.

FALK It is, dear friend. It doesn't have to be this way. How
different would this scene which he seems to have performed

here with Herr Gley have appeared to you, how much less horrible, indeed, how merry or grandiose, perhaps, would the fellow have seemed to you —

SOPHIE If I deserved him.

FALK That will never be the case, of course, — cannot ever be the case, of course. You would remain who you are in any event. One always does. But you would not have taken some things as hard. That you're such an incredibly decent person, that's what it is that brings a false note into your relationship with Herbot; and that you're not even able to enjoy this decency properly in the deepest reaches of your soul, that doesn't make things any better. If you were married to such a noble-minded Herr Gley, for example, — yes, to deceive, as we say, a human being like that, that is very ugly of course, because for these Herr Gleys, being deceived is something very substantial, undeserved and humiliating, and can occasionally drive them to suicide, these Herr Gleys. With the Herbots it's a completely different matter. The Herbots might act as if they noticed nothing; even to themselves they'd act this way; but they would recover.

SOPHIE You're speaking like a proper sophist.

FALK Only as a theater director, my dear friend.

SOPHIE *smiling* In theatrical affairs, I am merely — I am no longer available for consultation. Excuse me, I have to pack. He mustn't find me here any more.

FALK You seriously intend — and this very night? But that's not possible.

SOPHIE It is possible, believe me.

FALK Fine, but what shall I tell him?

SOPHIE That I was too moved by his big scene with Herr Gley today to be able to endure *Hamlet* as well.

FALK That — that he will not understand.

SOPHIE So, tell him the truth — that I —

FALK — love him!

SOPHIE Hate him! And that I will never again — as sure as

I'm alive —

FALK Hush! No oaths, one shouldn't burn any bridges behind one. One only ends up with the inconvenience of having to build them again from scratch.

SOPHIE *towards the left* Good-bye!

FALK I don't want to keep you any longer, Frau Sophie. Best of luck on your journey. But if you ask me where to, I'd say, not into solitude, but — somewhere else —

SOPHIE You are truly —

FALK Look, it doesn't obligate you to anything. Not even to coming back. You can stay there. Maybe that's where your happiness lies. It is possible. Of course, I don't believe it. Take a look down there by the way! An ocean of carriages! Yes, the man must be forgiven some things!

SOPHIE I would, too, as theater director.

FALK You must do so all the more as a woman. It's practically your profession.

SOPHIE Oho!

FALK To forgive — and to take revenge. The latter is known to be especially sweet. I'll see you, Frau Sophie — I'll see you soon. *In response to her glance* Well, yes, maybe — in the Styrian woods. I've been invited to the hunt too, you know. Or at least to a game of chess. A telegram will suffice, I'll come down, if only to fetch you — to bring you back to one who, fight it as you may, just happens to be your destiny. There are lesser ones, Frau Sophie. *The door in the background opens. Herbot enters wearing his not entirely closed coat over his Hamlet costume.*

FALK Tell me, have you gone completely mad?

HERBOT Say, what's the matter? Where are you hiding, Sophie? I'm looking through the peep-hole into the box and you're not there —

SOPHIE *merely stares at him.*

FALK *goes up to him, grasps his shoulder* Say, now will you — It's five minutes past seven.

HERBOT   Let them wait! I'm not going on until Sophie is
sitting in her box.

SOPHIE   But — but — I'm not even dressed yet.

HERBOT   Doesn't matter. Come with me as you are.

FALK   *to Herbot*   See to it, first of all, that you get on with it.

HERBOT   Sorry. I'm not moving an inch without her. I know,
I know. She didn't want to come at all. The — the boy was
here. She probably told you about it. The memories rose up
again. Well, just look at her, Falk. Isn't she standing there
like a marble ghost? But do come to your senses. The past is
dead, you know, stone dead. Do you still not understand that,
sweetheart? Don't think any more about the little trollop.
What do other people concern us anyway? You know I never
loved anyone but you. If you don't come along then I won't
play. Then our friend can close up the theater for all I care.

FALK   Six-thousand five-hundred marks. You will of course
answer for that.

HERBOT   You hear, Sophie? If someone else plays Hamlet he
won't fill half the house. And if you don't sit in your box
tonight then I won't play tonight or tomorrow or ever again,
in fact, and Addio dramatic art! *He throws down the sword
he had been holding in his hand.*

FALK   *who had been standing by the window*   His Highness has
just driven up.

HERBOT   I don't give a damn! Let him drive home again, your
Highness. There is only one here — *He is suddenly on his
knees before Sophie. There is a knock at the door. The Stage
Manager enters.*

STAGE MANAGER   Excuse me, Herr Herbot, it's ten after
seven. His Royal Highness — the audience —

FALK   *to the stage manager*   Have them give the signal.

HERBOT   *to the stage manager*   He said it, not I.

FALK   Give the signal!

STAGE MANAGER   *exits.*

SOPHIE   Do get up!

HERBOT Are you coming?

SOPHIE *does not answer, only her look expressing her assent.*

HERBOT *stands up, puts his arm around Sophie's waist, takes back the sword, which Falk had picked up* Was ever woman in this humor. . . .

FALK That's not Hamlet, that's Richard.

HERBOT Well, then, Arm in arm with you. . . .

FALK That's also from somewhere else. You'll end up all confused yet.

HERBOT Does it have to be just Hamlet? *Pressing himself impetuously on Sophie* Isn't it a glorious thought —

FALK Wili you please? *He pushes them both out the door. When the door opens, several hotel guests become visible walking by in the corridor; they regard the group in astonishment. Falk turns out the light, goes out also, and closes the door.*

Curtain

THE BACCHANALE

CHARACTERS

FELIX STAUFNER, *a writer*
AGNES, *his wife*
DR. GUIDO WERNIG
RAILROAD PORTER
WAITER
BUFFET MISTRESS
PASSENGERS
RAILROAD EMPLOYEES

The action takes place in the train station waiting room in Salzburg.

A waiting room with restaurant. In the background, three glass doors leading out to the platform. To the right, a wide stairway going down. To the left the buffet. Above it a clock. A number of tables, some of them set, with chairs. A blackboard to the right of the middle glass door. On the wall next to the staircase, timetables, maps, advertisements. The buffet mistress is at her post behind the buffet. A few people at tables. The PORTER *is standing along the open middle door. A train has just arrived as the curtain goes up. Passengers enter from the platform and go through the restaurant and down the stairs to the right. Agnes and Guido are standing to the left, almost motionless, glancing intently at the door, obviously waiting for someone. When the last passengers have gone through the room,* GUIDO *steps to the door and looks out; He takes a step towards the platform but is turned back by the porter.* AGNES *also goes closer to the door.*

GUIDO There's no one else coming.

AGNES Strange.

PORTER *shuts the door.*

GUIDO Excuse me, that was the train from Innsbruck, wasn't it?

PORTER No.

GUIDO No?

PORTER That was the Bavarian. The one from Innsbruck is supposed to get in at 5:20.

GUIDO Why do you say "is supposed to"?

PORTER Because it's late most of the time. But we've had no notice yet.

GUIDO That it's coming?

PORTER No, that it'll be late. *Exits to the right, down the stairs.*

GUIDO *looks at the clock* So, then we've got another eight whole minutes ahead of us. *He lights a cigarette.*

AGNES Eight minutes. *Comes forward, sits at a table.*

WAITER *approaches, skulks around her.*

GUIDO *after a short pause, goes over to Agnes and remains standing behind her* Agnes —

AGNES Guido —?

GUIDO *sits down beside her* I wonder if it weren't smarter after all —

WAITER What would you like, please?

GUIDO Thank you, we just had something here.

WAITER *shrugging, slightly offended, exits left.*

GUIDO I mean, if it really wouldn't be better if I waited for him alone.

AGNES Why this — now? Suddenly you don't trust me to have the necessary determination? Or do you think, maybe, that face to face with him —

GUIDO No, no, I'm sure of you. But I repeat, there is absolutely no way to predict how he'll take the news. And therefore —

AGNES *spirited, stands up* No. We'll do as planned, we'll wait for him together. That way the situation will be clear to him at once. That in itself is a tremendous advantage. It'll hardly require too many more words. And besides, it's the only way that's worthy of us — and of him. We owe him that. I owe it to him at any rate. *The whistle of a locomotive is heard. She starts slightly but does not turn around.*

GUIDO *stands up. A railroad employee enters from the platform, carefully locks the door behind him, and writes on the blackboard: "Train No. 57 from Innsbruck will be 44 minutes late." He bars the entry to the platform to a woman with two children while carefully locking the door again behind him. Guido and Agnes have not turned around. The whistle of the locomotive dies away.*

GUIDO *close to her* Agnes, do you love me?

AGNES I adore you. And you?

GUIDO You know. *Hastily* And in one hour it'll be all over.

Hold that thought! By this time tomorrow we'll be far away.
You must keep that in mind when you're face to face with
him. And together for all time.

AGNES *somewhat mechanically* For all time. . . . *Without
turning around* Isn't it here yet?

GUIDO *turning towards the back* The eight minutes are up.
The porter has returned. Guido sees the notice on the board
Oh!

AGNES What's the matter?

GUIDO A delay! Forty-four minutes' delay!

PORTER It'll end up being an hour, all right.

GUIDO It clearly says forty-four minutes. Forty-four! It's
obviously been calculated quite precisely.

PORTER *coldly* Well, yes, if she doesn't come in sooner.
*Slowly goes to the buffet, exchanges a few words with the
cashier, and exits soon after. Guido and Agnes look at each
other.*

AGNES An hour —

GUIDO Let's go back outside in the meantime.

AGNES But it's still pouring.

GUIDO Of course.

AGNES But if you feel like taking a walk — I can stay here
while you go. I'll look at some magazines. *She sits down
and picks up a magazine.*

GUIDO *goes closer to the buffet, compares his pocket watch
with the clock.*

AGNES *follows him with her glance, smiles* He'll be good and
impatient too in his compartment.

GUIDO *closer to her* How — how do you mean that, Agnes?

AGNES Well, as you know, he telegraphed me that he'll be
arriving here from Stubai at 5:20. Naturally, he thinks I'm
coming to meet him and that I'm waiting for him after this
six-week-long separation — and that we'll be taking the train
back together to our villa in Seewalchen. And I am waiting

for him, too. Only he is picturing it a little differently, most likely.

GUIDO I would feel a whole lot better if you viewed this in a somewhat less sentimental way.

AGNES Sentimental?! Me?! Would I be here if I were sentimental? *Short pause.*

GUIDO *merely in order to say something* You'd have missed the six o'clock train in any event.

AGNES There's another one at seven.

GUIDO Do you think he'll be on it?

AGNES Why not? I would want him to. And he is surely the man — *breaking off* He'll find everything at home the way he left it. I told Therese she should get everything ready, as if —

GUIDO That was superfluous. If he ever loved you he will never again cross the threshold of a house in which he spent five summers with you — *bitterly* happy summers.

AGNES He will. He loves the little house and the landscape so much. These haven't changed.

GUIDO Surely he won't be going there any more this year.

AGNES If he has any sense, he'll be home again by tonight.

GUIDO In a house that holds such memories for him?

AGNES *to herself* Hopefully, he'll already start to forget me on the way home.

GUIDO You imagine —?

AGNES Well, isn't it the best thing we can wish for him? *She picks up a newspaper and appears about to become absorbed in it.*

GUIDO *looks at Agnes, then walks back and forth, compares his watch to the clock again, then comes closer to Agnes* Maybe we could have a little something after all. *He raps on the table, takes up a paper as well, leafs through it hastily, looks across the table at Agnes, who seems completely absorbed in her reading, then calls out angrily* Waiter!

WAITER *appears, still somewhat offended* Yes, please.

GUIDO Bring me — *to Agnes* What would you like?

AGNES I really don't care.

GUIDO Well, then, bring us two lemon sodas.

AGNES Raspberry for me, rather.

WAITER *withdraws. Another pause.*

GUIDO *looks at Agnes.*

AGNES *continues to read, smiles* Why, there's something about you in here.

GUIDO About me?

AGNES Yes. "Regatta on the Attersee" — First prize, Baron Rumming on his sailboat "Storm" — second prize, Doctor Guido Wernig on his sailboat "Watersprite."

GUIDO True. You see, nobodies like me also get their names in the paper sometimes. On correspondingly unimportant occasions naturally — and even then only for second prize.

AGNES It'll be the first before long — on a different lake.

GUIDO You are too kind. But, I wonder, could it be a sign of fate after all?

AGNES *questioning glance* The second prize?

GUIDO The delay, I mean. You have a chance to reconsider one last time. *Goes closer to her in response to her warding off gesture* Maybe it isn't as simple as you imagine, after having been the life companion of a great man for five years, to continue life as the wife of a quite ordinary doctor of chemistry —

AGNES *quickly interrupting him* First of all, your family's factory is just as famous in its way as the collected works of my husband.

GUIDO What have I got to do with the factory? My father founded it, he runs it. I'm only the son —

AGNES And then, I did not love Felix because he's a "great man," as you put it. Who had actually ever heard of him, back when I married him?

GUIDO But you had an inkling.

AGNES An inkling, yes —

WAITER *enters with their order, puts the glasses down. Agnes and Guido remain silent. The waiter withdraws. Pause.*

GUIDO Why don't you say something, Agnes?

AGNES *as if to herself* How mysterious life is. It's been six weeks, no more than six weeks since I sailed across the lake with him in the little white steamer, since I said good-bye to him here, almost on the same spot. And how the whole world has changed in this short time. If he — if we had foreseen, on that clear summer day —

GUIDO Do you regret it Agnes? There is still time.

AGNES *as if awaking* I regret nothing, nothing. Everything that happened had to happen. Do you think I don't feel that, Guido? And everything that's happened was for our happiness. And most likely for his as well.

GUIDO For his?

AGNES He'll probably be thanking me soon for *smiling* giving him back his freedom. People like him —

GUIDO People like him?

AGNES Everything has its deeper purpose. It's good, perhaps it is even a profound necessity, that he'll have his solitude again from now on.

GUIDO Solitude — if that's what you want to call it.

AGNES *looks up* What do you mean by that?

GUIDO Nothing but what you're probably thinking yourself.

AGNES Stop being evasive! You've already made one such strange allusion today.

GUIDO What do you mean? When?

AGNES On our way here, on the train —

GUIDO I don't think my hints are the least bit necessary, given your forebodings. The thought that it wasn't only his play that kept him in the Stubaital for six weeks instead of the projected three is not one that has struck you today for the first time. You're smiling?

AGNES I find it a little odd that you obviously have a mind to make me jealous.

GUIDO Far from it. But, if you'll forgive my saying so, I see no good reason for you to — always try to crown your former husband with some sort of halo. With all due respect, when all is said and done, he is a human being like everyone else. In certain regards he's probably not a hair better than I and —

AGNES *smiling* "And you," you were going to say. Very kind.

GUIDO Will you please not misunderstand me.

AGNES Oh, I understand you perfectly. You want to make me believe that this Miss X —

GUIDO Bianka Walter —

AGNES — who added her signature to his last picture postcard, has somehow had a part in keeping my husband —

GUIDO Your former husband, Herr Felix Staufner —

AGNES — in keeping Felix in the Stubaital.

GUIDO I don't want to make you believe anything. I'm merely stating.

AGNES One doesn't state anything without proof. Without proof one only suspects. Besides, it'll come out shortly.

GUIDO How, if I may ask?

AGNES He too will tell me the truth.

GUIDO It's unlikely that you'll have time to interrogate him. Aside from which, it should be completely immaterial, indeed, if anything, even welcome to you, if my suspicion and — your inkling are confirmed.

AGNES I would be happy, even. I don't have to tell you that. There's nothing I'd rather have happen than — than for him to get off the train with this Miss Bianka or with some other woman.

GUIDO I'm afraid you picture life to be too simple, Agnes. It's not going to be made that easy for us. Miss X —

AGNES Bianka —

GUIDO — will not come along. She will have stayed in Stubai

— for now.

AGNES With her mother.

GUIDO Why with her mother? What do you care about the mother, of all people?

AGNES Why, she signed the card too. I'm afraid we're doing the young lady a terrible injustice, all in all, and are celebrating too soon! She is undoubtedly a respectable girl from a good family, an admirer of my — my Felix Staufner — exactly like her mother. *She takes a card from her purse and reads* "Isabella Walter, who, like her previously undersigned young daughter, does not wish to miss the opportunity to send her grateful, respectful greetings to the wife of the esteemed master."

GUIDO Somewhat roundabout.

AGNES But very much beyond suspicion.

GUIDO You're carrying the card with you?

AGNES I didn't have time to file it yet.

GUIDO You intend to keep it?

AGNES But why not? It's the last one, after all. It arrived four days ago. And it's surely the last he's written to me as my husband.

GUIDO *takes the card; as she offers some slight resistance, he says, offended* I suppose one is still allowed to touch it. *He reads* "I hope to be finished with my work in three days. You'll still get a telegram in any case. Your Felix." Did you answer this card?

AGNES Only one word.

GUIDO What word, if one may ask?

AGNES "Good-bye!" *Guido bites his lips* Well, is anything wrong? I didn't write I'll be seeing you, or I hope to see you again; simply, good-bye!

GUIDO And did you write him any letters too — in all this time?

AGNES A single one.

GUIDO So, I was right!

AGNES That was still before things had been decided between you and me. In the evening, an hour before you suddenly stood in my garden — beneath my window — and called my name into the night. Yes, that's how one writes a farewell letter sometimes, without suspecting it! How mysterious life — *Guido has the card in his hand, apparently on the point of crumpling it* What are you doing, Guido?

GUIDO You still love him.

AGNES *sincerely* No, Guido. I love no one but you. I have never yet — not even Felix have I loved as much as I love you! *Takes his hand* But I will never cease to *lets his hand go again* admire Felix Staufner — to revere him — to feel spiritually close to the writer Felix Staufner. In a certain sense — how many more times must I tell you, Guido — relationships like the one between Felix Staufner and me cannot be changed — never ever. That we were married, that's the least of it. Even if I were never to see him again, if we remained miles apart from each other —

GUIDO *interrupting* Yes, if only you remained miles apart from each other! That would of course be lovely. Then everything would be fine, then I wouldn't have the slightest objection to your spiritual relationship either. But unfortunately I can't spend my life traveling with you. I have to return to the yoke, that damned yoke, and. . . .

AGNES It goes without saying. I would absolutely not allow you to give up your profession. You must work, even if you don't need to. I would not want to live with an idler.

GUIDO I have no intention of giving up my profession. But all the same, I could practice it elsewhere. I'm going to speak with my father. As it is, he's been thinking for a long time about opening a branch in Germany or in America.

AGNES Or in Australia.

GUIDO The further, the better.

AGNES Guido!

GUIDO I simply cannot bear the thought of your running into your ex-husband later on.

AGNES *determined* Guido, you mustn't go back on all our arrangements now, at the last moment. You know Felix is not any ordinary person — *in response to Guido's gesture of despair, she goes on with even greater determination* He always recognized that the love between him and me could come to an end at some point. But that made him doubt all the less that everything else that connects us and which constitutes the real essence of our relationship will remain indestructible and imperishable. He knows, above all, that no one understands him to the depths of his soul as I do, — that is to say, that he will never have a better friend than I have been to him — and am — and will remain.

GUIDO A few minutes ago, Agnes, you expressed the wish that he might forget you as soon as possible — before the end of the day — forget you on the way to Seewalchen!

AGNES The lover, the wife, yes. But what I've been to him besides — and can remain —

GUIDO It will cost him some effort, in the beginning at least — to draw such a nice distinction.

AGNES I'll grant you that. But — we will become friends again some time or other.

GUIDO You really imagine that he won't find another — friend very soon?

AGNES A friend? No. Never. A lover — certainly! And whether her name is Bianka or something else — I only hope I'll be able to approve his choice!

GUIDO Why do you hope that? Do you by chance intend to associate with the future lover of your former husband?!

AGNES If things should turn out that way. . . .

GUIDO They will not turn out that way. Because I am telling you right now that I intend, as soon as our situation is settled unequivocally, which I hope will soon be the case, to run a respectable household. And I assure you, this entire rather interesting but also somewhat dubious society of artists and

actors of both sexes that was accustomed to going in and out
of your house will not cross the threshold of mine.

AGNES All the same, any dubiousness notwithstanding, it was
all right for you —

GUIDO That's different. A genuine passion explains and
excuses everything. And besides, your husband deserves his
fate.

AGNES Oh!

GUIDO One must guard a woman like a priceless treasure. One
does not leave a young woman alone, completely alone
among young people, in the summer — on a lake —

AGNES He simply trusted me, for all his doubts. That belongs
among the contradictions of his character.

GUIDO A man does not trust a woman he loves. He trembles
for her. He fights for her. I will never trust you. Even after
we've been together for years. Even when we have children
— and we will have children — I will always tremble for
you. To feel secure in a woman means, practically, to insult
her!

AGNES Nor did he do that. He was jealous, more often than
you think. Even of you.

GUIDO Even! Well — I would've thought —

AGNES But that was still before he had the slightest reason for
it. Just then. How mysterious —

GUIDO Life is.

AGNES — We hadn't yet spoken to each other three times! He
didn't say anything, naturally, but I could tell. Only I
couldn't understand it. After all, you were sailing around on
the lake all day long — in the beginning. Only in the evening
did you deign to sit next to us for half an hour on the hotel
terrace and to talk all sorts of nonsense that really didn't
interest me in the least.

GUIDO Nonsense. . . . Well —

AGNES I only mean to say that it was all quite harmless those
first days. Admit it, you really didn't pay any attention to me

either. The little Baroness Fellah was more important to you than I was! And God knows who else! But he — he saw it coming! I could tell from his glances. He sensed it right away, that you — that you of all people —

GUIDO And still he left you alone? Saw it coming, and went on a trip?

AGNES That's how he is. When he's seriously occupied with a piece of work everything else fades away.

GUIDO And he flees *pointedly* to his solitude.

AGNES *ignoring the allusion* In any event, he stops concerning himself with other people then, — at least with those people whom — he loves.

GUIDO He's left you alone frequently, then?

AGNES Sometimes. But that wasn't even the worst of it. It was much eerier when he stayed home and left me alone anyway. When my voice no longer reached him. When, to some extent, I became a ghost for him — paler, less alive than some characters he had just created, when I felt myself being extinguished, as it were, — for him —

GUIDO *taking her hand* For me you will never be extinguished, — never, Agnes.

AGNES *as if awaking* That's true, isn't it, Guido? You'll never leave me alone! You will never go off by yourself and forget me for days — for weeks — the way he did. It isn't good to leave us alone — you're right, Guido, it's dangerous — it's — *There has been some activity in the room for the past few minutes. Passengers are coming up the stairs. The porter enters from the right, goes towards the door to the platform.*

GUIDO What is it? *Looking at the clock over the buffet* We have another twelve minutes yet.

PORTER *opens the door.*

AGNES It does seem —

GUIDO *quickly up to the porter* The Innsbruck train?

PORTER Yes.

GUIDO Isn't it supposed to be another ten minutes —?

PORTER She made up some of the lost time.

GUIDO *to Agnes* You're pale. Wouldn't you rather — *A number of passengers pass through the room and out to the platform.*

AGNES *shakes her head vehemently* We had better go out.

GUIDO Out on the platform?

AGNES Yes. It's better than waiting in here. Let him already see us from the train.

GUIDO I don't know —

AGNES Come!

They make for the platform.

PORTER Platform tickets, please.

GUIDO Oh, God! *Reaches into his change purse* Here you are — *offers to give the porter money.*

PORTER Over there in the vending machine, please.

AGNES But the train will come in the meantime.

PORTER There's time yet.

GUIDO *goes to the vending machine, inserts coins, pulls on the lever in vain* It's not working.

PORTER *goes to the machine, tries likewise in vain to make it work, shakes his head* Sometimes she just doesn't want to.

GUIDO This is really —

PORTER Ah, there it goes. *Hands Guido two tickets, returns to the door, which he had locked before, and opens it again* Here she comes now. *Sounds of the arriving train.*

AGNES Your hand, Guido.

They go hand in hand through the door to the platform. Just as they're going out, FELIX *appears from the right, having come up the stairs. He sees Agnes and is about to go after her but notices at almost the same instant that she is not alone and sees her disappear out onto the platform hand in hand with Guido. He stands still for a moment, then makes as if to follow, but stops again at the door; he then goes to the closed platform door on the right and evidently follows the two with his eyes as they walk towards the train. He steps back, passes his hand over his forehead and looks out through the glass door again. The two have evidently disappeared from view. The train has stopped and the passengers are leaving the platform. Most of them go through the waiting room and down the stairs; a few sit down at the small tables, some step up to the buffet and receive food and drink. Felix goes as far as the center of the stage, the stream of passengers rushing past him; he has to get out of their way. He then steps up very close to the open platform door again, searching for Agnes and Guido. He spots them and looks out tensely. Then, as if suddenly afraid to be noticed by them, he steps back, his features expressing his complete understanding of the situation. He rushes abruptly towards the stairs, as if he had taken a sudden resolve to flee. Here he stops a moment, shakes his head, hurries back to the closed platform door and looks out. The last of the passengers leave the platform. Felix leaves the door, comes to the very front, puts a controlled expression on his face, then smiles somewhat distortedly, becomes serious again, then sits down in an easy manner at the same table at which Agnes and Guido sat earlier, automatically picks up a newspaper and looks over it to the platform door. The porter had locked the door already; now he opens it again. A previously delayed lady emerges with a great deal of hand luggage, then a station official, and finally Guido and Agnes. They cannot see Felix behind the newspaper.*

GUIDO Strange —
AGNES Is there another train from Innsbruck today?
GUIDO Let's take a look at the timetable. *They go up to the timetable on the wall next to the stairs; Guido studies it carefully.* 9:12 — no, that's coming from somewhere else. If only it were possible to figure this out. Yes, wait —
FELIX *puts the paper aside, stands up, remains still a while,*

then quickly crosses the stage to Agnes and Guido, who are studying the timetable. He stands motionless behind them a while, then says, in an innocent-joyful tone Here you are, Agnes! *Agnes and Guido both turn around, but neither is at first able to utter a sound. Felix, apparently not noticing, continues quickly* You see, I came on the earlier train, at noon. I'm afraid there wasn't any more time to send you a telegram. It was sort of a sudden decision. I happened to wake a little earlier this morning, my things were packed, and so I thought, you might as well take the first train and just stroll about in Salzburg for a few hours. Well, how are you, Agnes, how are you, my dear Agnes. *Shakes both her hands* Good day, Doctor. What are you doing here? On your way to Vienna? *Offers him his hand* Vacation over already?

GUIDO *has taken Felix's hand only after some hesitation* No, I'm not going to Vienna. I took the liberty of accompanying madame, that is to say, madame allowed me — indeed, it's a question of —

AGNES *gives him an anxious look, which Felix notices.*

FELIX *quickly interrupting him* That is very nice of you, Doctor. My wife loves to chat. It's very kind of you to have kept her company. When a person has traveled a route like that thirty or forty times, all the charms of nature will fail to hold their interest in the long run. *Quickly* So, Agnes, let me have a look at you. We haven't seen each other in a long time! Six weeks! I don't think we've ever experienced that before in our five years of marriage. Am I right?

AGNES You're looking very well, Felix.

FELIX Am I? Yes, so I'm told. You too, by the way. It even seems to me that you've put on some weight. And tanned, very tanned. Spent a lot of time outdoors, right? Well, the weather was beautiful. Except for today — of course. It's really very nice that you came to meet me —

AGNES Well, you did —

FELIX I only wanted to let you know, just in case. I wasn't counting on it by any means. After all, it is two and a half hours from Seewalchen to here. And one has to change trains too. It makes me all the more glad. All the same, it is quite a trip, even in the most amiable company.

GUIDO As far as my company is concerned, I would like to —

AGNES *interrupts him, quickly to Felix* You were here at twelve already? So what did you do with yourself until now?

FELIX I'll tell you in a minute. *Indicating a table* But why don't we — I could really do with a cup of coffee. And you? Or maybe you've had one already? Waiter! Waiter! What did you ask me before? What I did in the couple of hours I had here? Well, since I was here by noon, naturally, I had lunch in the city, very good, at the Nürnberger Hof. *Sits down* So, Doctor, won't you join us?

AGNES *sits down.*

GUIDO *with a glance at Agnes* I really don't know — that is, I —

FELIX *quickly* No ceremony, Doctor. Please. *To the waiter, who has just arrived at the table* Bring us *to Agnes* Coffee — right? One large. And you, Doctor?

GUIDO *who has sat down on a signal from Agnes* I've just —

AGNES *quickly to the waiter* Three melanges. *The waiter begins to go.*

FELIX Pretty dark for me. And say, wait a minute — do you still have that Gugelhupf maybe, that excellent one, the kind we got here six weeks ago?

AGNES *smiling* You still remember?

FELIX You did enjoy it too! *To the waiter* So, bring us each a piece of Gugelhupf with the coffee. — *The waiter exits.* So, what were we talking about? Yes, right. I ate at the Nürnberger Hof, then I strolled about —

AGNES In the rain?

FELIX Oh, that doesn't bother me. On the contrary. After the sultriness of the morning it was truly a relief. By the way, I also dropped in on Sebastian Schwarz for a half hour.

AGNES *to Guido, explaining* That's the antiques dealer, you see.

FELIX You're not interested in antiques, Doctor?

GUIDO I don't understand enough about them. However —

FELIX *quickly, to Agnes* He's got a couple of pretty things. Very good value in part.

AGNES You probably spent a pile of money again, didn't you?

FELIX Not so much. I've already had a few things sent to the villa in Seewalchen, as a matter of fact. A hanging lamp among other things, like we've been looking for such a long time.

AGNES For the dining room?

FELIX Yes, one could hang it in the dining room too. Also a very beautiful pendant. Baroque. Truly original. Aquamarine linked by a thin silver chain; wait till you see it. I have it in the valise. And when did you actually get here? I assume at four, right?

AGNES No, I was here by noon also —

GUIDO We were both here by noon.

AGNES *continuing* — had lunch in the station here and —

FELIX *quickly* Then strolled about the city too, of course. Strange that we didn't run into each other.

GUIDO We went for a drive.

AGNES In view of the bad weather, the Doctor was kind enough —

WAITER *brings their order. Felix shifts his chair so violently that the table and the glasses shake. The waiter looks somewhat astonished. Felix and Agnes put sugar in their coffee. Guido hesitates at first, then does so with nervous haste. Felix stirs his coffee with a spoon. The waiter exits with newspapers.*

GUIDO *with sudden determination* Herr Staufner, I must ask you for the kindness —

FELIX *quickly* Oh, do finish your coffee first. And let me enjoy mine. Then you may ask me for any kindness you please. You see, I find afternoon coffee to be the nicest meal of the day. I could sooner do without lunch than without my coffee.

GUIDO Herr Staufner — You asked me before whether I'm on my way to Vienna. Well. . . .

FELIX *quickly* Forgive my question. I did notice it was awkward for you. I don't want to be indiscreet. What you do with the rest of your vacation is your own affair, naturally. Rejoice in your life, for as long as — and so forth. I suppose you'll be taking over the management of the Hollenstein factory soon, won't you? Once your father retires —

GUIDO My father is still very vigorous. He has no intention of retiring yet. *He attempts to catch Agnes's glance but she avoids him.*

FELIX How old is he, if one may ask?

GUIDO Sixty-two. But as I was saying —

FELIX All the same, the principal burden will soon be on your shoulders. Therefore, enjoy your life while there is time. Travel. Yes, indeed, above all, travel.

AGNES The Doctor has traveled a great deal. He's already been to America.

GUIDO Yes, I've been to South America.

FELIX So, to South America. And do you know Japan?

GUIDO No, I haven't been to Japan yet.

FELIX Now Japan, that's attracted me for a long time. Wouldn't you like to go there too, Agnes?

AGNES There are still so many places close by —

FELIX That's not the point. One can't really go through the world in order like that, right? *Quickly* By the way, what's that hat you're wearing, Agnes?

AGNES You've seen it before.

FELIX The red band is new.

AGNES Yes, that is new.

FELIX · A proper summer color. It glows and sparkles. *He repeats, but in a tone of almost uncontrolled fury* It glows and sparkles! *Agnes looks at him, startled, then throws a quick glance at Guido, who has reflexively struck a pose. Felix looks up quickly and suddenly continues in an entirely cheerful tone* You're probably not yet interested in ladies' hats, Doctor, are you?

GUIDO *as if now perceiving an occasion to make a connection* Not in general. But I am interested in this one, Herr Staufner. And not only —

AGNES *looks at him in fright.*

FELIX Not only in this hat but also in its wearer. That's obvious. Me too, Doctor. Of course, this hat would be a matter of complete indifference to us if, for instance, it were hanging on that hook over there.

PORTER *enters, calls out* First call for the passenger train to Schwanenmarkt, Vöcklabruck, Atnang, Linz, Vienna.

GUIDO *moves back as if he wanted to stand up* Herr Staufner —

FELIX Yes, of course, that would be your train if you want to go back to Seewalchen. You can make a connection. *To Agnes, who is looking at him in total confusion* Ours too, you think? But you're mistaken, Agnes. It is not ours. More about that later. But I can understand perfectly well your being drawn back to the scene of your triumphs. Yes, indeed, your triumphs — *Smiling oddly* I'm sure you'll allow me to offer you my somewhat belated heartfelt congratulations.

GUIDO *taken aback* What for?

AGNES *looks at Felix, stunned.*

FELIX You've — *pause* won the regatta.

GUIDO *with an involuntary sigh of relief* Oh. Very kind of you. It was only the second prize, by the way.

AGNES *likewise as if saved* How do you know?

FELIX Why, it's in the paper.

AGNES You read the sports news? Since when?

FELIX Not all. But those from Seewalchen, they interested me, naturally. Especially on the train, when one's even read the editorial already. *To Guido* Have you been sailing long?

GUIDO For many years. Mostly on the Ostsee earlier on.

FELIX Isn't it actually supposed to be more difficult on lakes?

GUIDO One can't really generalize.

FELIX I'm afraid I don't understand a thing about it.

GUIDO I don't imagine you do much in the way of sport on the whole, Herr Staufner.

FELIX Oh, I do, I do. As a tourist, principally. I climb a lot. I even went on a few beautiful excursions in Stubai recently.

AGNES By yourself?

FELIX The longer ones, yes. Once in a while I had company on the shorter ones. There happened to be a couple of ladies there. Mother and daughter. The younger one was a pretty good walker.

AGNES Miss Bianka Walter?

FELIX How —? Oh, of course!

AGNES I take it she was blonde. That is your favorite color.

FELIX Yes, she was blonde, in fact. Do you want to know more? Budding actress. She even recited something for me. Maid. — Of Orleans, I mean.

AGNES Pretty?

FELIX Yes. Come to think of it, I must still have her picture on me.

AGNES Her picture? You have her picture on you?

FELIX Yes. *Takes it out of his breast pocket* She gave it to me as we were saying good-bye. I should show it to some director when I get a chance. She would like so much to get an engagement in Vienna. She thinks it requires only a word from me. Naive is what these women are! The mother wasn't bad either.

AGNES Isabella.

FELIX Isabella? Oh, I see! Yes. The mother's name was

Isabella.

AGNES And the daughter's Bianka.

FELIX The mother's name was Isabella and the daughter's Bianka. Sounds like the start of a ballad almost. *To Guido* Don't you think so?

GUIDO *icily* I am not an expert.

AGNES But, actually, wasn't it your intention to make no acquaintances there, and to devote yourself exclusively to your work?

FELIX Oh, I've been most industrious anyway. You'll be quite satisfied with me, I hope.

AGNES *with some effort* Are you finished?

FELIX Finished? Not quite.

AGNES It was — under these circumstances — hardly to be expected otherwise.

FELIX My, how malicious you can be, Agnes! No cause whatever, I assure you! It's really only a question of a trifle. With any luck, I can have it over and done with in three, four days. Only, I need your advice.

AGNES *unintentionally happy* My advice?

FELIX Yes. Indispensably. I have to talk the work over with you before anything else. I also have to read you the whole thing, as much as there is. That's why we don't want to go back to Seewalchen for now. I want to go back there again only after I've gotten everything completely cleared up. And I know from past experience that here, in Salzburg, it's always particularly easy for me to work. That's why I want to stay a few days.

AGNES We should stay here? This comes as quite a surprise, of course.

FELIX For me too. I mean — I only thought of it myself on the trip over here. You do agree, don't you? We'll simply telegraph our good Therese she should forward the essentials to us, and a few superfluous things too, of course; and whatever you — need right away — we can still buy today.

Or might you perhaps have had a hunch — and brought your charming little crocodile valise along?

GUIDO *feeling like the loser, not without malice but outwardly simply* I myself had the good fortune of bringing the charming crocodile valise to the check room for safekeeping.

FELIX Is that so? Why, that's excellent. Then everything's in perfect order, isn't it? And you're glad to be staying here, aren't you? Isn't that so, Agnes? And you'll see, it won't be three days and every difficulty will be overcome, and even before we return to our little country house I'll put the finishing touches on — *he hesitates* the Bacchanale.

AGNES *astonished* The Bacchanale?

FELIX Yes. Why are you surprised?

AGNES You're writing the Bacchanale?

FELIX Yes.

AGNES But when you left you had a totally different plan, didn't you?

FELIX Yes. But on the way to the Stubaital it already became clear to me that I had to write the Bacchanale before anything else. There are reasons for it, I imagine. It's all governed by such mysterious laws, you know.

GUIDO Yes, life is very mysterious.

FELIX Life — no. Not especially. But art. Yes, art is most — Something like this prepares itself within — ripens somewhere in the depths — one knows nothing of it — up here *indicating his forehead* — yes — *breaking off; in a different tone* As I said, two acts are completely finished. Only in the third, that's where the story turns, — well, you'll hear, and I'm sure you'll think of something reasonable.

AGNES If you think —

WAITER *enters and stands at their table.*

FELIX *noticing him* Oh, yes — So —

GUIDO I have one melange —

FELIX I won't hear of it, Doctor — *to the waiter* Three

melanges and three pieces of Gugelhupf.

GUIDO Four, — that is, I had two.

FELIX *laughing* Oh, I see. All right, four.

WAITER Five.

FELIX Five?

AGNES You crumbled one.

FELIX Is that right? I did that? Really! All right, five.

WAITER Two crowns forty.

FELIX *pays* Here — that's fine.

WAITER *discreetly to Guido* That still leaves two sodas.

GUIDO Of course — *wants to pay.*

FELIX *notices* What's this? Oh, I see. *Gaily* Allow me — *offers to pay as well.*

GUIDO I will not —

FELIX Oh, stop it. Two sodas? So, here. *Pays, then takes out his cigarette case and offers it to Guido.*

GUIDO *hesitating, takes a cigarette* Thank you. *Felix lights it for him, then lights a cigarette for himself as well.* And now, if you don't mind, I will say good-bye.

FELIX Good-bye, Doctor, and bon voyage — on whatever road you decide to travel.

GUIDO Thank you. Good-bye to you, dear lady. *He does not extend his hand to her yet* I hope I will soon have — if not before — *he is visibly pleased with his idea* then I will have the pleasure at the premiere of your husband's new play.

AGNES I will be glad to see you.

FELIX You are in no way obligated, Doctor.

GUIDO Oh, who's talking about obligation? I've never yet missed one of your premieres. So it goes without saying that I won't miss the Bacchus either.

FELIX Bacchanale, Doctor.

GUIDO I'm sorry.

FELIX But — it's no mythological drama, nor is it in verse either, in case you should be afraid of that.

GUIDO Oh, not at all.

FELIX The word is only used figuratively, of course. With the real Bacchanale I'd have probably had trouble with the censor, as you may imagine.

GUIDO I must confess, to my shame, that I don't even know what it is, a Bacchanale.

FELIX Oh, you don't know that? The Bacchanale was a custom peculiar to the ancient Greeks — a religious custom, one might say.

GUIDO A — religious custom?

FELIX *in a purposely incidental manner* Yes. Once a year for one entire night, at the time of the grape harvest, if I'm not mistaken, the people were granted unrestricted freedom — in a certain regard.

GUIDO Unrestricted freedom?

FELIX *very coolly now, as if reporting* In a certain regard. For this one night all family ties, all commandments concerning morality were simply suspended. At sundown, men, women, young girls left the house whose peace surrounded and protected them at other times, and betook themselves to the sacred grove — there was a considerable number of such groves in the country — in order there to celebrate the divine festival beneath the protective veils of night.

GUIDO The divine festival?

FELIX The divine festival.

GUIDO Beneath the veils of night?

FELIX Yes.

GUIDO And if the moon were shining?

FELIX That didn't make much difference. At break of day the festival was over, and every participant was duty-bound to forget with whom he had celebrated the divine festival. Duty-bound. That belonged to the religious custom — as much as the celebration itself. To recognize each other again would have been considered bad form, impiety even. And as the myth tells us, the participants are said to have returned home somewhat tired at times, but refreshed nonetheless, indeed, to some degree, purified.

GUIDO   And one had a stimulating topic of conversation at home   . . . until the next festival.

FELIX   It was not permitted ever to speak of the festival at home. Nor would it have made any sense. Because there was as little individual responsibility for the experiences of this one night as — for dreams. *Pause.*

GUIDO   But didn't it happen occasionally that a couple who had found each other in the grove did not wish to part again right away . . . and that neither one of them came home?

FELIX   Impossible. The penalty for that was death.

AGNES   Death?

FELIX   Yes. Death. They had to part, before the sun came up. The ritual was very strict.

GUIDO   Since the penalty was death —

FELIX   Of course, there was one mitigating circumstance.

GUIDO   Oh?

FELIX   *emphatically*   If two individuals who had found each other beneath the veils of night still felt a longing for each other the following night — this happened less frequently than one might think — then nobody, neither husband nor wife, nor mother nor father, was permitted to hold the lovers back; and they met again at the same place where they had parted in the morning. But from this second night — and here we must truly admire the wisdom of the priests — from this second night, which was no longer a Bacchanale — there was no return. Their former homes were closed to both of them for all time, and they were thrown upon each other for the rest of their lives. That is why so few are said to have felt the desire to leave the house — on the second night. *Pause.*

GUIDO   You've made a thorough study of mythology, Herr Staufner, for your new comedy.

FELIX   That wasn't even necessary. Nor, for that matter, if you happen to want to look it up, will everything be completely accurate. Because, as I said before, the Bacchanale is only a symbol for me. My play takes place in the present, and the present is lacking pretty much all the conditions necessary for the revival of so beautiful, simple, and pure a celebration as the ancient Bacchanale. People have become too irreligious. Instead of experiencing what is natural naturally, they spoil it with their damned psychology. There are no Bacchanales any more nowadays because our love life is spoiled, indeed, poisoned by lies and self-deception, by jealousy and fear, by impudence and repentance. Only occasionally — and only in pious souls, does a duller or brighter reflection of that wonderful magic flash forth at times, of the kind that surrounded those distant Bacchanales. In pious souls. And this reflection represents, perhaps, an even more exalted form of magic. But who among us may boast of true piety? Who among us?

PORTER *enters* First call for the express to Freilassing — Rosenheim — Munich — Paris.

FELIX *in a different tone* Isn't that your train, Doctor?

GUIDO *perplexed* My train?

AGNES To Paris! Of course it's your train, Doctor.

GUIDO *stands up* I suppose it is at that. And now I have to hurry to see to my luggage. Dear lady — *Agnes extends her hand to him. Guido hesitates an instant then kisses it. He bows to Felix. Felix extends his hand; Guido presses it very quickly and then exits down the stairs. Pause. Commotion of passengers on the platform with luggage carriers, etc. Felix seems to be observing the bustle, without looking at Agnes.*

AGNES *watching him, after a longer pause* And — what sort of reflection is it? *Felix turns his glance to her as if he didn't understand her* The reflection in pious souls which you spoke of just now, which is supposed to signify an even more exalted magic than the wonderful festival itself, which we no longer celebrate nowadays?

FELIX *almost roughly* This magic is called — forgetting. But I don't imagine either one of us believes in it.

AGNES You may be right there. But maybe there's another one, in which one can believe more readily. *Felix looks at her questioningly* Understanding. *She has the picture in her hand and crumples it. Felix laughs curtly.*

GUIDO *enters from the right carrying two valises and comes to the table again* I must beg your pardon. But since I checked both bags together for the sake of convenience, I took the liberty —

AGNES *anxiously* Thank you very much. If you'll just put it down here.

GUIDO Yes, of course. *He places Agnes's valise on the chair in which he had been sitting earlier.*

FELIX *standing up abruptly* Doctor Wernig —

GUIDO *understanding, very correctly* If you wish, Herr Staufner, I can also postpone my departure —

AGNES *quickly, determined* You will leave on this train, Guido!

FELIX *looks at her.*

GUIDO *hesitates. Pause.*

FELIX Go!

GUIDO *bows and goes out to the platform. Felix sits down, follows him with his glance, his face distorted; he gets up again halfway, as if he wanted to go after Guido. Agnes holds him by the arm and he sits down again. Agnes tears Bianka's picture into little pieces.*

FELIX *bitterly* If only it were all done with that!

AGNES *with a soft little laugh* Let's be — pious, both of us.

FELIX *with a sudden dull explosion* I hate you.

AGNES And I hate you a thousand times more — *with a new expression of tenderness* my lover!

Curtain

FINK AND FLIEDERBUSCH

Comedy in Three Acts

CHARACTERS

At the daily "Times"

LEUCHTER, *Editor-in-Chief*
FRÜHBECK, *Managing Editor and Editor of local news*
FÜLLMANN, *Political Editor*
OBENDORFER, *Features Editor*
ABENDSTERN, *Theater reviewer*
FLIEDERBUSCH, *Parliament reporter*
KAJETAN, *free-lance contributor*
HANAUSCHEK, *typesetter*
SERVANT

At the weekly "The Elegant World"

LEODEGAR SATAN, *Editor-in-Chief*
EGON, *his son*
STYX, staff writer
WÖBL, *staff writer*
SERVANT

COUNT GISBERT NIEDERHOF, *Member of Parliament*
PRINCESS PRISKA WENDOLIN-RATZEBURG
DOCTOR KUNZ
MAN-IN-WAITING TO THE PRINCESS
LADY-IN-WAITING TO THE PRINCESS

The play takes place in Vienna at the beginning of the century

FIRST ACT

In the Editorial offices of the "Times."
A spacious room. Three doors: one in the rear to the hallway,
one right to the Editor-in-Chief's office, one left to another
editorial office (to the right and left of the audience). Two desks
with telephones in the center, facing each other. One writing
standing each at the right and left walls. At the rear, on each
side of the door, a large cupboard, one of them open to reveal
portfolios and newspapers. Atop the cupboards, bundles of
papers. In the compartments atop the writing stands, books in no
particular order, some still wrapped. Above the desk on the
right, a map; above the desk on the left, a wall calendar. A
simple brass chandelier with three lights. It is past ten o'clock at
night.

FRÜHBECK, HANAUSCHEK

Frühbeck, around forty, lean, with brown hair, beardless,
wearing a pince-nez and smoking a cigar in a long white holder,
is at the desk to the left, a pencil in his hand, examining galley
proofs. Hanauschek, the typesetter, broad, with a blond, shaggy
mustache, is standing behind him.

FRÜHBECK *has a superior, often mocking tone, and a slow*
manner of speaking But what's this, my dear man? The little
feature would begin only on column nineteen this way and the
theater review not until the twenty-second.

HANAUSCHEK *speaks slowly, phlegmatically, which some-*
times has the effect of appearing impudent If we leave two
columns open, then right after the lead story we would have
to —

FRÜHBECK After the lead story?

HANAUSCHEK Well, because of the obituary for Ebenstein! The Editor-in-Chief just now phoned down.

FRÜHBECK *to himself* For Ebenstein! The day before yesterday he was still the Herr Doctor. Sic transit —

HANAUSCHEK Gloria mundi.

FRÜHBECK *over his shoulder* You think so too?

HANAUSCHEK We're all sorry about Doctor Ebenstein. Down in the print shop too. Such legible handwriting — I'm sure you'll forgive me, Doctor — we won't see in a man again.

FRÜHBECK You should have written the obituary, Hanauschek. *More to himself* It would have been sincere at least. *At work again* Parliament five, telegrams seven, features two and a half, Ebenstein — Again?

HANAUSCHEK Funeral.

FRÜHBECK One and a quarter — how come?

HANAUSCHEK The Chief wants the eulogies in large type too.

FRÜHBECK, HANAUSCHEK, *then* OBENDORFER

OBENDORFER *(who has entered from the left a bit earlier) around thirty-six, parted hair, mustache, slim, trousers with wide stripes, fancy vest, dark jacket, light-colored tie with pin; altogether of a somewhat provincial elegance.* What do you think, Frühbeck, aren't we doing just fine with the paper as soon as we're six feet under?!

FRÜHBECK *still occupied with his papers* Patience, Obendorfer, patience. You'll be just as well off one day too.

OBENDORFER Sentimentalist!

FRÜHBECK For you we'll even treat ourselves to a lead article. "He is gone, the singer of the golden Viennese heart, the best of the new wine, small theaters —"

OBENDORFER *waving him off* Enough, enough. *Standing at the desk to the right, looking through some papers that are lying there* By the way, what else is new in the world? Any more shooting up at Strakonitz?

HANAUSCHEK We have nothing more downstairs about the strike. It's possible something will come yet.

FRÜHBECK But it's already quieted down. All the shafts are being worked since the day before yesterday.

OBENDORFER What do you say, Frühbeck, to the Socialist interpellation in the Imperial Council? *To Hanauschek* Right, Hanauschek, it makes your comradely heart laugh, doesn't it?

HANAUSCHEK *shrugs.*

FRÜHBECK Theater two. Did you leave enough room for the premiere.

HANAUSCHEK Doctor Abendstern said he will express himself concisely.

FRÜHBECK He always says that — and then it turns into a filibuster.

OBENDORFER What premiere?

FRÜHBECK Kajetan's new comedy.

OBENDORFER *at the desk, rummaging* Yes, right — it'll be a pretty bit of rubbish!

FRÜHBECK Really, I must say. In your experience, has a staff member of the "Times" ever written any rubbish? One's co-workers are always talented. *To Hanauschek* Parliament looks pretty lousy again.

HANAUSCHEK Fliederbusch phoned, he's bringing some-thing else.

FRÜHBECK *coarsely* Herr Fliederbusch! Do you understand what I'm saying, Hanauschek? *That one* is still alive. *Looks at his watch* A quarter to eleven!

HANAUSCHEK Maybe he's already downstairs — *ironically* Herr von Fliederbusch.

FRÜHBECK In which case he might be so kind as to exert himself sufficiently to come up here. I have to talk to him.

HANAUSCHEK *about to go.*

FRÜHBECK *calling after him* Telegrams!

OBENDORFER *at the desk to the right again* And I would like to read my feature, Hanauschek.

FRÜHBECK *to Obendorfer* In which desire you differentiate yourself from our subscribers — whether to your advantage or not I prefer to leave undecided.

HANAUSCHEK *has exited to the rear.*

FRÜHBECK, OBENDORFER

OBENDORFER Jokes —

FRÜHBECK *still proofreading and otherwise occupied* I'm just reading what you said at the cemetery. Moving.

OBENDORFER *has sat down at the desk to the right, his legs stretched out underneath* Well, yes, as it happens to come from a man's heart.

FRÜHBECK When one considers that you actually couldn't stand him —

OBENDORFER But you — Frühbeck?

FRÜHBECK What does it get you! Ebenstein really was a decent human being.

OBENDORFER I don't deny it. An honorable man. But always those spinach stains on his vest! Sometimes it was scrambled eggs.

FRÜHBECK He had other things to worry about.

OBENDORFER Don't start with his five children. I have three of them too, and I'm only counting the legitimate ones. Ha, look at me.

FRÜHBECK Thanks. By the by, you'll be interested to know that our esteemed chief has settled a pension of three thousand gulden per year on the survivors.

OBENDORFER *has gotten up, walked right, and turned again* Three thousand! Well, yes. Let's not fool ourselves,

Ebenstein was really the only one of us all whom Leuchter truly liked. The rest of us are really only his slaves.

FRÜHBECK   Surely one can understand the attachment! Childhood friends! Went to school together. Immigrated to the imperial capital forty years ago, arm in arm, so to speak!

OBENDORFER   And from Szegedin at that.

FRÜHBECK   *coolly* Temesvar.

OBENDORFER   On foot!

FRÜHBECK   *parodying* What do you mean on foot?! — with torn boots.

OBENDORFER   And yet he wasn't out at the cemetery today.

FRÜHBECK   He can't risk that — with his heart. You know.

OBENDORFER   I know. By the way, who's in there with him so long?

FRÜHBECK   Füllmann.

OBENDORFER   Ah, Füllmann. I can imagine. Most likely he wants to take over the domestic department too.

FRÜHBECK   Thrift, thrift, Horatio!

OBENDORFER   Just between you and me, he hasn't approached you yet, our esteemed chief?

FRÜHBECK   What for? He knows I have no aspirations beyond my department. And my department, as everyone very well knows, is the vine louse.

OBENDORFER   Na, you needn't be all that modest!

FRÜHBECK   Politics? Leave me in peace! There are more important things. Five o'clock tea with the Chinese ambassador. — First conquest of the Winklerturm from the north side. — The battle of the flowers. — A double suicide. — The flight of attorney X with his clients' estates. — The crash of a furniture wagon with a court carriage in which His Highness was riding. — The reappearance of the vine louse. — These are the things in which people are interested. Who really cares about politics? Ministers, diplomats, stock brokers, princes, members of parliament, journalists, bank presidents — in short, those concerned for business reasons.

Of course, if there is some slaughter or rape committed somewhere in the name of politics, then the other people also fancy that they're interested in politics. But that is only fancy. Take from the events their deceptive aroma of future world history and what remains? The vine louse.

FRÜHBECK, OBENDORFER, KAJETAN

KAJETAN *over thirty, small, agile, curly black hair, wearing a smoking jacket, overcoat, and top hat, carrying a briefcase; in a hurry, as always* Good evening, gentlemen, how are you? Anything new? May I see the Chief? *Goes to the door on the right.*

FRÜHBECK Hold it! Someone's in there.

KAJETAN *he has the habit of repeating quite mechanically the last words of the person speaking before him* Someone's in there! — Is that bloody Abendstern here yet?

FRÜHBECK But he's at the theater watching your play.

KAJETAN Your play — Over long ago.

OBENDORFER Well, how did it turn out?

KAJETAN Colossal! Smash hit! Called out countless times. Loud applause! Will be played on every stage.

FRÜHBECK Congratulations. *Shakes his hand.*

OBENDORFER Likewise. *Shakes his hand as well* And you still honor us with your presence today?

KAJETAN Only in passing. Have to go to the Bristol. Banquet in my honor. Director, cast. Tewele was splendid. But still have to quickly proofread my short piece.

FRÜHBECK *telephones to the print shop* Kajetan's short piece. — And what's holding up the telegrams? — Is Fliederbusch here yet? — Not yet? — Outrageous!

OBENDORFER *to Kajetan* With what are you bringing joy to our readers this time?

KAJETAN This time — Small talk. Princess's park.

OBENDORFER What princess?

FRÜHBECK There is only one for us. The Princess Wendolin.

OBENDORFER *to himself* Not a spring chicken any more either.

KAJETAN Splendid woman!

OBENDORFER And what actually does one hear about the Prince?

FRÜHBECK *to Kajetan* By the way, do you have the obituary with you?

OBENDORFER Has he died, the Prince?

KAJETAN Wouldn't dream of it. Won't ever die. Lives in the South. Mallorca. Wonderful area. Been there. Date palms, rattlesnakes, first-class hotels.

OBENDORFER So who died then?

KAJETAN *takes a manuscript page from his briefcase* Here. *Gives it to Frühbeck.*

OBENDORFER *glancing at the page* What — the Minister of —?

FRÜHBECK *interrupts him* Shh —

OBENDORFER Surely it won't be a secret when a Cabinet Minister kicks the bucket.

FRÜHBECK *to Kajetan* But he's not even sixty yet —

KAJETAN Sixty yet. Doesn't matter. Fainting spell yesterday! Sugar! Six-and-a-half percent! Can't hold out much longer. Have spoken to his family doctor. Discretion a point of honor. A matter of certainty. I'm all finished with those between sixty and seventy.

OBENDORFER Oh, you write obituaries in advance —

KAJETAN Death treads apace to meet the human race.

OBENDORFER I must say, this is the height of frivolity.

FRÜHBECK On the contrary. *Pointing to his desk* I've got thirty-five of these lying in there. We haven't needed one yet. It's almost a kind of life insurance for a person when Kajetan writes an obituary for him.

KAJETAN — tuary for him — And the fee doesn't fall due until after the decease of the party concerned. What do you think?

OBENDORFER An obscenity.

FRÜHBECK No, not until after the funeral. One could merely appear to be dead.

HANAUSCHEK *brings galley-proofs again.*

FRÜHBECK Is Fliederbusch here yet?

HANAUSCHEK No.

FRÜHBECK Unbelievable fellow!

KAJETAN *has taken one sheet from Hanauschek* My article? Not even half. How come?

FRÜHBECK I've taken the liberty of making deletions. We all know the birds chirp and the lilacs are fragrant in the Wendolin Park. If you want to be poetic, Kajetan, then write poetry.

KAJETAN Poetry — I do that anyway. Lirum larum — third edition with Pierson, two marks, bound two-fifty. Much too cheap.

OBENDORFER How is it that you happen to know the Princess, Kajetan?

KAJETAN Why not? Come and go there as I please.

FRÜHBECK Kajetan is like the child of the house there.

KAJETAN Child in the palace — Haha. This by the way is the press release. *Takes a piece of paper from his briefcase and gives it to Frühbeck; to Obendorfer, by way of explanation* A great charity gala shortly. Bazaar. Lottery. Tableaux vivants. Ladies and gentlemen of the highest aristocracy taking part.

FRÜHBECK Is that so? — The aristocracy now visits the Princess Wendolin too?

KAJETAN Haha. I'm writing the connecting text. Mythological. Then Renaissance. Next Baroque, then Biedermeier. Closing tableau: triumph of the modern.

OBENDORFER Triumph? You won't have much luck with that.

KAJETAN Or maybe downfall. It depends. It'll turn out.

OBENDORFER But they're not quite the same I've been told.

KAJETAN To a certain extent, yes. Death and life, vice and virtue, wisdom and simple-mindedness, art and nature, somehow identical. New discovery. Or ancient truth. As you wish. Soon to be common property. Philosophical work in progress: Identity of Opposites.

OBENDORFER You're nuts!

FRÜHBECK *has torn up the paper Kajetan gave him and throws it in the waste basket.*

KAJETAN Haha. On to you already. *He takes a second paper from his briefcase* Copy. Has to appear. Chief in agreement. Princess has written him in her own hand. By the by, she was in the theater tonight also. Laughed herself half to death.

OBENDORFER Then you'll just have to write half an obituary.

KAJETAN Applauded like mad. Count Niederhof likewise. Was in her loge. Cousin. They have a relationship, the two of them.

FRÜHBECK That's long since over.

KAJETAN Long since over — What's keeping Abendstern? He's doing the review of my play.

FRÜHBECK He usually writes his reviews at the "Silver Fountain."

OBENDORFER And if the roast doesn't taste good, then the play was bad.

KAJETAN Was bad — Haha! *Has sat down on the right and reads proofs* "And thus the quiet, else so secluded garden of the Princess Proska — *corrects* Priska, — in which oft, for many moons —"

FRÜHBECK "Moons"? Months would serve as well.

KAJETAN   *reading on*   "the sacred-profane bustle of the metropolis is heard only in dying bones — *corrects* tones —"

FLIEDERBUSCH *comes in, a handsome twenty-three-year-old, beardless individual, neatly but rather modestly dressed.*

OBENDORFER, FRÜHBECK, KAJETAN, HANAUSCHEK, FLIEDERBUSCH

FLIEDERBUSCH Good evening, gentlemen.

KAJETAN Hi, Fliederbusch.

FLIEDERBUSCH Good evening, Herr Kajetan. Permit me to congratulate you on your great success.

KAJETAN Did you see it?

FLIEDERBUSCH Unfortunately, professional obligations kept me from it. But I heard people speaking of it already.

FRÜHBECK *ironically* If you happen to have a little time left over for me, Herr Fliederbusch —

FLIEDERBUSCH I am entirely at your disposal, Herr Doctor.

KAJETAN   *gives Hanauschek the manuscript*   Here. The headline reads: From a noble park of old Vienna. And Priska, not Proska.

HANAUSCHEK *exits with the galley-proofs.*

KAJETAN *looks at his watch* Eleven o'clock! And Abendstern is still stuffing himself! *To the writing stand, busies himself with the books, opens a package, turns a few pages, and so on.*

OBENDORFER *at the writing stand on the left, reads galleys.*

FRÜHBECK *leaning back, to Fliederbusch* What I have to say to you, my dear Herr Fliederbusch, is the following. Namely, things cannot go on this way.

FLIEDERBUSCH *standing opposite him, rather unmoved* Herr Doctor thinks so?

FRÜHBECK   I certainly do. If the Chief hadn't been so indulgent with you up to now, out of consideration for your family circumstances —

FLIEDERBUSCH   Herr Leuchter has indeed been very kind up to now.

FRÜHBECK   But he is gradually losing his patience too and — *to Kajetan, nervously* What are you doing there, Kajetan? Would you leave that alone? They're review copies.

KAJETAN   *putting books in his briefcase* Exactly. For reviewing. I'll bring the reviews in a few days.

OBENDORFER   *going up to him, takes one of the books* But you don't understand this, this is in Croatian.

KAJETAN   Child's play. Very similar to Slovenian.

OBENDORFER   Since when do you understand Slovenian?

KAJETAN   Don't understand it either, haha!

HANAUSCHEK   *brings galley-proofs again.*

FLIEDERBUSCH   Am I in there maybe?

HANAUSCHEK   *hands him a sheet without a word.*

FRÜHBECK   Let me see. This is it? *To Fliederbusch* You call this an eyewitness report, Herr Fliederbusch? The news service could supply this much too.

KAJETAN   *goes to the Chief's door, listens, shakes his head* I'm going to phone the Bristol. *Exits to the rear.*

FRÜHBECK   *to Fliederbusch* There must have been something to say about the Social-Democratic interpellation! You know our Chief wants us to take a position. Where has the position gone? The personal touch, Herr Fliederbusch?!

FLIEDERBUSCH   Whatever I add of my own to my parliamentary reports is almost always deleted. Just recently —

FRÜHBECK   You ridiculed the Minister of Justice. Obviously, we couldn't print that.

FLIEDERBUSCH I didn't think that an independent paper would consider the personality of a minister to be a priori inviolable.

FRÜHBECK There are no general rules here. As a journalist one must have a sense when one may offend a minister and when not. Well — and today nothing but shorthand minutes of the proceedings again?! There is no way I can put this on the Chief's desk.

FLIEDERBUSCH I must leave that entirely to your discretion, Herr Editor.

FRÜHBECK *somewhat surprised* As you say, Herr Fliederbusch. But under these circumstances Herr Leuchter might feel compelled to dispense with your further efforts on behalf of the "Times."

FLIEDERBUSCH That would not work out all that badly.

FRÜHBECK How so?

FLIEDERBUSCH I also came here today with the intention of suggesting to Herr Leuchter a dissolution of our relationship.

FRÜHBECK *surprised especially over Fliederbusch's tone* What do you mean?

FLIEDERBUSCH Yes, indeed, Herr Editor.

FRÜHBECK *after a short pause* Well, as you please. I'll tell the Chief — you know, he does not hold anyone who wants to leave.

FLIEDERBUSCH May I ask for the galley in the meantime? Perhaps I can add a few more lines, — as a swan song, so to speak. *To the writing stand left with the galley.*

FRÜHBECK *glances after him, screws up his mouth, and busies himself.*

ABENDSTERN *enters.* FRÜHBECK, FLIEDERBUSCH, OBENDORFER

ABENDSTERN *between forty and fifty, stout, thick blond hair somewhat speckled with gray, mustache, wearing a hat and an overcoat; a Virginia cigar in his mouth. During his first words he takes off his hat and coat and hangs them up.* You've got it good, gentlemen. Good evening. You can sit quietly in your office and write about reasonable things, and not have to lock yourselves up on a lovely spring evening in a so-called art institute to see what in reality is a wretched company, and have a so-called comedy performed for you which is, in point of fact, the greatest trash, the most deplorable rubbish. *He has in the meantime sat down at the desk right.*

OBENDORFER So it really was a success?

FLIEDERBUSCH *from his desk* Good evening, Herr Doctor.

ABENDSTERN *waving to him* Hello, Fliederbusch. Why don't you write bad plays? The best business, if one is related.

OBENDORFER To whom?

ABENDSTERN Doesn't matter. *He begins to write* Who actually is this Kajetan?

FRÜHBECK An intimate friend of yours, as far as I know. *Stands up.*

HANAUSCHEK *enters, goes to Frühbeck, brings him galley-proofs.*

ABENDSTERN Friend?! That was true once. And I stay on familiar terms with him because one can tell someone the truth better that way. This nobody! This zero!
Frühbeck and Hanauschek have exited to the rear.

OBENDORFER Don't yell like that. He's in the house.

ABENDSTERN Who is in the house?

OBENDORFER Kajetan. In there with the Chief.

ABENDSTERN So? That won't help him either. This boy! *He writes. Obendorfer exits left with his galleys. Fliederbusch and Abendstern are consequently alone on stage.*

ABENDSTERN *writes.*

FLIEDERBUSCH *goes to the writing stand right and takes several pencils and pieces of paper from a drawer, puts them in his pocket; glances at Abendstern occasionally, finally steps closer to him.* Herr Doctor —

ABENDSTERN What is it? Oh, it's you —

FLIEDERBUSCH I'm disturbing you.

ABENDSTERN Not at all. *Indicating the paper in front of him* Actually, two words would suffice: brain atrophy. How may I be of service?

FLIEDERBUSCH I wanted only to bid you a most humble farewell, Herr Doctor.

ABENDSTERN Farewell, how come?

FLIEDERBUSCH Herr Frühbeck has just indicated to me the likelihood of my dismissal. In all probability I will not set foot in these offices again. And you always treated me with so much friendliness, Herr Doctor —

ABENDSTERN Oh, nonsense. But they can't just — without ado —

FLIEDERBUSCH But they can, Herr Doctor. I'm only working on a per line basis.

ABENDSTERN What, still? But you've been with us for almost a year.

FLIEDERBUSCH To be sure, Herr Frühbeck has repeatedly — Herr Leuchter too, personally —

ABENDSTERN Well, then. Talk to him again. Or would you like me to? I can't guarantee anything, of course. Any number of things would be different around here if they paid attention to me.

FLIEDERBUSCH Thank you very much, Herr Doctor, but I would ask you most urgently not to trouble yourself in the least on my behalf.

ABENDSTERN Nonsense. It's not on your behalf. It's for the sake of the thing itself. You are a talented young person. We can make excellent use of you here. You represent the only hopeful element in this conventicle of worn out and broken lives. In time you will also learn how to write. That is to say, you do not know how to write yet. But that will come in time. What you do have is your own personality, which naturally you will lose later on in this brothel, — *with sudden interest* or do you have something else lined up already?

FLIEDERBUSCH Oh God, something will turn up for me all right.

ABENDSTERN Well, yes, — You have plenty of time.

FLIEDERBUSCH How so, Herr Doctor?

ABENDSTERN You're living here in the bosom of your family, it's easy enough for you to act the proud gentleman — even if your father is probably not independently wealthy. I, at your age — But what can happen to you in the end? You have your home —

FLIEDERBUSCH Home! That sounds more beautiful sometimes than it appears close up. My home! Do you by any chance know the Kleine Schiffamtsgasse, Herr Doctor?

ABENDSTERN Unfortunately I haven't had —

FLIEDERBUSCH Say rather, thank God, Herr Doctor. I live there you see, at number — But that's besides the point, because in this neighborhood one house looks exactly like the next, gloomy on the outside and on the inside. On the stairs it smells of cabbage — at every hour of the day — in the halls women stand around in grease-stained dressing gowns —

ABENDSTERN *professionally* You describe this most vividly!

FLIEDERBUSCH From behind every door, out of every window, resounds the yelling of children. And the fact that my own siblings are yelling along does not make it sound any more pleasant to me.

ABENDSTERN You still have such young siblings?

FLIEDERBUSCH The youngest is three. There are six of us all together. I'm the oldest.

ABENDSTERN So. This is certainly — And if I may ask — Your father — What profession —?

FLIEDERBUSCH As you guessed so very accurately, Herr
Doctor, he is not a man of independent means. To be sure,
he has come very close to becoming one at times. I vaguely
remember a time when we didn't live on the Kleine
Schiffamtsgasse. That's quite long ago. He's a merchant, you
see. Don't ask me what he buys or sells, Herr Doctor. I don't
believe there is anything from shoe buttons to Ringstrasse
palais that has not passed through his hands in the course of
the past twenty years. The only unfortunate thing is that shoe
buttons have been preponderant lately.

ABENDSTERN *amused, laughs* Look, Fliederbusch, here —
here is where your future may lie.

FLIEDERBUSCH *waving him off* Well —

ABENDSTERN I don't mean in shoe buttons. In the humorous
sketch. Write something of that kind sometime, like our so-
called human interest feature writer Obendorfer, only better
of course, more realistic.

FLIEDERBUSCH Do you find them especially humorous, Herr
Doctor, these details of my personal life which I've permitted
myself . . . . That would be a mistake. Nor, incidentally,
would I want you to misunderstand me, Herr Doctor. My
father — I admire him actually. He's a highly gifted
individual in a sense. He believes in himself. To this day he
believes in his future. An enviable individual. But for that
very reason he is very difficult to get along with at times.
Especially for my mother.

ABENDSTERN *sentimentally* You still have a mother, you
lucky fellow.

FLIEDERBUSCH A wonderful woman. A truly — But this
would go too far. I'm already taking up too much of your
time as it is, Herr Doctor —

ABENDSTERN A temporary advantage for Herr Kajetan,
merely. But anyhow, I gather from all this that your private
circumstances — I would in your place think it over
carefully, in any case, before I —

In the meantime, Obendorfer and Kajetan have appeared at the door in the rear speaking with each other. Somewhat earlier Frühbeck and Hanauschek have entered. Füllman enters from the right out of the Editor-in-Chief's office.

KAJETAN *seeing him* Well, finally. Hi, Füllmann! *Picks up his briefcase and goes quickly into the Editor-in-Chief's office.*

HANAUSCHEK *exits to the rear.*

FRÜHBECK, OBENDORFER, FLIEDERBUSCH, FÜLLMANN, ABENDSTERN

FÜLLMANN *over forty, rumpled graying hair, dark full beard, pince-nez, in a somewhat worn frock coat, excitable, occasionally screaming.* This is outrageous, outrageous! *Sits down at the desk.*

FRÜHBECK *across from him, left* What's the matter?

OBENDORFER *at the writing stand, right* Can't you see? He's been given his walking papers again.

FÜLLMANN *gloomily* I ask you, gentlemen, *leans back* are we a voice for democracy or not?

OBENDORFER It says so right in the paper. What are you asking such silly questions for?

FÜLLMANN *after a disparaging gesture* I ask you further, gentlemen, do you take me for a revolutionary, for a bomb-thrower?

FRÜHBECK *barely looking up from his work* No one can accuse you of that, Füllmann.

FÜLLMANN Thank you. And now permit me, gentlemen, to read you my article which our esteemed Chief does not want to publish because he finds it too biting. *Silent resistance on the part of the others* I cannot release you from this, gentlemen. You must hear for yourselves. And after you've heard, I will ask you whether you'll declare your solidarity with me, solidarity against the criminal in there.   *Points to the right.*

FRÜHBECK   *cool*   Restrain yourself.

ABENDSTERN   But he has a point.

FÜLLMANN   Biting!   *Straining his voice*   This article biting! And what if it is. I ask you gentlemen, when else should we be biting if not at an occasion such as this one? Blood has flowed at Strakonitz, human blood, innocent human blood. Let's not inquire which side is to blame. Far be it from me to be the spokesman for revolution, for sedition. You know me, gentlemen.

OBENDORFER   Far be it from you.

FÜLLMANN   But we must not allow it to pass without contradiction when a representative of our reactionaries stands up in Parliament and maintains clear as day that the lives of workers, of citizens, are not worth a straw.

OBENDORFER   Who said anything like that?

FÜLLMANN   Count Niederhof.

OBENDORFER   Isn't he the one who shot Baron Napador in a duel a couple of years ago?

FLIEDERBUSCH   *informed*   The same.

FÜLLMANN   Not a straw — a human life!

FLIEDERBUSCH   Excuse me, Herr Füllmann, I was present at the session, — I don't recall the Count's saying that —

FÜLLMANN   It was the sense of his words, young man! The principle of the state's authority, this is how he spoke, stands in every instance higher than the life of any one individual, whoever he may be. Did he say so or didn't he? Well, then! Go ahead and fire into the rabble if it shows any fight! And if an innocent boy is struck by a fatal bullet on the occasion, what does it matter?! Do stop making such a fuss about a few drops of human blood! The principle has been preserved. Did he say this, Count Niederhof, or not?

FLIEDERBUSCH   *hesitating*   In a sense — nevertheless —

FÜLLMANN   Well, then. And that's why —

FRÜHBECK *interrupting* But Füllmann, please, who is this Count Niederhof, really? No one takes him seriously!

FÜLLMANN You think so?

OBENDORFER Since when is he a politician anyway? A jockey is what he is! As recently as last year, gentlemen, he rode in the great steeplechase.

FRÜHBECK When he began to get fat he had himself elected to Parliament.

FÜLLMANN He is the coming man, I tell you. A year from today he'll be Prime Minister. *Obendorfer and Frühbeck laugh* Shall we bet? He goes in and out of the Palais Nepomuk. This is the man who will govern Austria one day.

FRÜHBECK But for the time being nobody cares what he says in Parliament. The worker's paper disposed of him in a few ironic lines.

FÜLLMANN That's just it. That's the misfortune of it. The socialists are ironic and we — we liberals keep our mouths shut — as usual. It couldn't be more absurd. And it will catch up with us. It is already catching up with us. Because the others, they do talk. They proclaim Count Niederhof as the herald of their ideology, they're blowing the fanfare.

OBENDORFER Has anyone heard anything?

ABENDSTERN Who's blowing the fanfare? *Continues writing.*

FRÜHBECK What *are* you talking about, Füllmann?

FÜLLMANN Has none of you gentlemen read "The Elegant World," then?

FRÜHBECK The gossip sheet?

OBENDORFER One could say scandal sheet as well.

FÜLLMANN That was true once. Herr Satan is developing political ambitions.

OBENDORFER Ah, Satan! Is he still having an affair with the Negedy woman?

FÜLLMANN What do I know? You concern yourself with that sort of thing. Whether he is still having an affair with the Negedy woman, that's what interests you people. Oh my dear

Austria! But that Herr Satan is shortly going to publish a large clerical paper, of that you know nothing!

OBENDORFER Wouldn't be the end of the world either.

FÜLLMANN Oh, my dearest Herr Obendorfer, do try not to misunderstand me.

OBENDORFER *teasing* Far be it from you.

FÜLLMANN Yes, indeed, far be it from me to speak out for atheism or anarchy, but the latest issue of "The Elegant World" is preaching not order and faith, against which I would certainly not have the least objection, but reaction —

FLIEDERBUSCH Reaction?!

FÜLLMANN Darkest reaction in every sense of the word.

FLIEDERBUSCH *with increasing interest* You really think so, Herr Füllmann?

FÜLLMANN I do, young man. Have you read the article?

FLIEDERBUSCH Fleetingly.

FÜLLMANN Read it carefully. All of you, gentlemen, should read it. This article is in many ways symptomatic. What Count Niederhof has managed to utter in Parliament in an incidental, to some extent aphoristic way, most likely under the influence of a champagne breakfast, those very words are being defended by a gentleman who signs himself Fink and who for several weeks now has been working his nuisance in "The Elegant World" — Fink, remember the name, gentlemen. Did I say defended? they are being praised, — made over into a system! And it ends up in a hymn to everything we're fighting against and in scorn for all that is dear to us. Listen for yourselves. Only a few prominent passages. *He reads* "We too lament the victims of Strakonitz, all the more so because the truly guilty parties are not to be found among them but among the people who for years, for decades have been using their terroristic slogans to carry on their irresponsible but unfortunately also unpunished agitation — agitation and incitement directed not only against property owners, indeed, against the peaceful and satisfied population in general, but also against property as such, against property in the wider and higher sense! Because in this connection we wish to designate as property not only material values, but also ideal ones which, when all is said and done, it is the duty of each one of us to respect, to preserve, to defend: God and Country!"

OBENDORFER What is it you want, that's not all that silly?!

FÜLLMANN Silly? I wasn't saying that at all. Quite the contrary. It is very cunning, very denunciatory and very — But it gets better, gentlemen, just hold on — *searching* down here. *He reads* "Let us say it openly for once, that it has always been our country's old, hereditary landowning families in whose illustrious scions the idea of the state has found its purest and noblest expression, that it was neither the upstarts of finance and industry nor the so-called intellectuals, but always our much maligned landed gentry, who — in a higher sense than Mister Tailor or Glovemaker" — that's the middle class, gentlemen! — or "a certain international union of professors" — Do you notice anything, gentlemen? — "or even our democratic-liberal press would ever be able to grasp, who furthered the cause of progress, though certainly not of rebellion; of development, not of revolution; the cause of freedom, not of democracy, thank God!"

FLIEDERBUSCH *stands behind him, reads along, with growing excitement in his face* Outrageous!

FÜLLMANN Isn't it?

ABENDSTERN Sophistry without equal.

FLIEDERBUSCH Worse than that.

FÜLLMANN Falsehood!

FLIEDERBUSCH Knavery!

FÜLLMANN And now for the conclusion. Bear with me this much longer, gentlemen. "But we, loyal to the tried and true principles of our paper, side with Count Niederhof and here repeat the courageous words he spoke in Parliament three days ago: Sentimentality becomes the politician as little as it

becomes the soldier! And who has a greater right to coin such a
phrase than a man whose ancestors were ready at all times to
offer their blood and lives for God, Emperor and Fatherland."
*Leuchter enters through the door right, Kajetan right behind
him. Fliederbusch disappears at the same instant through the
door left.*

LEUCHTER, KAJETAN, OBENDORFER, FRÜHBECK,
FÜLLMANN, ABENDSTERN

LEUCHTER *between fifty and sixty, stocky, bald, with a long,
gray hanging mustache; he has an apparently good-natured,
almost patriarchal disposition, occasionally quite abrupt and
turning to almost brutal rudeness relative to Füllmann; genial
to the others* Hasn't he calmed down yet? We're supposed to
respond to that twaddle. What do you say to that, gentlemen?
OBENDORFER Simply ridiculous.
LEUCHTER *coarsely* We wouldn't think of it.
KAJETAN Hi, Abendstern.
ABENDSTERN Good evening. My pleasure, Herr Editor-in-
Chief.
LEUCHTER You've come from the theater, Abendstern?
Kajetan has just been telling me about his great success.
ABENDSTERN Success? That is a matter of opinion, Herr
Editor-in-Chief.
LEUCHTER *turning away from Abendstern again right away;
to Frühbeck* Nothing new from Strakonitz?
FRÜHBECK All quiet. They're working in a number of shafts.
LEUCHTER As I predicted. So, let's let the dead rest in peace.
FÜLLMANN This has long since stopped being a question of
Strakonitz, Herr Leuchter. It is a question of ideology!
ABENDSTERN *to Kajetan* What are you hiding behind the
Chief for? Won't help you a bit. Your play is a piece of
garbage, and nothing in the world will prevent me from
saying so.

KAJETAN *laughs.*

ABENDSTERN Don't laugh so stupidly, you won't be laughing tomorrow.

KAJETAN Laughing tomorrow. Won't be all that bad. Sorry, no more time. Expected at the Bristol. My pleasure, Herr Editor-in-Chief. *Exits.*

LEUCHTER *to Frühbeck* The eulogies are in Borgis?

FRÜHBECK Yes, Herr Editor-in-Chief. And take quite a bit of space.

LEUCHTER So print them Petit.

FRÜHBECK *nods, telephones to the print shop.*

LEUCHTER *to Füllmann* Moreover, we are not here to give publicity to "The Elegant World." We have never mentioned it by name, nor will ever mention it, and as long as we do not mention it, it does not exist. Write about the disorders in Albania. You're more at home there. With domestic politics — do you think Ebenstein fell from heaven a polished master? Ask Frühbeck how often I deleted entire pages. Well — de mortuis nihil nisi bene. And remember, Füllmann, *in a fatherly tone* in domestic politics, everything depends above all else on moderation. We are not here to sharpen conflicts, we are here to smooth them over. This strikes me as the noblest task of a truly democratic publication.

FÜLLMANN *has been wanting to cut him short for some time* Absolutely right, without a doubt. But even if we want to disregard the article in "The Elegant World," a speech like Count Niederhof's must not —

LEUCHTER Count Niederhof is a clown.

OBENDORFER A jockey.

LEUCHTER *who does not like to be corrected* A clown.

OBENDORFER *beaten* A clown.

FÜLLMANN Granted, Herr Editor-in Chief. But in spite of his being a clown, or perhaps just for that very reason, he is persona gratissima in certain circles. He goes hunting with the Archduke Nepomuk.

LEUCHTER *good-naturedly* So let him go hunting with Nepomuk. *To the others* What harm has Nepomuk done him this time? *Suddenly in a coarse tone* Case closed. *As if he were about to leave, to Abendstern* I want to see your review before it goes down to the print shop.

ABENDSTERN Herr Editor-in-Chief, I regret having to declare in advance —

LEUCHTER I know, you find Kajetan is no Shakespeare.

ABENDSTERN To be sure, I will not be able to avoid stating something of the sort. Because I hold it to be my sacred duty in my capacity as critic, unmoved by my personal friendship with an author, to follow my innermost conviction and write the purest truth —

LEUCHTER My dear Abendstern, I have never yet prevented one of my staff from expressing his convictions. *Turns to the others* Or have you gentlemen perhaps — *to Abendstern* But the truth is something very relative, and in any case it allows itself to be expressed in a variety of ways, sharply or mildly, and it still always remains the truth. One can find gold nuggets even in quartz, and to point out those gold nuggets does not contradict any sacred duty, as you were pleased to express yourself before. *Seems to be about to leave again; to Frühbeck* I want to see my article about Ebenstein.

FRÜHBECK *telephones* The commemorative piece. *To Leuchter* Right away.

LEUCHTER I'm quite curious what you'll think of it, gentlemen. No easy matter, I assure you, to write this sort of article. And this is not my first of the kind. Last year Breitner, three years ago Wagenstein — yes, yes. But what is one to do, gentlemen? A journalist is like a soldier. He has just enough time to shake his fallen comrade's hand, — and then back into the field of battle. *Pause* So, Füllmann, write me a nice Albanian article. But don't insult the Crescent too much. One never knows. *Signals Frühbeck to come closer* Have you spoken to Fliederbusch?

FRÜHBECK Yes, I have, Herr Editor-in-Chief.

LEUCHTER Well?

FRÜHBECK He seems to have expected it.

LEUCHTER How come?

FRÜHBECK Evidently it offended him that we deleted his remarks about the Justice Minister recently, and I'd have to be very much mistaken if he didn't already have something else lined up.

LEUCHTER So. We don't hold anyone here by force. We won't hold him either.

FRÜHBECK We certainly have no need to.

LEUCHTER But you should not have let the matter go this far, Frühbeck.

FRÜHBECK In no way did I —

LEUCHTER Pity. I had plans for him. I feel something in him. You know I have a sixth sense for that sort of thing. *Exits right with Frühbeck.*

OBENDORFER *has in the meantime exited to the rear.*

ABENDSTERN, FÜLLMANN. *Abendstern at the desk right, writing. Füllmann at the writing stand left, writing. Pause.*

FÜLLMANN *abruptly* I can't. I don't give a damn about Albania.

ABENDSTERN *tearing a piece of paper* This boy! I'm surprised he's not ashamed of himself. What do you want to bet, Füllmann, that he's creeping about at the "Daily Mail" right now and crawling. But that's the way to get ahead.

FÜLLMANN *who has not been listening* Shall I tell you something, Abendstern? *Close to him* Something is going on. This whole business doesn't sound right to me.

ABENDSTERN What do you mean?

FÜLLMANN We've been betrayed, Abendstern.

ABENDSTERN What are you talking about? You don't know Kajetan very well if you think that. He'll settle more cheaply.

FÜLLMANN Who's talking about Kajetan? I'm talking about the paper. He didn't always smooth over conflicts as he would like to do now, our Chief. We're turning. We're turning ever further to the right. That's why we mustn't write anything against Count Niederhof. Niederhof is the coming man, and we're becoming officious, to put it mildly.

HANAUSCHEK *enters* Can I have the review now, Herr Doctor?

ABENDSTERN Go to — You can damn well wait for it.

HANAUSCHEK *exits.*

Abendstern and Füllmann continue to write.

FÜLLMANN This Mortimer died on him with striking convenience.

ABENDSTERN *his writing disturbed, somewhat angry* How's that? What?

FÜLLMANN Ebenstein had his stroke very much a tempo.

ABENDSTERN *laughing* I say, Füllmann!

FÜLLMANN What are you laughing about? Ebenstein embarrassed him.

ABENDSTERN He could have fired him.

FÜLLMANN Fired? Leuchter never fires a member of his staff.

ABENDSTERN *laughing* He'd rather kill him?

FÜLLMANN And if he really did have a stroke, whose fault is it? *With a gesture to the right* His, only his. The treachery of his old friend struck Ebenstein down.

ABENDSTERN Have you heard? He's giving the widow three thousand a year pension.

FÜLLMANN He's buying off his conscience with that. His business! But I won't be a party to that. I have no intention of renouncing my past. I will not remain with any officious paper. I'll go somewhere else.

ABENDSTERN Easy to say. Don't you think I'd like to also? But where? Where?

FÜLLMANN I dare say something can be found for the bloody Abendstern.

ABENDSTERN Yes, if I were still the old bloody Abendstern. But I am nothing more than his shadow now.

FÜLLMANN Well —

ABENDSTERN Who can stay bloody in the long run at a paper where one loves everybody who's made his mark? Where one is on friendly terms with most of the people who are still on earth?

FÜLLMANN There's always the dead.

ABENDSTERN *furious* Too few. And besides, it doesn't give me the least pleasure to annihilate people who can no longer feel mortified.

FÜLLMANN Listen to me, Abendstern.

ABENDSTERN Leave me in peace now, Füllmann, I have to compose a hymn to Kajetan. Otherwise I can go begging tomorrow. Leave me alone. *He writes* "Since Shakespeare, Molière, Holberg" — do you know anyone else, Füllmann?

FÜLLMANN *next to him* The two of us should start a paper, Abendstern.

ABENDSTERN The two of us?

FÜLLMANN A paper in which we could write what we want. A paper against the living. — Against the living in politics and art. All evil comes from the living.

ABENDSTERN Who will give us the money for it?

FÜLLMANN We'll get it.

ABENDSTERN From where?

FÜLLMANN You have some money, don't you?

ABENDSTERN I have money?

FÜLLMANN You did inherit something two or three years ago.

ABENDSTERN Inherit? Enough so the interest barely pays for my mid-morning snack.

FÜLLMANN It wouldn't be so bad for you to kick that habit. But in all seriousness, Abendstern, we'll find some rich backers too as soon as the people see that we ourselves are prepared to risk our few pennies!

ABENDSTERN We? Do you have anything?

FÜLLMANN That's all the same. If we're in business —

ABENDSTERN And if I have to lay down my pen today or tomorrow?

FÜLLMANN What are you talking about, you with your forty-two or forty-three —

ABENDSTERN Forty-seven, Füllmann.

FÜLLMANN Your best years.

ABENDSTERN Not if one has had to drudge all his life as I have. Yes, my dear Füllmann, from my sixteenth year on I've had to write for my daily bread. If I had had it as good as other people, if I —

LEUCHTER *enters from the right with some handwritten pages in his hand. Abendstern, Füllmann, Leuchter. Then* FRÜHBECK, OBENDORFER, FLIEDERBUSCH. *Later* KAJETAN.

LEUCHTER Frühbeck! Where is Frühbeck?

ABENDSTERN *getting up, calls* Frühbeck!

FRÜHBECK *entering from the left* Herr Editor-in-Chief —

LEUCHTER *indicating the pages* Do you know this handwriting, Frühbeck?

FRÜHBECK Fliederbusch.

LEUCHTER *incredulously* How's that?

FRÜHBECK It is Fliederbusch's handwriting.

LEUCHTER Get Hanauschek up here. *Shaking his head* How does Fliederbusch come to —

FRÜHBECK *phoning down* Tell Hanauschek to come up.

OBENDORFER *enters from the rear.*

LEUCHTER *to Füllmann, genially* Well, how is Albania coming along?

FÜLLMANN I'm lacking the inspiration, unfortunately, Herr Editor-in-Chief.

LEUCHTER I am going to tell you something, Füllmann, I'd almost rather you write without inspiration. Inspiration can be a very dangerous thing in foreign politics.

HANAUSCHEK *enters* Herr Editor-in-Chief —

LEUCHTER What kind of scribblings have you stuck in with these galleys here, Hanauschek?

HANAUSCHEK Well, Flie — Herr Fliederbusch says to me I should bring it along up here. I reckoned you, Sir, know —

LEUCHTER *shaking his head* Go ahead and read it, Frühbeck. *Gives him the pages* Where is Fliederbusch?

HANAUSCHEK He was down in the print shop just now, but on the point of leaving.

LEUCHTER If he's still here send him up to me immediately, Hanauschek.

HANAUSCHEK *exits.*

LEUCHTER So what do you say, Frühbeck?

FRÜHBECK It's not clear to me yet.

LEUCHTER Let Füllmann read it.

FRÜHBECK *goes over to Füllmann; they read together.*

FLIEDERBUSCH *enters, in his overcoat* Herr Editor-in-Chief wanted —

LEUCHTER You had Hanauschek put in a manuscript for me —

FLIEDERBUSCH I took the liberty.

LEUCHTER What kind of mysterious business is this? Are you Houdini? Why didn't you hand it to me in person?

FLIEDERBUSCH I wanted to leave it to chance, so to speak —

LEUCHTER *harshly* Really? Is this stuff actually yours?

FLIEDERBUSCH Herr Editor-in-Chief, who else should —

LEUCHTER Since when do we pay you to write political articles?

FLIEDERBUSCH *in a somewhat more saucy tone* Actually, you are no longer paying me at all.

LEUCHTER *purposely ignores this* And who actually gave you the order?

FLIEDERBUSCH No one, Herr Editor-in-Chief. Nor would anyone have had the right to do so. It was an experiment. If it failed, please excuse my boldness.

FÜLLMANN *to Frühbeck* But that is my — please, that is exactly the same as I — *to Leuchter* I wish to point out, Herr Editor-in-Chief —

LEUCHTER *to Fliederbusch* When are you supposed to have written this stuff?

FLIEDERBUSCH Just now, Herr Editor-in-Chief.

LEUCHTER What do you mean, just now?

FLIEDERBUSCH In the past hour. *Pointing to the left* Next door here.

LEUCHTER But what gave you the idea? Tell me.

FLIEDERBUSCH *hesitant at first, but then increasingly sure of himself* A while ago, Herr Füllmann read to us several excerpts from the article in "The Elegant World" to which I refer. I had already read it in fact, as I take it to be my obligation to keep informed in every respect. But I must confess, it made scarcely any impression on me in my fleeting perusal. Not until Herr Füllmann read the most salient passages, in a tone of noblest and most righteous indignation —

FÜLLMANN *makes a warding-off gesture.*

FLIEDERBUSCH Only then did all the equivocation, all the meanness of the opinions gradually reveal itself to me from one word to the next. The session of Parliament during which Count Niederhof took the floor suddenly emerged again before me. I saw him standing before me in all his reactionary arrogance. You should have seen him, Gentlemen! My indignation knew no bounds. I believe I would have choked on it if I hadn't sat down right away and written some sort of reply. I ask you again, Herr Editor-in-Chief, if my boldness —

LEUCHTER Well, gentlemen, what have you to say to this?

FRÜHBECK Very spirited, to be sure. But not entirely unobjectionable in some regards.

LEUCHTER And what is your opinion, Obendorfer?

OBENDORFER I cannot declare myself to be in absolute agreement with the intent.

LEUCHTER You're altogether a reactionary, Obendorfer.

OBENDORFER *laughs* But not at all badly written. The only question is whether Herr Fliederbusch is inclined personally to stand behind what he —

FLIEDERBUSCH It goes without saying that I'm prepared to sign with my full name.

LEUCHTER *energetically* That is not customary with us. The paper will stand behind it.

FRÜHBECK I am the Managing Editor, however.

LEUCHTER We've published worse, in the early days.

FRÜHBECK *cautiously* In the early days —

FÜLLMANN *suddenly screeching* And it still doesn't touch on the crux of the matter.

FRÜHBECK *indicating the page* Here, for example —

FLIEDERBUSCH I will personally answer for every word.

LEUCHTER *to Frühbeck* Which passage do you mean? Read it aloud. It might be a good idea, so the effect —

FRÜHBECK *reads* "Whether or not it seemed necessary to fire a live salvo on a crowd including women and children that had perhaps been led astray but which, in any case, was extremely excited and no longer in control of its senses, will be for the announced inquiry to determine. Whether it was politically wise might be shown as early as the next elections.

And, since a temporary calm seems to have returned to the place where these events took place, we could refrain from any more general considerations were it not that the eulogy — more original than delicate — delivered in Parliament for the pitiable victims of Strakonitz demands a modest contradiction. It remained for Count Niederhof —"

LEUCHTER We know the speech. Down there — *Points to a place on the page.*

FRÜHBECK *reads* "But we ask, who may presume to pass judgment on the worth or lack of worth of a human life into whose ultimate mystery —"

FLIEDERBUSCH *takes the pages from Frühbeck's hand and reads himself*— "whose ultimate mystery he must necessarily be unable to know. And who will decide which side of the scale will spring upward when we lay the so questionable and often abused concept of the state's authority on one and let the tears of a mother who has had a son murdered trickle on the other."

FÜLLMANN *dishevels his hair.*

FLIEDERBUSCH *continues reading* "For our part, we have always taken the position that men who live by their manual labor, that even the poorest of the poor who are obliged to earn their scanty crust of bread in the darkness and danger of the coal mine, are to be considered just as useful members of human society as the greater part of Count Niederhof's upper-class companions who wander at their leisure on the sunny side of life. And at the risk of being laughed at by him over our sentimentality, we would like to consecrate an entirely unpolitical tear to the dead of Strakonitz, whom we view as victims not only of their own unruliness, but also, to some extent, of a social order that does not offer equal benefits to all individuals; above all to the twelve-year-old boy —"

FÜLLMANN Fourteen!

LEUCHTER Twelve-year-old is much better in this context. Leave twelve.

FLIEDERBUSCH *continuing* — "above all to the ten-year-old boy —"

FRÜHBECK *to himself* What a talent!

LEUCHTER *smirks with satisfaction.*

FLIEDERBUSCH *continuing* — "who may have been ordained — for who knows the ways of providence? — to render more important services to his fatherland than those to which the newly elected representative Count Niederhof seems called, much as we are inclined to do justice to his great accomplishments in the breeding of thoroughbreds in Austria and in the advancement of the fine arts, especially with regard to the ballet."

FÜLLMANN But these are personal invectives.

LEUCHTER *to Fliederbusch* Go on.

FLIEDERBUSCH *reads* "Although our deepest feelings are repulsed by a phenomenon such as Count Niederhof, whose heart beats no stronger at the bier of a sacrificed, guiltless child of the working class than it does when a race horse breaks down, — what may be able to reconcile us with him and his ilk is the consideration that he represents his side in this matter, foul as it is, and that he, like his fellow aristocrats, would be prepared at any time to confirm their theory of the unworth of an individual life by risking their own. Our more profound, not so much political as human aversion is directed not against the Niederhofs of this world, whatever their names, but against their voluntary fellow-travelers, against the deplorable retinue that clings to their tracks or sings hymns to them, in the manner of that sweet enthusiast, perhaps, who allowed his finch-like voice —"

FÜLLMANN *disparagingly* Really —

LEUCHTER Pretty good!

FLIEDERBUSCH *continues* — "to resound in a much-read sporting paper."

LEUCHTER   Why "much-read"? In a little-read sporting pamphlet.

FLIEDERBUSCH   *revises*   Little-read sporting pamphlet. *Continues to read*   "Our aversion, indeed, our disgust is directed at the snob, the foolish, undignified snob who is always to be found where he has no business and who acts as if he too belonged there; the snob, who is at all times prepared to deny both mother and father for a condescending smile from someone of higher birth, and whose just reward is to be mocked and despised by those very same people before whom he humbles himself."

LEUCHTER   Very good. With what he's saying here Fliederbusch has courageously put his finger on a cancer that is devouring the marrow of our middle class. Go on.

FLIEDERBUSCH   — "The snob, however, for all his nullity, is not a harmless creature by any means. Because it is not the man who is lined up against us face-to-face who is our worst enemy, the real enemy is the turncoat, and therefore —"

FRÜHBECK   *interrupts*   I must ask you to consider —

FÜLLMANN   That business about the hymn — that's what I said before!

FRÜHBECK   There may be subscribers, Herr Editor-in-Chief, who may be offended precisely by these last remarks.

LEUCHTER   A subscriber is never offended. You may rest quite easy on that score, gentlemen. We will run the article.

FÜLLMANN   In order to — to — smooth over the conflicts?

LEUCHTER   How's that? *Remembers*   Sometimes they have to be smoothed over, sometimes they have to be stressed. It all depends on the form they take. — The article is certainly no masterpiece, it clearly shows the beginner, even, but it takes a stand; and we need to take a stand, gentlemen, especially in such a politically turbulent time. Hence we're running the article — right after mine about Ebenstein, in fact.

FRÜHBECK   And how will we make room for it, Herr Editor-in-Chief?

LEUCHTER *picks up the dummy* Albania goes.

FÜLLMANN How's that, Herr Editor-in-Chief?

LEUCHTER Albania is not urgent. Our readers can wait for it.

FÜLLMANN In that case, Herr Editor-in-Chief, I must ask —

LEUCHTER *does not listen to him* Come, Fliederbusch, I want to have a few words with you before — *Exits right with Fliederbusch.*

FRÜHBECK *telephones down* Send Hanauschek up.
>   *Pause.*

OBENDORFER I think our esteemed Chief's mettle has played a trick on him this time.

FRÜHBECK Congratulations, Abendstern.

ABENDSTERN Why's that?

FRÜHBECK Your protege is moving up.

ABENDSTERN What do you mean, protege? We are going to make fools of ourselves with that article.

FÜLLMANN Now you talk! Why didn't you open your mouth before?

ABENDSTERN What do I care about the political section? Do I always have to bail you out?

KAJETAN *rushes in with his briefcase* Good evening, gentlemen.

FRÜHBECK Already over, the banquet?

KAJETAN Not yet. Carriage downstairs. *Gives him a piece of paper* Short insert. For the morning edition. My play just translated into English. *About to go in to the Editor-in-Chief.*

FRÜHBECK Hold it! Someone's in there.

FÜLLMANN Gentlemen, we cannot put up with this. Albania must appear.

KAJETAN Albania — why so?

FÜLLMANN *going up to Frühbeck* Frühbeck, I insist that Albania appear.

FRÜHBECK *shrugs his shoulders, points to the right, inviting Füllmann to go in himself.*

KAJETAN *turns questioningly to Obendorfer.*

FÜLLMANN *takes a few steps to the right and stops again* I am asking you for a vote of confidence, gentlemen. What I have just experienced could happen tomorrow to any one of you. I must know whether I can count on you, gentlemen. Will you declare your solidarity with me? *Pause, then pleading* Gentlemen — *silence* — *then pleading, to Abendstern* Abendstern, you —!

FRÜHBECK But of course he declares his solidarity with you, Füllmann. He's not quitting either.

KAJETAN *still not understanding* Solidarity — not quitting either —?

Curtain

SECOND ACT

The editorial office of "The Elegant World." It resembles a fairly elegant study. Dark red wallpaper. In the middle of the room a medium-sized desk. Upon it a telephone, framed photographs, a calendar, electric lamp, ink stand, newspapers, letters. Moved up against the desk, a divan with a Persian cover and numerous pillows. To the right, a door to the anteroom which extends to the rear in such a way that a person standing there cannot immediately look into the office. To the left a door covered by a portière. In the background a window. Along the wall left, a fireplace with a mirror above it. In the back a bookcase. To the right a kind of filing cabinet which does not fit the decor and which is pretty well concealed by a curtain. On the walls, photographs of actors, actresses, and so on, as well as sporting scenes in the English fashion. At right front, a small smoking table with smoking supplies; next to it a rocking chair.

The stage is empty. The door to the right opens. A liveried SERVANT *appears. Immediately thereafter* LEODEGAR SATAN. *Perhaps fifty, dressed with somewhat exaggerated but not entirely obvious elegance. Blond hair, parted in the center, a blond mustache, narrow mutton chops. Light gray summer suit, light yellow shoes, light tie, a white carnation in his buttonhole. Takes his coat off upon entering, the servant helping him. He hands the servant his hat, gloves, and walking stick.*

SATAN *while taking his coat off* Has my son been here already?
SERVANT Not yet, Herr Editor-in-Chief. *Pause.*
SATAN Has Herr Styx shown his face by any chance?
SERVANT Not so far, Herr Editor-in-Chief. *Pause.*
SATAN Very well.

SERVANT *exits.*

SATAN I have to do everything myself. *Sits at the desk, picks up the letters, then, somewhat disgusted, lets them fall again, lights a cigarette, opens a couple of the letters, skims through them, and throws them down again, bored; the third letter appears to surprise him. The door to the right opens again. The servant stands in the doorway, Styx in the anteroom. Forty-five years old, very slim and tall, black hair parted on the right, a small, black mustache; and a monocle continuously in his eye. His is a crumpled elegance; he wears fashionable striped slacks, black jacket, dark coat, worn patent leather shoes. His bearing is more natural and distinguished than Satan's. He is smoking a cigarette.*

SATAN, STYX

SATAN *picks up his galley-proof.*

STYX *still in the anteroom* Herr Wöbl here yet?

SERVANT No, Herr Styx.

STYX *somewhat flippantly* The young man, perhaps?

SERVANT Not yet, Herr Styx.

STYX *has also handed his overcoat, etc. to the servant, then dusts his shoes off with his handkerchief.*

SATAN *both amused and annoyed* Good morning.

STYX Oh, you're here already? Good morning. *Continues dusting his shoes, then shakes out his handkerchief, puts his cigarette out in the ashtray, takes another from the cigarette case on the small smoking table and lights it. The servant has exited.*

SATAN *as above* Don't let me disturb you.

STYX Certainly not. *Picks up a newspaper, sits down in the rocking chair, and reads. From behind the paper* I predicted that Feverish Dream couldn't possibly win the race.

SATAN It's not a question of Feverish Dream.

STYX *unperturbed* I advised you to bet on Mezzanine. If I'd still had five gulden to my name I'd have put them on Mezzanine.

SATAN It's not a question of your five gulden.

STYX To some extent it is. That is, I want to ask you for an advance.

SATAN You've drawn advances for a year and three quarters' worth of your salary.

STYX I sent an article to the print-shop yesterday that will cause a sensation.

SATAN *busy with the proofs* I'm just now reading it.

STYX Well?

SATAN It will not cause a sensation.

STYX Huh?!

SATAN That is, it will not appear. You do know that I no longer intend to publish such society and backstage gossip. Why do you keep bringing me this stuff all the time?

STYX You intend? Egon intends.

SATAN We intend.

STYX *rises, then goes slowly to the desk, finally stopping across from Satan* Yesterday you had a meeting with Radlmann. The consortium that wants to buy "The Elegant World" consists of the brothers Borgmann and the Banker Veit. But behind them stands none other than Prince Wendolin-Ratzeburg and his cousin, Count Niederhof.

SATAN *somewhat coarsely* My, but you are marvelously informed!

STYX That shouldn't surprise you any more. I know everything.

SATAN Everything? No. That Count Niederhof is calling here in person at eleven thirty, that, for example, you did not know.

STYX Count Niederhof — in person? A great honor!

SATAN As far as I know you were friends once —?

STYX   Friends?! He was my comrade — like a few dozen others. One of those who had more luck than I did. Ah — *lightly* let's not talk about him. The important thing is that you really seem to have the intention of turning a hitherto amusing, even original paper into one that will be exactly as boring as the hundred others in which politics are taken seriously.

SATAN   Boring? That's a matter of opinion. It is just since our paper has taken a more distinct political tinge that it has been going up again, while during the past two, three years, as you very well know — *shrugs his shoulders.*

STYX   Because you lost your courage. Because you thought it right to cross out the spiciest parts of my articles. If we had used our — my material properly —

SATAN   We took enough risks in the early days. Fortunately, that is no longer necessary.

STYX   You think —?!

SATAN   By the way, what did you think of our little Fink's article?

STYX   *shrugs contemptuously.*

SATAN   It was brilliant. Egon too — *breaking off* You have something against Fink!

STYX   How could I? I hardly know him — for the time being. None of us knows him. A new kid on the block. One fine day, in comes a puppy like that, brings you a mood piece about the horse races —

SATAN   A very fine one.

STYX   The next time some society small-talk —

SATAN   Very witty.

STYX   But without a clue. And now his political chatter. —

SATAN   Our audience likes it.

STYX   That does not — *a gesture to indicate "mean much"* By the way, did you read how he's taken to task today, your little Herr Fink, together with the noble Count?

SATAN   Taken to task?

STYX Dispatched!

SATAN   In what way? Where? You know I only read newspapers in the most dire emergencies.

STYX *brings him the paper* Here, my dear Leodegar.

SATAN *skims through the paper.*

STYX *takes another cigarette* What kind of brand is this you bought? A sign of the new politics?

SATAN *reading* This does attack rather sharply. Who do you think — maybe old Leuchter himself?

STYX Not his style.

SATAN Well, have no fear, our little Fink will come up with the right answer, I'm not worried on that score.

STYX And Herr Fink will not be the only one who might feel attacked. Your son too —

SATAN What do you mean?

STYX Well, aside from the more general observations about snobbism, which I don't find all that bad, at least with regard to his friendly relationship with Herr Fink. Yesterday they rode to the racetrack together. Fiacre number 714.

SATAN I went by train!

STYX Oh, yes, the sons have it better. Egon even used the opportunity to introduce his friend to Princess Wendolin, who had graciously deigned to address him in her usual condescending manner.

SATAN Why shouldn't he? And — as to the Princess, I have something to tell you.

STYX Oh, of course, you were summoned to an audience on Sunday. Well?

SATAN The Princess is sending us a number of pictures one of these days which are to appear in "The Elegant World" in connection with her impending gala. Interiors, photographs from the park, portraits of ancestors, and so on. I wanted to ask you to write the accompanying text. But if I might make one request — *hesitates.*

STYX I know, I know, without enumerating her past lovers. I will simply say, our paper's limited space unfortunately does not permit —
Egon Satan enters; a handsome, young man of twenty-one, dressed with intentional but altogether impeccable elegance. His tone is sometimes childishly haughty.

EGON, SATAN, STYX

EGON Good morning, Papa. *Shakes hands with his father and greets Styx with only a slight nod.*
STYX Good morning.
EGON Herr Fink hasn't been here yet?
SATAN Not yet. Why do you ask?
EGON Have you read the "Times," Papa?
SATAN Indeed.
EGON Well, what do you say?
SATAN *unsure, with a glance at Styx* As a journalist one must always be prepared for such attacks.
EGON *after a short pause* I looked for Herr Fink in the coffee-house but unfortunately — Maybe you have his home address, Papa?
SATAN No, I don't. Up to now it's never — Do you happen to know, Styx?
STYX No. *To Egon* But before I introduce my friends to a most serene Princess I really would first inquire where they live and, above all, whether they really are who they claim to be.
EGON I'm not sure I understand, Herr Styx.
STYX There are three parties named Fink listed in the directory. Matthias Fink, gentleman's tailor, Margaretengürtel 15, has a married daughter but no son. Privy Councilor Fink, Wollzeile 17, a childless bachelor. Then Walpurga Fink, homemaker, captain's widow, has two sons, one seven, the

other five. There are no other Finks registered with the Vienna police. *Pause.*

SATAN *somewhat puzzled* You went to all that trouble, Styx?

STYX A hobby. One could almost say craft.

EGON *to his father, without looking at Styx* A craft which Herr Styx may perhaps, in the future, practice with greater success somewhere other than in the editorial office of "The Elegant World."

SATAN Egon!

EGON Where henceforth we might not require informers or spies.

STYX *coolly* Silly boy!

EGON Sir —

STYX Don't trouble yourself, young man. It's been a long time since I've been able to give satisfaction in a duel. Just as long, approximately, as I've been part of the staff of "The Elegant World." A fortuitous coincidence — But otherwise I am still in possession of all sorts of useful qualities from former days. *Looks at Egon.*

EGON *shrugs and turns away.*

STYX So long, Leodegar. I'm going down to the print-shop. *Exits.*

SATAN, EGON

A short pause.

SATAN *embarrassed, attempts to sound severe* Dear Egon, you're allowing yourself —

EGON *energetically* No, Papa. You mustn't tolerate this person in your company any longer.

SATAN You are being unjust to him. Fine, he was down on his luck once. Under different circumstances —

EGON One simply does not gamble beyond one's means when one is an officer, although I could sooner forgive him that of all things —

SATAN I have the right to demand of you, my dear Egon — you're young, you lack the insight —

EGON But Papa, you'd prefer that we get rid of him too, if we could. You're only afraid, not entirely without reason, unfortunately, that certain dark details in the past of "The Elegant World" would then —

SATAN What do you mean dark details?

EGON Oh, God, Papa —

SATAN My son, you're taking a little too much pride in having once had the opportunity, sword in hand, to defend our paper's honor —

EGON I'm not proud of that, Papa. But that I did it so to speak against my own conviction —

SATAN Nobody asked you to do it. Certainly not I.

EGON Nevertheless, you can hardly say, Papa, that my interceding did our paper any harm.

SATAN That — that — I will freely admit to you. Yes, my son. *In a milder tone, going up to him and placing his hand on his shoulder* It will probably interest you to learn that our negotiations are proceeding the way we wanted.

EGON I'm glad to hear that. But aren't you being a bit too optimistic again?

SATAN I don't believe so. I have an important conference ahead of me this very morning.

EGON With Veit?

SATAN No. With Count Niederhof. *Looks at his watch* He'll be here in ten minutes.

EGON *involuntarily* Here?

SATAN *slightly hurt* Listen, this place should do just fine for Count Niederhof. He's hung around in some of worse repute.

EGON Nevertheless — I suppose you have Herr Fink to thank for the Count's visit —

SATAN You know that informal conversations with people who are very close to the Count have already —

EGON Fink's last brilliant article tipped the scale, without a doubt.

SATAN Could be. But what do you say to Styx's information concerning —

EGON It doesn't particularly surprise me. I haven't believed for a long time that we're dealing with any Herr Fink. In my opinion, we're dealing with —

SATAN Well?

EGON An undercover agent —

SATAN What?

EGON The people who want to buy the paper have placed him on our staff to examine the conditions at their source.

SATAN And what makes you come to that conclusion?

EGON Did you observe him yesterday, perhaps, while the Princess was speaking to him? And she herself, the way she looked at him — her entire demeanor? I have no doubt she's known him for a long time.

SATAN An undercover agent, hmm. And if it were as you say, how do you explain — *hesitating* Earlier I received a letter here by pneumatic post, which I purposely didn't mention to Styx, in which your undercover agent urgently requests me to have his honorarium ready for him this morning.

EGON Why shouldn't an undercover agent experience financial difficulties?

SATAN Herr Fink's demand amounts to thirty-seven crowns and forty heller. For an undercover agent —

EGON If someone's playing a role he has an obligation to see it through. Precisely this ploy — By the way, I want to check the Cafe Dobner again. *Looks at his watch* In case Herr Fink should turn up in the meantime, I assume you'll be kind enough to keep him here, Papa. *Prepares to leave.*

SATAN That I will. And use the opportunity to sound him out a little better.

EGON *at the door* I advise you to be careful, Papa!

SERVANT *brings a card.*

SATAN It's him.

EGON Count Niederhof?

SATAN Yes. Show him in.

COUNT NIEDERHOF *enters. Short bow.*

SATAN This is a particular honor, Count. Permit me to introduce you to my son, Egon —

COUNT My pleasure.

EGON *bows. He is standing at the door ready to depart* Count —

COUNT I hope I am not the reason for your —

EGON Not at all, Count, I had just said good-bye.

Repeated bow; exits.

COUNT, SATAN

The Count is approximately forty, but younger looking, although he appears somewhat worn out; blond, elegant, of an occasionally haughty amiability.

COUNT So grown-up a son already, Herr Satan? One couldn't tell by looking at you!

SATAN Twenty-two years old, Count. Lieutenant in the reserve, — with the Thirty-Fourth Dragoons.

COUNT *nods, as if approving, then asks incidentally* Have we met before, Herr Satan?

SATAN I had the honor on the occasion of a reception at the American Embassy four years ago —

COUNT Of course, I remember very well. Well, I'm pleased to be able to renew our acquaintance under such very promising circumstances.

SATAN *invites him to take a seat* My view entirely, Count.

COUNT *sitting down* Is it you, perhaps, whom I must thank for the excellent article which appeared in your paper in connection with my much misunderstood speech in Parliament?

SATAN Unfortunately I am not in a position to lay sole claim to so flattering an acknowledgment. The article comes from the pen of one of our younger collaborators by the name of Fink.

COUNT Fink, yes. I thought that was a pen name. It seems to me I've seen it a number of times already.

SATAN We've used the young man for a number of months now. It's only seldom that I find time to take up the pen myself, unfortunately. Most of the time I have to content myself with making suggestions, providing a sense of direction —

COUNT You're the spiritual leader, yes, that's what I thought. Still, to get to the point. As you know, Herr Radlmann has given me to understand his inclination in principle to sell "The Elegant World," and he has attached to the sale, among others, the condition, which is very welcome to us, of course, that you as incumbent Editor —

SATAN For the past twenty years.

COUNT — should continue your association with the paper —

SATAN *somewhat quickly* My contract, which has three years to run, gives me the right, indeed, obligates me —

COUNT Of course, that is what I just wanted —

SERVANT *enters.*

SATAN *nervously* What's the matter? You can see — Please excuse me, Count. *Stands up, goes up to the servant who has remained standing near the door.*

SERVANT Herr Fink wants to know whether Herr Satan has left something for him?

SATAN *recalling* Oh, yes. He should be so kind — a little later — I'm busy now.

COUNT Did I hear correctly? Fink? Himself?

SATAN The young man can wait. *Waves the servant off, comes back* Count —

COUNT But why? Do have him come in, Herr Satan, unless it's awkward for you. I will be very interested to meet him in person.

SATAN With the Count's permission — *Waves to the servant.*

SERVANT *exits.*

COUNT *looking around the room, casually* You've established yourself very comfortably here.

FLIEDERBUSCH *enters, somewhat more elegant than in the first act, almost foppish, but not excessively by any means. He is wearing a monocle* Beg pardon, I had no idea —

SATAN Permit me, Count, to introduce our youngest collaborator, Herr Fink —

COUNT I am very pleased to make your acquaintance, Herr Fink. *Shakes hands with him, holds his glance* But where have I — you seem so familiar to me.

FLIEDERBUSCH Maybe from yesterday. The Count strolled past me at the race track. I had just had the honor of engaging in conversation with her Highness the Princess Wendolin.

COUNT Right. You were standing with my cousin under the judge's box. I had pictured you as being older, actually, from your literary accomplishments. I was just taking the opportunity of remarking to your Chief about your article — isn't that so, Herr Satan? — excellent, really excellent!

FLIEDERBUSCH I'm happy, Sir, if my modest attempt has met with your approval.

COUNT You may soon have more ample opportunity for such "attempts." Since "The Elegant World" — Herr Satan won't object if we continue our conversation in your presence —

SATAN *invites Fliederbusch to sit; all three are sitting.*

COUNT *continuing* — Since "The Elegant World" will before long — if we come to terms in everything else — appear as a daily —

SATAN Herr Radlmann has already given me to understand that such a plan —

COUNT *with growing conviction* A weekly would be of no use to us. And solely in order to get over certain growing pains typical of newly established newspapers as quickly as possible, it was decided in the inner circle of our party to contact an existing concern. I took the liberty of directing my friends' attention particularly to your paper, the ideology of which, if I may say so, our new paper intends to advocate with total commitment.

SATAN May I mention, perhaps, in this connection, that "The Elegant World" is popular not only in court, aristocratic, and high finance circles, but also, as can be gathered from our list of subscribers, among members of the high and highest clergy. *Gives the Count a notebook that had been on the desk.*

COUNT *turning the pages fleetingly, nods* This is very nice. Now the point will be not only to hold on to this circle of readers but also to broaden it appropriately. After all, gentlemen, we cannot hide from ourselves the fact that for the time being our political opponents have a better funded as well as a better organized press at their disposal, and it really seems high time that the journalistic industry displayed by the other side be offered effective resistance in equal measure by means of an appropriate effort on our part. And even if the areas in which your paper has been the leader up to now — sports, fashion, high society — are by no means to be neglected or even eliminated in the future, still we hold it to be most desirable that the reformation of "The Elegant World," its politicizing, if I may call it that, should attain the clearest possible expression, beginning with a new name.

SATAN I was so well prepared for this possibility, Count, that I've already thought about such a change and taken the liberty of writing down a few names for you to choose from, if you please. *Goes to the desk again, brings the Count a sheet of paper.*

COUNT *reads* Niniche — Miss Harriet —

SATAN Pardon — those are tips for tomorrow's races. *To the desk again, searches among the papers.*

COUNT *objectively* Miss Harriet for the great steeplechase?

SATAN Herr Count doesn't think so? After the race last Sunday —

COUNT That means nothing. That was a sham.

SATAN And may one ask —

COUNT I believe only in Feverish Dream.

SATAN Feverish Dream?

COUNT Butters is riding him. I'm not infallible, of course, as I've often had occasion to discover to my chagrin, but — *in a more serious tone* but I believe we've drifted a bit from our subject. You were going to offer us a choice of names.

SATAN Yes, here. *Stands at the desk with a small piece of paper in his hand* What would the Count think of "Pious Souls"? Or even more to the point, "The Christians," or quite simply, "The Catholic World"?

COUNT *smiling unintentionally* I don't underestimate your profound understanding of our endeavors, but I'm afraid that the names you've suggested lack sufficient drawing power — in the journalism-business sense, I mean. Add to this the public's tendency, however unfair, to connect with your suggested designations concepts which, however estimable they may appear to an ethicist, are not as relevant to political struggle; concepts such as leniency, humility, and the like. I want to make no secret of it that we intend in the new paper to emphasize just those articles of a certain sharper, so to speak militant tone, articles, say, of the sort that may be especially in the line of *courteous gesture towards Fliederbusch* your young colleague.

FLIEDERBUSCH *glowing* Consider me fully at your disposal, Count.

COUNT Thank you, Herr Fink. A wide field will lie open to your talents. Our opponents, as I've already said, have up to now been more energetic and more successful than we. If we view the matter historically, their phrases, as hollow as they are seductive, have been resounding through the world since the days of the French Revolution. Liberty, equality, fraternity — Where is the Neanderthal who doesn't believe he understands these words, the poor wretch to whom they do not seem to signify deliverance from his misery, — where is the tribune of his people who is not able to captivate his audience with them? As it does so often, shallowness achieves the more far-reaching success here. And to these indestructible phrases, if I may call them that, are joined the catch-words of the moment, political and philosophical, which complement one another and to which I — *to Fliederbusch* need not begin to direct your attention in detail.

FLIEDERBUSCH I am absolutely burning for the next opportunity to elaborate in more extensive and bolder modulations the principal themes I was able to touch upon in the article you were so kind to notice.

COUNT I'll just mention at random a few of the words that the opposing party loves to display on its banner: free public education, civil marriage —

SATAN *laughs scornfully.*

COUNT Individualism, individual rights and so on. I'm sure you have a sense of the abundance of themes, Herr Fink, which offer themselves to an argumentative spirit who is truly determined to take a stand on the side of those tendencies which we may designate, in a word, as supportive of the state, in contrast to the other, destructive ones.

FLIEDERBUSCH I hardly know how to thank you for all these valuable suggestions, my Lord.

COUNT I hope for an early opportunity to learn they've fallen on fertile soil.

FLIEDERBUSCH Our next issue will — *with emphasis* God willing — prove it to you.

COUNT —?

FLIEDERBUSCH It has probably escaped your notice, Count, that I — please forgive my boldness — that both of us, you, Count, and I, have been quite rudely attacked because of my last article.

COUNT Is that so? But where?

FLIEDERBUSCH In the "Times."

COUNT Oh? I'm not in the habit of reading it.

SATAN Hardly worth the effort this time either.

FLIEDERBUSCH Now that — *gesture to complete the thought: "may be open to argument"* — In any event, it's my intention to write a sharp response, and this response will at the same time embody a program — the program of your, of our new paper, as well, if I may say so, as the battle cry of our party.

COUNT But that is splendid. This can really —

STYX *enters* I beg your pardon.

COUNT Oh! *Recognizes him, stands up, goes over to him.*

STYX *calmly* You're mistaken, Count, it's not me. My name is Styx.

SATAN A distinguished staff member of many years' standing in "The Elegant World."

COUNT *with a barely perceptible smile* Glad to meet you, Herr Styx.

STYX Herr Radlmann has just driven up and is waiting for you gentlemen in the print-shop.

SATAN Shall we have him —

COUNT *with a warding-off gesture* In the print-shop? That's most convenient. I'd be interested in getting to know these areas too. Perhaps we could go down right away, if you have no objection, Herr Satan. We can then discuss any further —

SATAN As you please, Count.

COUNT So, my dear Herr Fink, we'll talk again soon — and at length. I'm very eager to see *with emphasis* your reply, your program — how did you put it? — your battle cry, and I hope to get to see it before it is printed. That way we could still consult on some of the details, perhaps.

FLIEDERBUSCH Count —

SATAN *in a sweet-sour tone* Good-bye, dear Fink.

The Count exits first, then Satan; Styx follows them, turns around at the door, looks at Fliederbusch with a strange, half skeptical, half cunning glance, then exits too.

FLIEDERBUSCH *alone* A fascinating individual! Isn't this a twist of fate? When I think that I set foot in this building an hour ago only to pick up my money — which by the way I still do not have — never to return! A twist of fate! Now I know where I belong. Here is my place, — with the elegant — with *hesitating* the Catholic world. Now it's been conclusively decided. And now let's immediately draw up the program, the battle cry. Ah, here is — *He picks up the "Times" which Satan had left lying on the desk, reads to himself, shakes his head* This is too silly! *Reads aloud* "Where he has no business . . . acts as if he too belonged there —" Who acted? What impudence! — "Prepared to deny both mother and father . . . just reward is to be mocked and despised —" Who is being mocked? Just wait! You'll be sent about your business in fitting fashion! Flieder — how's that? Why, I don't even know the fellow's name. Doesn't concern me either. An anonymous — a cowardly anonymous — *He reflects, then begins to write zealously.*

STYX *enters* Forgive me if I'm disturbing you, Herr Fink.

FLIEDERBUSCH *makes a polite gesture of denial.*

STYX A response to today's attack in the "Times," I imagine?

FLIEDERBUSCH A few lines. It won't take a minute.

STYX "Snob" — "Foolish, undignified snob!" Strong words!

FLIEDERBUSCH *somewhat irritated* I — am replying just now. *Continues writing.*

STYX You desired the payment of your outstanding honorarium — thirty-seven crowns fifty. Herr Satan takes the liberty herewith — may I kindly ask for your receipt? *Lays a piece of paper before him.*

FLIEDERBUSCH *signs.*

STYX *puts the paper in his pocket* Thanks. And you want — how much?

FLIEDERBUSCH *with a sour smile* I think, you yourself — thirty-seven crowns fifty heller.

STYX *counting ceremoniously* Ten, twelve, fourteen — You would, by the way, be doing me a favor if you would place perhaps half at my disposal by way of a loan.

FLIEDERBUSCH This is really not easy for me.

STYX Until tomorrow after the races, on my word of honor. I would also like to give you a tip.

EGON *rushes in, sees Fink but not Styx* Finally — *as soon as he sees Styx he stops.*

STYX *laughs; puts the rest of the money in his pocket as well* I may just as well place the bet for you, that's even easier. But now I have to leave, unfortunately. Investigations, my dear Herr Fink, always investigations. Sometimes really just as a hobby. *He exits.*

EGON, FLIEDERBUSCH

EGON I've been looking for you the past three hours, Herr Fink. Have you read the article in the "Times"?

FLIEDERBUSCH Sure. I am just now responding to it in the manner it deserves.

EGON What do you mean? Responding? Surely you're joking, Herr Fink.

FLIEDERBUSCH What do you mean?

EGON Need I tell you, Herr Fink, that it is scarcely fitting to respond to invectives of this kind?!

FLIEDERBUSCH You find —?

EGON I dare say there is only one appropriate response in a case such as this.

FLIEDERBUSCH —?

EGON Pistols for the fellow!

FLIEDERBUSCH What?

EGON A snob — forgive me for repeating it — they called you a foolish, undignified snob.

FLIEDERBUSCH *somewhat confused* Me?

EGON Something like that cannot be washed away with ink.

FLIEDERBUSCH Why not? It is only a matter of ink. You'll see, dear Egon, don't worry.

EGON I will not see, Herr Fink, because you will not write. You belong to the editorial staff of "The Elegant World," you will fight a duel.

FLIEDERBUSCH With an anonymous writer? That may involve some difficulties.

EGON We will, within the hour, have learned the name of the person who insulted you.

FLIEDERBUSCH How might that —

EGON You have friends, fortunately. Since we didn't find you in the coffee-house and we don't know your home address —

FLIEDERBUSCH *hastily* I'm in the process of moving, I'm living at a guesthouse in the meantime.

EGON Please, it's not my intention to pry into secrets whose deeper significance I may be able to sense. In any event, a delay in the matter, particularly at the stage "The Elegant World" finds itself in currently, does not appear opportune to us, hence we took the liberty of setting things in motion on our own.

FLIEDERBUSCH We?

EGON Our colleague Wöbl has already gone to the offices of the "Times" in order to bring the offending party's name to light.

FLIEDERBUSCH They won't identify him.

EGON Let's wait and see.

FLIEDERBUSCH They'll suggest a lawsuit. Really, think of it, a liberal, a democratic paper! That rabble doesn't fight duels.

EGON Then you'll just have to slap the fellow's face.

FLIEDERBUSCH The anonymous one?

EGON Or the managing editor, — whoever. In any event —

WÖBL *enters. Tall, strong, athletic, with a turned up black mustache, speaks in a broad, forced, correct language but falls easily back to dialect.* EGON, FLIEDERBUSCH

WÖBL Hi, Egon. My respects, Herr von Fink. It can begin, gentlemen. We've got him already, without a doubt. Fliederbusch is the scoundrel's name.

EGON Well, now, that went fast.

WÖBL Got a cigarette, Egon? Ah, here. *Takes a cigarette from the case, lights it.*

FLIEDERBUSCH They gave you the name just like that, Herr Wöbl?

WÖBL I wouldn't say just like that. But there was a gentleman present, fortunately, an old fraternity brother of mine; no sir, it wasn't sung to him in his cradle either that he'd wind up at such a Jewpaper, my friend Obendorfer.

FLIEDERBUSCH *to himself* Obendorfer.

WÖBL Anyhow, he reminded the gentlemen who first babbled something about editorial confidentiality that the author explicitly stated he would bear any consequences. Well, and then they simply changed their minds and declared to me that the author is named Fliederbusch and that he can be found in the office between one-thirty and two without fail.

FLIEDERBUSCH Without fail. So —

WÖBL At one-thirty.

EGON *looks at his watch* At one-thirty. *They both look at Fliederbusch, expectantly.*

FLIEDERBUSCH A nice lot, I must say.

EGON How's that?

FLIEDERBUSCH To betray a colleague, just like that? I find —

EGON Since the author himself expressly stated he would bear the consequences there can really be no talk of betrayal!

FLIEDERBUSCH Nevertheless —

WÖBL And it's all right with us in any case.

EGON It's a quarter to one, we await your instructions, Herr Fink.

FLIEDERBUSCH I thank you, gentlemen.

EGON Do you authorize us to deliver your challenge to Herr Fliederbusch?

FLIEDERBUSCH Yes, indeed. I authorize you, gentlemen.

WÖBL Know how to fence good, Herr von Fink?

EGON Sabers are totally out of the question in our case. I dare say you share my view, Herr Fink?

FLIEDERBUSCH Totally. Sabers are out of the question.

EGON Right you are! These journalistic duels have been accounted farces long enough. This finally has to end, at least when one dares to insult a staff member of "The Elegant World." And you have been insulted, Herr Fink! And all of us with you. — Only pistols can be considered.

FLIEDERBUSCH Absolutely, pistols.

WÖBL Without a doubt.

EGON Three shots each.

FLIEDERBUSCH At least.

EGON Distance thirty paces with advance to twenty.

FLIEDERBUSCH With advance to twenty.

WÖBL The other seconds will certainly have something to say too.

EGON Not much, we'll see to that all right. You give us complete authority, Herr Fink?

FLIEDERBUSCH Complete authority. Complete unrestricted authority.

EGON Will you wait for us here, Herr Fink?

FLIEDERBUSCH I will wait for you!

EGON We could be back again in an hour.

FLIEDERBUSCH I will not budge from this spot. I will not move so much as an eyelash.

EGON Good-bye, Herr Fink!

WÖBL We'll work it out, Herr von Fink.

FLIEDERBUSCH *shakes hands with both of them* Good-bye, gentlemen. *Egon and Wöbl exit.*

FLIEDERBUSCH *remains alone, as if transfixed at first. Laughs suddenly, then turns serious again. Goes to the window, waves down to the departing men, comes back into the room, smiles, grows more serious, reflects, goes to the door, stops, shakes his head* No, that would make — *gesture to complete the thought: "no sense at all"* In that case, I'd have to reveal my identity. And for that — *now it occurs to him* I would first have to know myself who I am. *Shakes his head, reflects* Perhaps I shouldn't have gotten so rough with myself right away. At any rate, for this sort of consequences I was not — *He laughs, then serious again* But now it's happened, and I must decide. Must I? Must I really? If not today, tomorrow — or the day after. And how will they — *thinks again* It was a joke. Yes. — But who made the joke? Fink or Fliederbusch? That is the question! A Fliederbusch who occasionally gets the itch to play a Fink —? Or a born Fink who came into the world as a Fliederbusch solely through an error of fate? Hmm. — And if it were not a joke —? Because it isn't one. But see if one can make these people — *gesture: "understand"* Not too hastily, that's the most important thing. And in any case, first I have to excuse my absence from the office of the "Times" somehow. *Goes quickly to the telephone; at this moment, before he places his call, the door to the right opens.*

PRINCESS PRISKA *appears, perhaps thirty-seven, attractive, not exaggerated in any way, either in her behavior or her dress. Behind her* FRANZ, *her man-in-waiting, with a package, and the* SERVANT.

PRINCESS *still in the doorway, to the office servant* They did tell me down at the entrance that Herr Satan —
FLIEDERBUSCH *goes up to her, bows deeply.*
PRINCESS *comes further into the room* Oh — *Does not recognize him at first.*
FLIEDERBUSCH *introducing himself* Fink! I had the good fortune yesterday, Your Highness —
PRINCESS Of course, at the races, now I remember. Isn't Herr Satan here?
FLIEDERBUSCH As far as I know he's down in the print-shop. I'll call at once —
SERVANT Herr Satan has just now driven away with the Count.
PRINCESS Well, that's a pity. Let me have the package, Franz. You see, these are the pictures that Herr Satan asked me for recently. Perhaps he has mentioned them to you already, Herr von Fink?
FLIEDERBUSCH Certainly, Your Highness. *He receives the package from her.*
PRINCESS It occurred to me down in the carriage that as long as I'm here I could go over the details with him in person.
FLIEDERBUSCH If Your Highness would like me to — I will convey all Your Highness's wishes down to the last dot.

PRINCESS Yes, that would do too. You can wait outside in the meantime, Franz.

Franz and the Servant exit.

PRINCESS, FLIEDERBUSCH

FLIEDERBUSCH *has placed the package on the desk* If Your Highness would perhaps — *offers her the armchair; he remains standing at the desk and opens the package.*

PRINCESS Yes, go ahead and open it, Herr von Fink. Tell me, with what Count did Herr Satan drive away? With Count Niederhof, most likely?

FLIEDERBUSCH Yes. Surely Your Highness is informed? There are significant changes in store for our paper.

PRINCESS Yes, I know. My cousin wants to go among the journalists now. Well, why not? Anyway, it's the only thing he hasn't tried yet.

FLIEDERBUSCH *still occupied with the package* I had the honor just now of being introduced to the Count. It will remain an unforgettable moment for me. A fascinating — *at first he wants to say "person"* Count — and a terrific, charming temperament. Our newspaper faces a great future under his aegis.

PRINCESS You think so?

FLIEDERBUSCH I am firmly convinced of it. And since His Highness Prince Wendolin also — it is no longer a secret as you know — is not completely removed from the transformation of "The Elegant World." —

PRINCESS That's right, he's supposed to provide money for that. *Interrupting herself* So, here are the pictures, Herr von Fink, which I promised Herr Satan. We're old friends, you know, Herr Satan and I. I like your journal, it's a very amusing paper. Especially the theater gossip, I always study it with great pleasure. A bit ambiguous occasionally, but — Do you write those by any chance?

FLIEDERBUSCH No, Your Highness, I write for the political section.

PRINCESS So — Politics? Well, yes, we need that too, I guess. *Picks up the pictures again* This is the front view of the palace. It can't be seen from the road. It stands far inside the park.

FLIEDERBUSCH A charming façade!

PRINCESS Built in 1760 by a student of Fischer von Erlach's, Matthias Bronner.

FLIEDERBUSCH *examining the picture expertly* Comes very close to the master.

PRINCESS He'd have turned out greater than Fischer von Erlach. But he died at thirty.

FLIEDERBUSCH *regretfully* Oh —

PRINCESS You needn't extend your sympathies. He'd be dead by now in any case. *Turns to another picture* Our performance will take place here, in the roundel.

FLIEDERBUSCH Outdoors?

PRINCESS Of course. *Pointing* The tableaux will be set up here, and here — these are yew hedges, you know — the audience will sit here. There was another theatrical performance almost a hundred years ago on this very spot. My great-grandmother Elizabeth Charlotte took part in that one. Dead too, already, like Bronner. But she lived to ninety.

FLIEDERBUSCH It is a truly noble decision on Your Highness's part to open the park to the people.

PRINCESS For a twenty gulden admission fee. Whether the people will get much out of it — Besides, if it were up to me I would have had the park open, completely open to the public a long time ago. After all, I live mostly at Strebowitz, when I'm not traveling, and the climate in Vienna is poison for the Prince.

FLIEDERBUSCH His Highness is infirm?

PRINCESS Resigned. For the past ten years now. But he's doing quite well. *With a new picture* Here I have the pleasure of introducing you to Elizabeth Charlotte, née Baroness von Eberswald. The one who took part a hundred years ago. Actually, she played a large role at the Congress of Vienna. The King of Denmark courted her. It's all right to talk about it now that it's been in the books for ages. She wasn't the only one. Nor he either. Kings and great-grandmothers are like that. *Laughs softly.*

FLIEDERBUSCH *laughs also.*

PRINCESS She doesn't look at all like a great-grandmother in the picture, don't you think? Fuggersburg painted her.

FLIEDERBUSCH *knowingly* Ah, Fuggersburg —

PRINCESS It's generally thought that I bear a striking resemblance to my great-grandmother. Do you think so too, Herr von Fink?

FLIEDERBUSCH Marvelously! Absolutely a trick of nature!

PRINCESS And I will be wearing the same exact costume at our gala. In the same colors even. Those you can't see here, naturally, for that you'd have to know the original. Do you understand anything about painting?

FLIEDERBUSCH A little.

PRINCESS Our small gallery is not generally open to people, but if it interests you, you can look at the collection some time.

FLIEDERBUSCH Your Highness —

PRINCESS And write a few lines about it maybe. My friend Satan wants to run an essay about the Wendolin palace and park anyway, on the occasion of our gala. He should simply send you, Herr von Fink.

FLIEDERBUSCH Your Highness, I would be happy —

PRINCESS The more publicity the better. We want to collect a lot of money for our charitable causes. In fact, something appeared today already. Very well written. By a certain Kajetan.

FLIEDERBUSCH Kajetan —

PRINCESS A very talented young author. He'll also be writing the connecting text for the tableaux vivants. *Pointing to another picture* This is a portrait of me. *The telephone rings* The most recent photograph.

FLIEDERBUSCH Excellent! *The telephone rings again.*

PRINCESS Please, don't let me disturb you.

FLIEDERBUSCH With your permission, Your Highness — *picks up the receiver.*

PRINCESS *stands up, goes back and forth in the room and looks through her lorgnette at the pictures on the walls.*

FLIEDERBUSCH "Elegant World" editorial office here. Fink, yes — Sure. — Oh, Herr Wöbl. What, he didn't appear? *To the Princess* I beg your pardon, Your Highness.

PRINCESS *indicates with a gesture that he shouldn't let her disturb him. In front of the pictures, still with her lorgnette; occasionally nods, as if remembering the original.*

FLIEDERBUSCH *on the phone* What? — Agreed? — In his name? — Settled? — Ah! — Obendorfer? — And who is to be the other second? — Füllmann? — No, where should I know the name from?

PRINCESS *becomes attentive.*

FLIEDERBUSCH Agreed at once? — They raised no objections to the pistols either? — All the better. — Why not? — Twelve noon? — Of course. *To the Princess* I beg your pardon, Your Highness. *On the phone* I don't understand — Prater — Oh, I see, Prater meadows — That's all the same to me — Yes — Of course I'll wait here — Thank you. — Good-bye. *Hangs up, then, with contrived ease* Again, a thousand pardons, Your Highness. So, to get back to the illustrations — it's going to be a matter —

PRINCESS Weren't you talking about pistols?

FLIEDERBUSCH *smiling, incidentally* Among other things.

PRINCESS *also smiling* A duel?

FLIEDERBUSCH *as if he did not understand* Why, Your
Highness —? Oh, because of the pistols. Absolutely not, it
has to do with a sporting competition. *Lightly* I think that
Your Highness's portrait should appear on the first page,
since the entire issue so to speak —

PRINCESS *interrupts him, interested* So, it's a duel you've
—?! And what mischief have we done? Alienated a wife from
her jealous husband or tempted an innocent maiden from the
path of virtue?

FLIEDERBUSCH Your Highness —

PRINCESS Forgive me, Herr Fink, I don't want to be
indiscreet, but under the circumstances I do not want to keep
you any longer, you'll have more important things to take
care of.

FLIEDERBUSCH Not at all, Your Highness. Nothing can be
more important to me than —

PRINCESS *putting him off* So, say hello to Herr Satan for me,
he should choose the pictures that suit him. Everything is at
his disposal.

FLIEDERBUSCH I have an idea, Your Highness. If the portrait
of Your Highness and that of — Elizabeth Charlotte were to
appear next to each other, one to the right, the other —

PRINCESS That might look very nice.

FLIEDERBUSCH And at any rate, I'll write the text before the
day is over.

PRINCESS There's really no great rush with the text. It's still
two weeks until —

FLIEDERBUSCH *gesture: "one never knows."*

PRINCESS *understanding* Oh, I see! — *Looks at him with
interest and pleasure* No, I really don't want to — Before
something like that — yes, you already told me — before
such a sporting competition one surely has all sorts of —

FLIEDERBUSCH I have nothing but my profession, Your
Highness, and I am happy that precisely this task is —

PRINCESS *smiling* Nothing but your profession? No friends,
— Girlfriends?

FLIEDERBUSCH *shakes his head.*

PRINCESS But — relatives? You probably still have your
parents, don't you? Not that I could imagine — quite the
contrary. I'm convinced everything will go splendidly — with
your sporting competition.

FLIEDERBUSCH *cheerful but reserved* Slight accidents are
never totally impossible during such events, Your Highness.
But as far as my parents are concerned, they don't live here.
They live in the country, on a small estate — a sort of farm.
Seven hours by train. So, much as I'd like to, there wouldn't
be enough time —

PRINCESS When is it supposed to take place, your
competition?

FLIEDERBUSCH Around noon tomorrow.

PRINCESS Oh, right, I did hear that. Well, then I'll wish you
— but one isn't supposed to do that on occasions such as this.
So I'll say simply — Good-bye, Herr von Fink!

FLIEDERBUSCH *shrugs his shoulders slightly* Good-bye,
Your Highness.

PRINCESS *extends her hand to him.*

FLIEDERBUSCH *kisses her hand, then, with a hasty resolve,
quickly* If I — if I might perhaps ask for a special favor:
permission to lay the text of my completed article before
Your Highness. — In case some slight changes prove to be
desirable — I have to rely on my imagination to some extent,
you know —

PRINCESS Oh, right, you don't know the park at all. So, come
today, maybe — no, this evening is unfortunately not
possible. Come tomorrow morning. I'm a very early riser.
And if I should happen to have ridden out already — I'll give
the order that you be shown everything, the park — and the
gallery too.

FLIEDERBUSCH Your Highness —

PRINCESS So, good-bye, Herr von Fink! *She exits.*

FLIEDERBUSCH *alone, takes a deep breath, as if he wanted to inhale the perfume which the Princess left behind* What a wonderful woman. And that glance as she was leaving. Should fate from this side too — It would be sad to have to die now. *Slaps himself on the forehead, laughs, shakes his head; then, in a different tone* Not bad at all, the gentlemen at the "Times"! Accept a duel in my name! A duel to the death! Oh, yes, that would suit them, that I — rather, that he — *goes to the telephone, hesitates, then goes to the door right, locks it. To the phone, calls* 774 please — Yes, Flie — *Softly* Fliederbusch here! Could I perhaps — Oh, it is you, Herr Frühbeck. *Quickly* I wanted to ask you to apologize to Herr Leuchter for me. What? I just wanted to let you know that I was unavoidably detained. *As if amazed* Oh — oh — You did throw them out the door, didn't you? How's that? — What? — Ha! — Füllmann and Obendorfer? — Oh, Herr Obendorfer, good afternoon — Because I said that I'd bear any consequences? — I meant the legal ones. — You're all of this opinion? — And the Editor-in-Chief? Ah! — You convinced him? — So! — You think so? I don't think so — Not in this case either. I am opposed to dueling on principle. I hold it to be an outdated, barbaric custom. — Why not? — Let him sue me! — Who says that? — What does Herr Kajetan say? — What is Herr Fink supposed to be? — Rado? — I don't understand. Oh, desperado! — Is that so? — Ah, Kajetan knows him? — This is really very interesting. Ha! — Capable of anything? — Sorry. My position is unshakable. — Perhaps towards evening. — No. One does allow oneself to have a private life. — My final word. — In this matter my final one. — I didn't ask you to, you know. — Then I'll shoot him down like a mad dog. Sorry. — That's my business. Exclusively mine. Finished. *Hangs up* Just wait! You'll make proper fools of yourselves.

I wouldn't dream of it. *Remembering again* Rather,
Fliederbusch wouldn't dream of fighting a duel. Fliederbusch
will back out! Fliederbusch will disappear! *In a different tone*
Because he has no choice but to disappear. But how? Flight?
A fairly miserable role — all in all. But what do I care about
that! What does Fliederbusch concern me? Nothing!
Absolutely nothing more! It's becoming ever more apparent
that I am Fink, after all. Fate itself — and now, in peace and
quiet, let's write our article about the Princess, or rather,
about the Wendolin palace and park — *He prepares to write,
takes the Princess's portrait and becomes absorbed in
contemplating it. A knock at the door.* Come in! *Someone
is turning the doorknob in vain.* Oh, right — *goes to the
door, opens it.*
STYX *enters.*

FLIEDERBUSCH, STYX

STYX Locked yourself in, Herr Fink?
FLIEDERBUSCH *unembarrassed* I was busy. An important
    article.
STYX Yes, of course.
FLIEDERBUSCH Not the one you think. Her Highness,
    Princess Wendolin was just here.
STYX The servant told me.
FLIEDERBUSCH At her expressed desire I'm writing an essay
    in connection with the forthcoming charity gala. I've been
    asked to appear at the palace tomorrow morning.
STYX You're writing the essay, Herr Fink! That works out
    quite well. I would no longer be in a position, unfortunately,
    to undertake the short assignment that Herr Satan requested
    of me, since — it is my intention to leave "The Elegant
    World" —
FLIEDERBUSCH Oh —
STYX And join another publication.

FLIEDERBUSCH And may one ask —?

STYX The "Times" — in place of a certain — Fliederbusch.

FLIEDERBUSCH *involuntary movement; embarrassed laugh.*

STYX *laughs also, silently.*

FLIEDERBUSCH That really is a most interesting piece of news.

STYX My investigations have been successful, as usual.

FLIEDERBUSCH You're coming from the offices of the "Times"?

STYX Calm down, Herr Fliederbusch. I have not shown myself there yet. But I will go there within the next half hour in order to offer the gentlemen my services.

FLIEDERBUSCH *taking a deep breath* And what makes you assume, Herr Styx — or whatever your name may be — that the "Times" will desire to avail itself of your unquestionably most estimable services?

STYX They will undoubtedly be glad to find an immediate substitute to fill a vacancy for which they could not have been prepared. And they probably don't care who will be writing the parliamentary report tomorrow or the day after. And since you yourself, Herr Fink — as you will be exclusively known from now on — will write a letter to your boss in which you recommend me in the warmest terms as your temporary substitute, there shouldn't be any further difficulties.

FLIEDERBUSCH And what leads you to the supposition, Herr Styx, that I actually have a mind to give up my, be it said, modest position at the "Times"?

STYX You're joking, aren't you, Herr Fink? Aside from the fact that it would cost me but a single word to make your position untenable not only there, but here as well, the most basic sense of propriety should prohibit you from ever setting foot in the offices of the "Times" again. Even if your colleagues don't know that Fliederbusch and Fink represent one person — you, Herr Fink, must surely know who wrote

the article in which you're called an foolish undignified snob
—

FLIEDERBUSCH *breaking in* I do not know. I am the
parliamentary correspondent for the "Times" — reporter if
you like — I don't concern myself any further with who —
STYX No matter. It won't, or wouldn't remain a secret to you.
And since I can't imagine that you could bring yourself to
shake hands with that colleague afterwards — or perhaps
even pay him your respects after he's made you appear
ridiculous and contemptible this way, even if unknowingly,
I should think you'd be grateful if I make it possible for you
to free yourself from an untenable position by supplying a
substitute immediately in an unobtrusive and relatively correct
manner. So — start writing, Herr Fliederbusch. *Prepares
paper, etc. for him.*
FLIEDERBUSCH What should I write?
STYX Whatever I'm going to dictate. My esteemed Herr
Editor-in-Chief — You're hesitating?
FLIEDERBUSCH It's — it is a big decision, after all, Herr
Styx. To move with such determination, as it were, from one
existence to the other. It's not such an easy thing, you know.
Stands up.
STYX It is quite easy — when one has no choice, Herr
Fliederbusch!
FLIEDERBUSCH Give me some time to think it over, Herr
Styx.
STYX What do you need to think for? Do you feel like being
thrown out two doors at the same time, Herr Fink and
Fliederbusch?! Write! — Or else —
FLIEDERBUSCH Do you know what this is called, Herr Styx?
STYX Of course. So: My esteemed Herr Editor-in-Chief —
FLIEDERBUSCH You will at least allow me to ask you a —
an informal question first, the friendly ·answering of which
may put you in the perhaps not unwelcome position of doing
me a small favor in return.

STYX —?

FLIEDERBUSCH I want to consult you — as an expert: how does one go about creating under a voluntarily assumed name a new, middle-class existence, a — how shall I put it — legally unassailable one?

STYX I understand. That sort of thing is by no means impossible. I'll be happy to assist you in your attempt —

FLIEDERBUSCH Truly, Herr Styx?

STYX We'll talk about it at the appropriate time. But first, the letter, if I may ask.

FLIEDERBUSCH *after a final hesitation* Let me hear what you have in mind. *He writes.*

STYX *dictating* My esteemed Herr Editor-in-Chief. Unforeseen family circumstances of an urgent nature force me to — to request a leave of absence of several days, and I take the liberty at the same time to recommend the bearer, Herr Styx, who is well-known to me personally, as my substitute. Moreover, Herr Styx desires to use this opportunity to offer the highly esteemed staff of the "Times" a private piece of information —

FLIEDERBUSCH *looks up.*

STYX — which should, as he assures me, be of great interest to you. With deepest respects — and so on — Fliederbusch. So, let me see. Fliederbusch — With which this name disappears from the world of German journalism.

FLIEDERBUSCH *still holding the letter* A private piece of information of great interest —?

STYX I could also have said — several private pieces of the greatest interest.

FLIEDERBUSCH And may one ask, perhaps —

STYX One may. Surely you wouldn't believe that my goal is to work as a reporter for the "Times" on a per-line basis. This is a first step, nothing more, in which you're helping me. For me it's only a question of using the happy coincidence that's been handed me to establish myself at the "Times" as quickly

as possible. Because my real intention, and it would be unfair
of me to keep it a secret from you, is to put myself at the
disposal of the "Times" as a comrade-in-arms.

FLIEDERBUSCH How am I to understand that?

STYX As fellow-fighter in a field that you entered in so
promising a way as well. This morning's article struck a tone
that finds a joyful resonance in my heart.

FLIEDERBUSCH —?

STYX At the risk of insulting you, Herr Fink, I feel compelled
to praise most highly the intent of this article in which you
are made to hear such personally unpleasant things — the
intent, I say — less so the execution. There is in this article
not only a somewhat naive as well as thoroughly sincere
hatred for the high-born and arrogant lot under whose
predominance, scarcely mitigated by our merely seeming
parliamentary system, our country has been languishing for
centuries, — but also the proper contempt for that pack that
not only puts up with this predominance, but is also studious
to encourage and promote it through their adoration and their
fawning. And the author senses quite correctly that
democracy would have finished feudalism off long ago if the
latter hadn't always had its indispensable as well as despised
ally rising on its behalf — the snob in his most diverse
manifestations — this deplorable mongrel bred from lackeys,
cowards, and renegades.

FLIEDERBUSCH Hmm. . . .

STYX It is that which the author of this article senses. But —
he is able only just to sense it. Because it's easy to see that he
obviously never had the opportunity to get to know close at
hand the people against whom his hatred and contempt are
directed. One proof of that among others is that he sees
Count Niederhof as representative of our reactionaries when
in reality he is little more than their jester, and that, in his
polemical zeal, a harmless, unimportant collaborator of "The
Elegant World" — you, Herr Fink! — becomes the

archetypal snob. I — without wanting to compare my journalistic gifts with the author's — have at any rate one advantage over him: I know the people with whom he longs to quarrel. I have lived among them, I have been part of them, I was — to some extent —born one of them —

FLIEDERBUSCH *nods, as if he were about to say something.*

STYX *cuts him off with a gesture* What's in a name? We both know how little that signifies, Herr Fink and Fliederbusch, right? What I was once and would still be today — outwardly — inwardly too, most likely, if something very human hadn't happened to me once, that is no longer relevant. I am Styx now, and that's that. But, of course, a Styx with memories, with knowledge, with insights, of the kind which the gentlemen at the "Times" have necessarily not been granted, and for which, if they are serious about taking a new, radical direction, they must pay with gold. As I was reading the article today it became clear to me: I am the man the "Times" needs, and I — I need the "Times." And with that, my dear Herr Fink, you see me on the way, with your letter, to install myself at this excellent paper, in order to — offer it my material.

FLIEDERBUSCH Your material?

STYX My closets at home are bursting with it. Up to now I have unfortunately been unable to use the best of the stuff I've been lucky enough to collect over the years. "The Elegant World" could not make use of it, understandably; the "Times" will appreciate it —

FLIEDERBUSCH You may be mistaken, Herr Styx, if you assume that the "Times" will be interested in a kind of gossip that "The Elegant World" formerly used to —

STYX These stories will be different from the ones I've told in "The Elegant World." No gossip, Herr Fink, but cultural history, world history. And if the gentlemen at the "Times" know how to use it properly, then within six months we'll have the revolution that will sweep the entire circus from the face of the earth, the Niederhofs together with the Finks.

FLIEDERBUSCH And it's for this that you want this letter from me? I find that original, to say the least.

STYX I could do without it if I had the time to lose. But I've already learned the hard way about myself that it would be a serious error for me to let my fire go out. And I am burning at last to employ my pen, which has been degraded and misused so long, in the service of a good and righteous cause. I want to be at my post by the time your response appears in "The Elegant World." Let's do battle with each other as honest foes and — I promise you I will not use my material about you in any way.

FLIEDERBUSCH *smiles* Even if you should succeed, in time, in completing it?

STYX I'll have more important things to do.
Wöbl and Egon enter.

STYX, FLIEDERBUSCH, WÖBL, EGON

Egon is disagreeably moved at finding Styx, and does not speak at first.

WÖBL *has a pistol case in his hand* My respects. Everything's in order. Oh, Herr von Styx —

STYX *carelessly return the greeting.*

WÖBL *comes closer to Fliederbusch, repeats with emphasis* Everything's in order.

STYX *to Wöbl* What have you got there, Wöbl?

WÖBL Won't be hard to guess, I'd say.

STYX A pistol case? What for?

WÖBL *to Fliederbusch* Say — doesn't Herr von Styx know, then —?

STYX You're fighting a duel, Herr Fink?

FLIEDERBUSCH *nods.*

STYX With the author of the article in the "Times"?

WÖBL Without a doubt.

STYX *to Fliederbusch* And — you could keep that from me?! *To Wöbl* He identified himself, *to Fliederbusch* and is prepared to give you satisfaction? Who is it, then?

WÖBL Fliederbusch is the scoundrel's name.

STYX Fliederbusch —??

WÖBL *indicating the pistol case* Spanking new! A pretty pair! Got it sealed up right off.

STYX Herr Fliederbusch is fighting a duel with you, Herr Fink?

FLIEDERBUSCH Why shouldn't he, Herr Styx?

STYX You're fighting a duel with Herr . . . Fliederbusch?

FLIEDERBUSCH Is there anything to disqualify him?

WÖBL Do you know him, Herr Styx?

STYX Of course I know him. And haven't you made his personal acquaintance just now?

WÖBL No, not so far. But his representatives have assured us in his name that he is prepared to render satisfaction of any sort.

STYX Of any sort — yes. That's just like him. An impudent little brute, gentlemen. But some talent! Has a great career in front of him. — So, with pistols?

WÖBL Yes.

STYX And who are the seconds?

WÖBL Two colleagues of his — Obendorfer and Füllmann. True, we still have a meeting with them this evening, but everything is actually as good as settled already. Three shots each, thirty paces, — advance of five —

STYX God damn it! This is splendid. *Drumming on the pistol case* I could almost get the urge myself again — And where exactly is this merriment to take place?

WÖBL In the Prater meadows. And, where precisely do you think, Herr Fink? On the exact same spot where Count Niederhof shot Baron Napador dead seven years ago.

STYX And the hour has already been fixed as well?

WÖBL   We proposed noon. Namely, because there's horse racing tomorrow too. That way we'll be close by at the same time, and it's most convenient for Doctor Kunz too —

STYX   Really, what are you troubling the man for? I don't suppose he'll have anything to do under these conditions.

WÖBL   Well — hey —!

FLIEDERBUSCH   Who is Doctor Kunz?

WÖBL   An excellent surgeon! And since he's also the racetrack doctor we arranged it this way. In between the shooting and the races we'll still have enough time left for a small lunch at the pavilion near the funhouse.

STYX   Funhouse? A somewhat optimistic choice of words, dear Wöbl. Well, my esteemed Herr von Fink, you are in good hands and I hope, I wish you —

WÖBL   Psst, Herr von Styx!

STYX   So — I'll see you, gentlemen, if not before, then at lunch tomorrow in the pavilion. I'm taking the liberty of inviting myself. You needn't even go to any additional expense, gentlemen, I'll pay in advance for the cover charge — the remaining one.

FLIEDERBUSCH   *points to the letter which is still lying on the desk* You're forgetting, Herr Styx —

STYX   Yes, right. Thank you, Herr Fink, I like you quite a great deal. Until tomorrow, then!

> *He exits.*
>
> *Egon, Wöbl, Fliederbusch*

EGON   *who purposely refrained from speaking during the entire previous scene, but who could hardly hide his annoyance at some of Styx's remarks* The tactlessness of this person really exceeds all bounds. It goes without saying that he will not take part in our lunch. I hope you haven't allowed yourself to be irritated any further, Herr Fink.

FLIEDERBUSCH   What can you be thinking about, dear Egon? So, everything is really in order? Not the slightest difficulties have arisen?

WÖBL No. Seems to be a very sharp fellow, this Fliederbusch.

EGON And Styx must know more than he revealed to us.

WÖBL What shape's your marksmanship actually in, Herr Fink?

FLIEDERBUSCH It seems to me you're a bit late inquiring about that.

EGON Even if you'd never had a pistol in your hand, Herr Fink, — there really would have been no alternative —

FLIEDERBUSCH You may rest quite easy, Egon.

WÖBL You know what, Herr von Fink, at home in our little garden I have a shooting range; it would be good in any case if you practiced your shooting a bit this afternoon.

SATAN *enters in his overcoat, in high spirits.*

EGON, WÖBL, FLIEDERBUSCH, SATAN

SATAN Good afternoon. Ah, Wöbl, — and to what does one owe this pleasure? Well, Egon — Gentlemen, I'm able to bring you the joyful news that the matter is as good as settled. We're signing tomorrow. The Count was charming. True, Radlmann behaved like a peasant but that didn't make any difference. From the first of July we appear as a daily, with the name —*at the desk* What's all this? Oh!

FLIEDERBUSCH Her Highness, Princess Wendolin was here in person and left the pictures for you to make your selection.

SATAN You've spoken with her, Herr Fink?

FLIEDERBUSCH She was very sorry not to find the Herr Editor-in-Chief and sends her cordial regards.

SATAN *looks at the pictures* Did you touch on the financial side, Herr Fink? We have a fixed fee in such cases, you know.

FLIEDERBUSCH I didn't dare offer the Princess an honorarium.

SATAN *smiles* That's not it, Herr Fink. That is, it's we who — Something like this involves expenses, after all.

EGON I dare say that will come to an end now too, Papa.

SATAN Of course. We won't be dependent on that any more now. And how is your response coming along, Herr Fink? The Count is really excited. Have you got any of it yet? — *he notices the pistol case* What's the meaning of this?

EGON Dear Papa, I don't think anything will come of the response. Herr Fink has naturally preferred to demand chivalric satisfaction and will fight a duel.

SATAN A duel? Are you all mad? With Herr Leuchter maybe?

EGON No, with Herr Fliederbusch.

SATAN Fliederbusch? Never heard of him. Who is that?

EGON *somewhat impatiently* The author of that insipid article.

SATAN He accepted the challenge?

WÖBL Without a doubt.

SATAN And I'm telling you, gentlemen, this duel will not take place.

EGON Papa, I really don't understand —

SATAN You will not fight any duel, Herr Fink.

FLIEDERBUSCH Herr Satan —

SATAN We cannot inaugurate this new era of our paper with a duel. *To Egon* Hasn't Herr Fink told you? Don't you know about the leanings of the new paper? Among the planks in our platform there is, among others, the fight against the folly of dueling.

EGON The folly of dueling?

SATAN Yes indeed. I've already discussed that with Count Niederhof too. We will attack the duel most sharply — and that from a religious standpoint. Even the single combat of the officer class, as a crime against —

EGON But for the time being we haven't reached that point, Papa. And so, let's hold on to the fair custom of chivalric satisfaction until further notice. You won't keep us from it, Papa.

SATAN I will keep you from it. As your Editor-in-Chief, Herr Fink, I forbid you to fight this duel.

FLIEDERBUSCH *shrugs.*

SATAN Besides, I don't have the least desire to have my —
one of my best men shot dead. That would be —

EGON It's not likely, dear Papa, that Herr Fliederbusch should
be more skilled in the use of weapons than Herr Fink.

SATAN In a pistol duel everything depends on chance. The best
marksman can be wiped out by a bungler.

FLIEDERBUSCH I suppose you're right there, but today more
than ever, Herr Editor-in-Chief, we may surely say, we are
in God's hands.

SATAN *not understanding at first* What do you mean? Oh,
yes. In God's hands — Yes, — but not with any certainty
until — after the first of July!

EGON Papa, one doesn't make jokes about such things.
Gentlemen, we still have all sorts of things to discuss for
which this is not the right place. Good-bye, Papa.

WÖBL My respects, Herr Editor-in-Chief.

FLIEDERBUSCH Herr Editor-in-Chief. *All three exit.*

SATAN Craziness. I will — In any event I will bear no
responsibility. *He is at the desk again, looks at the pictures
absent-mindedly* Beautiful woman — still. I'll write the
Count. — Hmm — *Rings the bell* Maybe Styx could —

SERVANT *enters.*

SATAN Have Herr Styx come up.

SERVANT Herr Styx has already left.

SATAN Already? Did he say when he's coming back?

SERVANT Not today.

SATAN All right. One has to do everything by himself! *He
angrily begins to open letters.*

Curtain

THIRD ACT

The Wendolin park. Along the left side, the small baroque palace, two stories high, with a small, usable balcony on the second floor. Three glass doors lead from the first floor, across a terrace, into the park.
In the center, towards the left, under a walnut tree, a table with chairs. To the right, a large park gate which remains closed; immediately adjacent to it a small, usable one. The table is set, the Princess is at breakfast. FRANZ has just finished serving her.

PRINCESS, *in an elegant morning dress, drinks coffee, puts the cup down, picks up a small notebook that had been lying next to her, and reads more or less to herself.*

PRINCESS Dressmaker at eleven, at eleven thirty the decorator — *to Franz* What time is it now?
FRANZ A quarter after eight, Your Highness.
PRINCESS *as above* Herr Kajetan at twelve — *to Franz* The luncheon at one!
FRANZ It's been arranged, Your Highness, as always on racing day.
PRINCESS *in thought* But still, it seems to me as if I'd forgotten something.
FRANZ If I may be permitted most humbly to remind you, Your Highness, Count Niederhof wanted to pick you up at eight for your morning ride.
PRINCESS No, no, that wasn't it.
FRANZ The Count will be here shortly in any case. *Glances at her morning dress.*

PRINCESS *more to herself* It's almost eight-thirty. There's someone out there at the fence. *Uses her lorgnette* Right! The young man from "The Elegant World."

FLIEDERBUSCH *greets her from the other side of the fence.*

PRINCESS *to Franz* Go ahead and open it, Franz. *To herself* One really should write everything down.

FRANZ *opens the small gate which had still been locked.*

FLIEDERBUSCH *enters the park and greets her again.*

PRINCESS Please, come closer, Herr Fink.

FLIEDERBUSCH *comes to the table, bows* Your Highness —

PRINCESS *extends her hand to him* So, you're really —

FLIEDERBUSCH *kisses her hand* Taking advantage of Your Highness's kind permission, I take the liberty of laying my manuscript before you.

PRINCESS *receives the pages* So. Thank you very much. This is really very good of you. *Fleeting glance at the pages* And for you to go to the trouble personally. . . .

FLIEDERBUSCH Your Highness gave me leave —

PRINCESS Of course.

FLIEDERBUSCH Also, I'm not fooling myself into thinking that the article isn't still fairly rough. Any number of things which only a first hand look — *He looks all around* I can already see — a short stay in the park, a walk through the palace insofar as it's open to view, will undoubtedly provide me with the welcome possibility of shedding some more light here and there.

PRINCESS Yes, but — will you have time for all that?

FLIEDERBUSCH *dignified gesture.*

PRINCESS You do have — something else planned for today, as far as I remember. Or did —

FLIEDERBUSCH Nothing has changed since yesterday, Your Highness. But until twelve noon I have nothing else left to do *with a fleeting smile* on this earth.

PRINCESS *laughs* Than to shed light. But won't you take a seat, Herr von Fink? Please!

FLIEDERBUSCH *sits down. Short pause.*

CHAMBERMAID *appears on the second-floor balcony.*

FRANZ *appears below.*

CHAMBERMAID *asks with a glance what is going on.*

FRANZ *gestures: "I don't know."*

PRINCESS *glances at the manuscript* Six closely written pages. That you could find the composure — the concentration, I mean, to do —

FLIEDERBUSCH I took it as a particular favor on the part of fate that I was allowed to devote myself to this particular task.

A PORTER *at the gate.*

FRANZ *takes a letter from him, brings it to the Princess.*

PRINCESS You'll excuse me, Herr von Fink. *Opens the letter* Kajetan —? Well, all right. Fine, tell the porter I'll expect Herr Kajetan at ten instead of twelve.

FLIEDERBUSCH *repeats automatically* Kajetan?

PRINCESS The young author who's writing the text for the tableaux vivants for me. I did tell you — You have no idea how much work goes into an event like this. But it amuses me.

FLIEDERBUSCH And the noble cause —

PRINCESS Of course.

CHAMBERMAID *comes across the terrace into the garden* Your Highness —

PRINCESS What's the matter?

CHAMBERMAID The hairdresser.

PRINCESS Oh! — I'll be right there.

CHAMBERMAID *exits.*

FLIEDERBUSCH *stands up* I don't want to disturb Your Highness.

PRINCESS I am so very busy today. You know what, Herr von Fink, I'll read your article while I'm getting my hair done, and in the meantime maybe you can take a short stroll through the park.

FLIEDERBUSCH With Your Highness's leave. I will try to capture this delightful morning mood.

PRINCESS Good. Afterwards Franz will take you to the gallery so you can see the Fuggersburg in the original.

FLIEDERBUSCH Your Highness will find a few words in these pages about that as well.

PRINCESS About my great-grandmother? Is that so? Now that I am really curious about. Well, I hope still to see you afterwards, — *Smiling* young hero! *Exits across the terrace.*

FLIEDERBUSCH *alone* Young hero! Actually, I strike myself as being a fraud. — But why? It's not my fault. I would be prepared. Oh, I — *Pantomime, gestures as if he held a pistol in his hand and fired on his opponent* Without batting an eye. One, two — *he suddenly recalls* with advance of — three! *Winces, holds his hand in front of his eyes as if his opponent had fallen* A pistol duel took place yesterday under difficult, under unusually difficult conditions, between one of our most gifted young journalists, a staff member of a rigorously conservative paper, and — *flippant gesture* Let us not speak of the other. He's been dispatched. The affair seems to be in order, for the time being. The gentlemen from the "Times" have not been heard from again, — and now Styx is to help matters along. *looks at his watch* Hmm. Nonetheless, under the current circumstances, it would be embarrassing to run into Kajetan here. The best thing for me would be — *about to leave.*

FRANZ *enters* Her Highness asks if you might find it agreeable to view the gallery now.

FLIEDERBUSCH   The gallery? — *checks his watch* Unfortunately — unfortunately — My time — Perhaps another time I could —

COUNT *in a riding suit, enters the park.*

FLIEDERBUSCH *hearing his steps, turns around.*

COUNT *not exceedingly surprised* Ah, Herr Fink!

FLIEDERBUSCH Count —

COUNT What are you doing here at such an early hour?

FRANZ *leaves.*

FLIEDERBUSCH, COUNT

FLIEDERBUSCH I have the honor of writing an article on the occasion of the forthcoming charity gala in the Wendolin park. Her Highness has just now been gracious enough to subject it to her reading.

COUNT So, you're still writing that sort of thing too?

FLIEDERBUSCH As an exception.

COUNT But tell me — *suddenly remembering, looking at his watch* Is the — affair in question settled then?

FLIEDERBUSCH Count — *Falters.*

COUNT *misunderstanding* Well, then I congratulate you. And nothing happened to the other one either, I hope?

FLIEDERBUSCH Nothing at all has been settled yet, Count.

COUNT *somewhat disappointed* So —

FLIEDERBUSCH But may I be so bold as to ask how the Count came to the knowledge —

COUNT Your boss found it necessary to assure me by letter that he advised you against fighting a duel. So the matter is to be settled amicably, I suppose?

FLIEDERBUSCH No, Sir.

COUNT So — when is it to proceed, then, this single combat?

FLIEDERBUSCH Today.

COUNT Today? And you're still —?

FLIEDERBUSCH Professional obligations, Count. It's not taking place until noon; not very far from here. And not entirely by coincidence, the spot chosen for the encounter is the very one where several years ago the Count and Baron Napador —

COUNT *disagreeably moved, interrupting* Oh, but that's a charming gesture. I suppose you want me to interpret it as —?

PRINCESS *appears on the balcony* Oh, it's you! Good morning, Gisbert.

COUNT Good morning, Priska. I'm a little late. You'll forgive me.

PRINCESS I'm not ready myself yet. The gentlemen know each other?

COUNT Of course. We're old acquaintances, Herr Fink and I.

PRINCESS *holding the manuscript in her hand* Very nice what you've written here, Herr Fink. And the way you describe the picture, it's really more of a declaration of love — to my great-grandmother.

COUNT Ah, — the famous portrait that looks so much like you.

FLIEDERBUSCH A quirk of nature.

COUNT You've seen the Fuggersburg already?

FLIEDERBUSCH I know only the copy for the time being.

PRINCESS If you gentlemen will excuse me for a few more minutes. *She disappears into the room.*

COUNT *smiling* Well, if you escape with your skin today, Herr Fink — which let us hope — I predict you will go far.

FLIEDERBUSCH The Count is very kind.

COUNT *offers him a cigarette.*

FLIEDERBUSCH *takes one.*

COUNT *lights it* By the way, as long as we've run into each other here, I'd like to tell you something right away that should not be entirely without interest for you. You know, Herr Fink, that I had yet another meeting with Herr

Radlmann yesterday. Well, to make a long story short, I find him just as impossible as I do your esteemed boss, Herr Satan. I have decided, therefore, after consultation with my friends, to cut off negotiations with "The Elegant World" at once and to found a paper on my own. And I want to use this opportunity to ask you whether I can count on your collaboration under these circumstances as well.

FLIEDERBUSCH I have no binding obligations whatsoever to Herr Satan or Herr Radlmann, and I am happy to be able to place my unrestricted services at your disposal.

COUNT I'm very glad, Herr Fink. But you'll be pressed for time now, I assume. Perhaps you'll do me the pleasure of having lunch with me today? Then we can discuss — At a quarter to two, all right? By then everything — *always in a very easy tone* Or perhaps you attach some value, after a finished — I mean afterwards — with your seconds —

FLIEDERBUSCH Not in the least, my Lord.

COUNT You may not be able to avoid it. The reconciliation meal has most likely been ordered already.

FLIEDERBUSCH Reconciliation meal?! Count! How can you believe —

COUNT Well —

FLIEDERBUSCH A reconciliation between me and Herr Fliederbusch is out of the question.

COUNT *backing down* Well — You're fighting with pistols?

FLIEDERBUSCH That's right.

COUNT Well, then I hope the matter will have been seen to — May one know the terms?

FLIEDERBUSCH Three shots

COUNT Oh!

FLIEDERBUSCH Thirty paces with advance.

COUNT And three shots? Well, I say! What sort of seconds do you have, Herr Fink?

FLIEDERBUSCH *simply, with composure* It was I myself who had to insist on these terms.

COUNT Still, if I may say so, Herr Fink, I find this somewhat excessive.

FLIEDERBUSCH Count — *about to raise an objection* Or is it possible that the Count has not yet read my opponent's article?

COUNT Of course I've read it. Yesterday, right after our conversation. It interested me, as you may imagine. But precisely because I read it — What's involved here, in the end? A difference of political opinion —

FLIEDERBUSCH Which nevertheless grew on my opponent's side to the point of personal invective against me — and a little against you too, my Lord.

COUNT Well, — but you yourself seemed willing to respond to this gentleman — what is his name, actually?

FLIEDERBUSCH Fliederbusch.

COUNT To respond to this Herr Fliederbusch in like manner, — well —

FLIEDERBUSCH Upon closer reflection it became clear to me that such a response would in the end only signify a delay.

COUNT —?

FLIEDERBUSCH Because the world is not big enough for the two of us — for me and for Herr Fliederbusch.

COUNT Are you serious, Herr Fink?

FLIEDERBUSCH I certainly am, my Lord.

COUNT *shaking his head* I really can't see any reason for this degree of — bitterness. In the end Herr Fliederbusch only represented his point of view, as you did yours, Herr Fink. In its expression he may have gone too far here and there; but his point of view has, in the end, as much justification — as yours.

FLIEDERBUSCH *surprised* And — yours, Count!

COUNT Well, yes. No less justification and no more. As you know, there are no absolute truths — not in politics. Or do you really believe —

FLIEDERBUSCH If I hadn't earlier, — ever since a certain speech in Parliament which I had the good fortune to hear and for which you now see me prepared, if I may say so, my Lord, to suffer martyrdom —

COUNT *declining* My esteemed Herr Fink — with all due respect for your determination and courage, I must decline any responsibility for what you may, on my behalf — Of course for you, Herr Fink, the only thing in question is the political idea, which, when all is said and done, you may see represented by any of two dozen of my fellow party-members as well as by me. But where do you get the notion that Count Niederhof, the person, has anything to do with the symbol which he happens to signify for you — or with the bugbear you prefer to make of him?

FLIEDERBUSCH You yourself, my Lord, have through your speech elevated yourself to a symbol. How many others have I already heard speak, in Parliament and in assemblies? And of the same mind as you, too! You are the first to have managed to win me over to your side. With you I first experienced the complete merging of a man's essence and message. The words which you slung at the multitude with such enthusiastic or, as others will perhaps find, with such shocking force, have turned me into a passionate follower of your cause; it was your own — fanaticism that grabbed hold of me and pulled me along. Thus —

COUNT *interrupting* And if I — were not a fanatic to the degree you believe, do you think, maybe, that the effect of my speech on you and on others would have been noticeably weaker?

FLIEDERBUSCH I do indeed venture to maintain that.

COUNT But why —? Logically one should assume that precisely a fanatic, — by that I mean, for example, a speaker who holds nothing of himself back, — who squanders his best strength on his enthusiasm for his own ideals, — on his ill will towards the errors of his opponents, — on his despair over the betrayal of his friends, — that just such a spiritually intensely involved politician would from the outset have to be at a disadvantage against another who is — not a fanatic — who might rather be capable of keeping his inner resources fully available for his — profession, for the technical aspect of his calling, — precisely without having to squander the greater part of these spiritual resources on sentimental side issues.

FLIEDERBUSCH *surprised* What — does the Count mean by — sentimental side issues?

COUNT *simply* That which we are also accustomed to calling by a more common term — convictions.

FLIEDERBUSCH Accustomed to calling —?!

COUNT But which in the overwhelming majority of cases have no right to lay claim to so honorable a designation.

FLIEDERBUSCH —?

COUNT *incidentally* Convictions —! My God — one is born somewhere, one aspires to get somewhere else, one has sympathies and antipathies, vanities, ambitions, — relationships created by chance; — out of all these elements and a few others I can't think of at the moment there develops a more or less neat mixture which you may for all I care designate party spirit — or pathetic and complacent sentiment; — but conviction —?! Where is the solid proof that true conviction exists in individual cases at all — and not one of its numerous, deceptively similar surrogates.

FLIEDERBUSCH *in a refined tone* There is one proof. Being prepared — to die for this conviction.

COUNT *smiling* I see. — But this is sometimes — I'm sure you'll forgive me, Herr Fink — sometimes, I say — also just a way of making the others — or oneself believe that one has had a conviction.

FLIEDERBUSCH It does almost seem, my Lord, that you want to deny the existence in the world of any convictions.

COUNT Not at all. But there where I discover, or think I discover one, — there the problem first begins for me! You will surely not deny, Herr Fink, that every side has its clever and its stupid adherents, its respectable people and its scoundrels; — the stauncher and firmer in his convictions a party man one is, the more he will be inclined to see on the other side only brawlers — and blockheads — *stops.*

FLIEDERBUSCH And from that — it would follow —?

COUNT That one would generally do better, perhaps, instead of speaking about convictions — to speak of fixed ideas.

FLIEDERBUSCH And you yourself, Count —! Your own position —What reason would you have had — in Parliament —

COUNT You would be doing me a particular favor, Herr Fink, if you finally kept my speech out of it. It would be most painful for me — I believe I've already indicated to you that I must decline any responsibility, if by chance I —

FLIEDERBUSCH Far be it from me to — push some responsibility on to you. But do you seriously expect me to understand your masterful speech not as political credo — but — how shall I say — as a kind of tour de force of fencing?

COUNT *somewhat perplexed at first, then easily* Would that necessarily have to be something inferior in every instance?

FLIEDERBUSCH Perhaps not inferior; but it would still be in every instance something — quite different, Count — and —

COUNT And if my views had been — known to you yesterday, then you'd have probably dispensed with — how did you put it? — suffering martyrdom for me — or my speech?

FLIEDERBUSCH *dignified* I know now, at least, that I must do so only for myself and for my conviction.

COUNT Nevertheless, — under these circumstances I couldn't blame you if you now regretted getting this deeply involved, and I realize more and more that I had the responsibility of clearing up in a timely fashion the misconception under which you were laboring concerning my "symbolic significance." I'll make you a proposition, Herr Fink — back out!

FLIEDERBUSCH —?

COUNT Back out of your duel!

FLIEDERBUSCH My Lord! —

COUNT I'll fight Herr Fliederbusch in your place.

FLIEDERBUSCH *indignant* Count — how can you —

COUNT Don't go thinking, Herr Fink, that the idea just hit me for the first time: — not the idea, exactly, of taking your place, — but also on my own behalf. — Last night, after reading his article, I already thought in passing of calling Herr Fliederbusch to account on my own.—

FLIEDERBUSCH And obviously changed your mind again —?

COUNT Yes.

FLIEDERBUSCH I suppose Herr Fliederbusch struck you as — an all too meager opponent? —

COUNT Not at all. Why should he? — But I decided at the very outset of my political career never to allow journalistic attacks to become reasons for affairs of honor. Where would it get me if I were that sensitive? And — where would it get the others? Since I — forgive me for speaking of it — am not entirely unadroit in fencing and similar tricks, such a proceeding would shift the balance all too much to the disadvantage of my journalistic-political opponent; it would not be fair play, people might find, for me to exploit such an advantage. But this one time — it shouldn't be said that I — send other people into the fire for me, — that I let my followers instead of —

FLIEDERBUSCH No one is saying that, my Lord. If you — should still entertain the desire after the conclusion of my affair, then — But if I may be permitted to voice my honest opinion, I must say, — that it — would certainly not be unfair — but downright immoral if you wanted to fight Herr Fliederbusch.

COUNT *almost merry* Immoral even?

FLIEDERBUSCH And that precisely — because you — you said so yourself earlier, you find his point of view to have as much justification as your own, — thus you can feel no sort of enmity whatsoever against him.

COUNT That's not the point in such cases, Herr Fink. One could almost say — on the contrary. I did not, after all — since you brought up the disagreeable affair earlier — entertain any kind of hostile feelings towards Baron Napador either; — indeed, he was — almost — a friend of mine, — and still I was obliged to fight him —

FLIEDERBUSCH And even — to — *He stops.*

COUNT Well — that — my dear Herr Fink — When a man stands face to face with another that way, — then he simply wants to be the one who — shoots better. That has nothing to do with hostility. One has nothing personal against the target one aims at either, you know, — one wants to hit it.

FLIEDERBUSCH Dead center — in the black. —

COUNT *shrugs.*

FLIEDERBUSCH As long as you hit — without hatred —!

COUNT *understanding* Oh, I see —! You, Herr Fink, obviously find it more respectable or grander — or God knows what, if one kills another human being out of hatred than — *he searches for a word* than —

FLIEDERBUSCH *calmly* Than for sport.

COUNT *at first taken aback* You mean —? *In a different tone* Very well. I accept the term. I am just — a sportsman. Indeed, I've been one all my life. Always — and everywhere. Most likely we have just the one choice with most things in life — sportsman — or — *he searches.*

FLIEDERBUSCH Or — monomaniac.

COUNT *almost joyfully* Yes. it really seems so. Rather — one doesn't even have the choice — one is organized this way or that. Quite right, Herr Fink. It just seems to be my calling to demand records of myself, — in all fields — in keeping with my years. Before it was all sorts of other things, now it's simply the turn of politics. Hopefully it'll turn out to be quite amusing.

FLIEDERBUSCH It looks very much like it.

COUNT *good-naturedly* Doesn't it?

FLIEDERBUSCH You were born under a lucky star, Count. Not everyone has the talent to take life — so cheerfully and easily.

COUNT Cheerfully ? I'll concede that, Herr Fink. But easily? Maybe I don't take it as seriously, as pedantically, as — other people. But does it therefore have less substance and especially, fewer dangers than for these other people? I don't think so. And who knows if my political — sporting career will not end with a couple of fanatics or pedants hanging me from a lamp-post?

FLIEDERBUSCH Let's hope not —

COUNT Very kind of you.

FLIEDERBUSCH But one thing is certain: you will, in your final moments, imagine that you're perishing for your conviction!

COUNT You're mistaken, Herr Fink. However it ends for me, I would depart this life in the comforting awareness that I've always been merely a sportsman, and not for a single second, not even the last — a monomaniac.

FLIEDERBUSCH Go ahead and say it: a fool.

COUNT Oh —

FLIEDERBUSCH After all, it's inescapable that people who are prepared to face danger and death, not out of a whim or sporting courage, but out of conviction, must in every case strike you as absolute fools.

COUNT *hesitating* A little. Yes. But what will perhaps astonish you, — I rather like them for all that, these fools, — whether they happen to be called Fink or Fliederbusch. And therefore I allow myself once more to express the hope that both of them will emerge uninjured from the fight.

FLIEDERBUSCH I, my Lord, can envisage that less than ever.

COUNT —?

FLIEDERBUSCH It's become increasingly clear to me just in the course of this conversation that one of the two must leave this world, — Fink or Fliederbusch.

COUNT You are obstinate, Herr Fink. What's to become of our lunch then? I mean, if the other — has better luck than you!

FLIEDERBUSCH *after a short pause* Have a second setting put on in any event.

COUNT I'm glad to see you so brave and confident.

FLIEDERBUSCH The Count misunderstands me perhaps; such confidence would be tempting fate. Rather, I assume, in view of the admirable objectivity you're displaying in your judgment of my — your opponent, that you don't particularly care with whom you'll have lunch today — and that Herr Fliederbusch would be no less welcome as your guest than I.

COUNT Have I offended you after all, Herr Fink? That would make me —

FLIEDERBUSCH Not in the least. But I would really have no objection to an arrangement whereby, if fate should decide against me today, Herr Fliederbusch would come before you, Count, to deliver my last greetings.

COUNT That would certainly be original!

FLIEDERBUSCH I'm not joking, Sir. Really I'm not. Whether the one — fool or the other — it's all the same in the end, right?

Egon Satan appears on the other side of the fence; he looks in, hesitates, makes a sign of understanding to someone who stands behind him to the right but who is not visible.

FLIEDERBUSCH *notices him; his glance grows fixed.*

COUNT What's the matter with you, Herr Fink? *He follows Fliederbusch's glance and notices Egon without immediately recognizing him.*

EGON *greets.*

COUNT He's greeting you. An acquaintance? Ah, the young Herr Satan — Obviously he wants to speak to you.

FLIEDERBUSCH It appears in point of fact — *With a quick resolve, goes up to the fence.*

COUNT *walks slowly in the same direction.*

FLIEDERBUSCH My dear Egon, are you looking for me?

EGON To be sure, Herr Fink. *He greets the Count again.*

COUNT *thanks him.*

EGON *remains standing outside* I beg your pardon, but a most urgent matter —

FLIEDERBUSCH *inside the park* That concerns me?

EGON Yes. And since we knew — *to the Count, who is still approximately three steps away* that Herr Fink had been asked to Her Highness's for today —

COUNT I don't wish to disturb.

FLIEDERBUSCH Oh — the Count knows all about it. Well?

EGON In a word, — the police have gotten wind of the impend- ing duel.

FLIEDERBUSCH How?

EGON We have it from the best of sources. It seemed to us more opportune, therefore, to fix the fight for an hour and a half earlier. The gentlemen on the opposing side are in agreement.

FLIEDERBUSCH *can hide his astonishment only with difficulty* Herr Fliederbusch is in agreement?

EGON If you are likewise, Herr Fink, then the encounter will take place at ten thirty instead of twelve, at the same place.

FLIEDERBUSCH *looks at his watch* Ten thirty —

EGON Otherwise we would be forced to postpone the whole thing until tomorrow or to an even later time, which under the prevailing circumstances had best be avoided.

FLIEDERBUSCH Quite right.

COUNT   And we'll move our lunch up likewise by an hour, which on account of the races alone would be quite agreeable. So, I'll expect you at one, my dear Herr Fink.

FLIEDERBUSCH   Count — I — or the other one will appear punctually.

WÖBL   *appears across the way and greets.*

EGON   *to Wöbl* Everything in order. *To Fink* The carriage is waiting at the corner. We'll drive straight there.

FLIEDERBUSCH   And may I perhaps ask, Count, that you convey my humblest apologies to Her Highness.

COUNT   I will do that. So — good-bye! *Gives him his hand. Egon and Wöbl exit with Fliederbusch.*

COUNT   *looking after them, after a while* Strange. *Lights a cigarette.*

FRANZ   *enters and clears the table* Your obedient servant, Count.

COUNT   *paces back and forth* How are you getting on, Franz?

FRANZ   Thank you for your gracious inquiry, Count, as well as can be expected. Seventy-five in August.

COUNT   No one could tell by looking at you, Franz!

FRANZ   Is it permissible to offer the Count my humblest congratulations?

COUNT   For what?

FRANZ   On your political debut.

COUNT   You're interested in politics too, Franz?

FRANZ   What's left at my age, Count? Of course, with the Count it surprised me a bit. But maybe it's only a passing fancy.

Kajetan appears at the gate carrying his briefcase.

KAJETAN, COUNT, *at the beginning also* FRANZ

KAJETAN   Good morning!

FRANZ   *Notices him only now, goes to the gate.*

COUNT *pays no attention to him, smokes.*

KAJETAN Her Highness is expecting me. *Gives Franz his card.*

FRANZ *exits with the card.*

KAJETAN *at the gate but already in the park* Beg to wish you a good morning, Count.

COUNT *reciprocates coolly.*

KAJETAN *closer, introduces himself* Kajetan. I had the honor once.

COUNT Of course, of course, Herr Kajetan. The day before yesterday I had the pleasure of seeing you on stage. — Congratulations on your success.

FRANZ *returns* Her Highness will appear in a few minutes. *Exits.*

KAJETAN Most charming of Her Highness. That is, I wasn't summoned here until twelve. But unforeseen circumstances, which is how it is with us journalists — At twelve I have to be somewhere else again.

COUNT You're terribly busy, Herr Kajetan?

KAJETAN Enormously. All over. Interesting profession. Heights and depths. Palace of the rich, hovel of the poor. Death and life. Fact and fiction.

COUNT *laughing* Quite especially the last.

KAJETAN Especially the last. At ten in the Wendolin park, spring breezes, birdsong, awakening nature, poetry and peace, — two hours later, forest gloom, blood and horror, struggle and victory, death and decay.

COUNT Well, I hope it won't be all that dangerous.

KAJETAN Be all that dangerous — Perhaps it will. Just between us: pistol duel!

COUNT Pistol duel? Witness?

KAJETAN Witness — I? No, not my case. Correspondent.

COUNT Correspondent at a duel — we have that too?

KAJETAN We have everything. Actually, even more.

COUNT I suppose you're talking about the journalist's duel that's taking place today? Between Herr Fink and —

KAJETAN And Fliederbusch. The Count is well informed. Should've known.

COUNT A coincidence.

KAJETAN Sensational affair. Colossal bitterness on both sides. Strike here — strike there. Ten paces, five shots each. If no result then continuation with daggers. No child's play. Tragic outcome not unlikely, expected even, am prepared in any case.

COUNT You?

KAJETAN Journalistically. Haha! Both obituaries over and done with. *Indicating the left and right sides of his briefcase* Here Fink — here Fliederbusch! Nothing can happen to me!

COUNT You can say that again, I'm sure. You know both of them?

KAJETAN Know both of them. Naturally. Fliederbusch personally, even.

COUNT And Herr Fink?

KAJETAN Sources. Former officer.

COUNT Ah —

KAJETAN Gambling debts. Desperado. First-rate fencer and marksman. Also writes under the name of Styx.

COUNT Styx? Might you not be mistaken, Herr Kajetan?

KAJETAN Never mistaken. Sources.

COUNT So. Hmm. And the other one, — Fliederbusch, do you know any details about him too, maybe?

KAJETAN Promising young man. Father a big speculator gone to ruin. Small garret, starvation. Seven siblings. Organ-grinding. Fliederbusch cared for all of them. Splendid fellow. Great future, if he's not shot dead. I'd be sorry. Just now drove past me with two gentlemen. Looks good as life itself. Subject to change. Ha! *The following very quickly.*

COUNT Who drove past you? Herr Fink?

KAJETAN Fink? Don't know him. Fliederbusch.

COUNT Drove past you with two gentlemen?

KAJETAN Our carriages crossed at the corner.

COUNT And you recognized the two gentlemen too?

KAJETAN Two gentlemen? No. Complete strangers.

COUNT They must have been his seconds.

KAJETAN Why? Friends. Only nine-thirty. Duel not starting for a long time yet.

COUNT The two gentlemen wore top hats?

KAJETAN Top hats.

COUNT The one gentleman very slim, the other tall and husky, black mustache —?

KAJETAN The Count saw them too? Smart carriage with two black horses?

COUNT Yes, he drove past here. So that was Herr Fliederbusch?

KAJETAN Was Fliederbusch. Last drive maybe.

COUNT Let's hope not.

KAJETAN Hope not. Can turn out well too. Nothing new under the sun. Nonetheless, if one — *interrupts himself.*

COUNT Pardon?

KAJETAN If one of them must fall, I'm more for Fliederbusch.

COUNT With whom you're friends?

KAJETAN Friends is overstated. Close acquaintance.

COUNT And wish for his death?

KAJETAN Don't wish it. But obituary is better than the other one. Written with life-blood. The one of Fink dull.

COUNT And for that reason you'd prefer that Fliederbusch —

KAJETAN That's right. That Fliederbusch fall.

COUNT But that is downright devilish, Herr Kajetan.

KAJETAN The writer's soul, a sinister spot. Haha! Nightspot without music. Sometimes with, too. *Takes out his notebook and writes* Could use that.

PRINCESS *comes from the house wearing a riding dress* Good morning!

COUNT *kisses her hand.*

KAJETAN I must ask a thousand pardons, Your Highness, for being early —

PRINCESS Doesn't matter. *Looks around* But where is —

COUNT *draws the Princess to the front* Herr Fink begs to be excused, unfortunately he couldn't wait any longer.

PRINCESS So —? Well, yes.

COUNT Most likely you know?

PRINCESS What am I supposed to know?

COUNT About the duel?

PRINCESS By sheer coincidence.

COUNT A very interesting young man. Very promising. It would be a pity — Do you know, it's a fight to the death?

PRINCESS Seriously?

COUNT Yes.

PRINCESS So it's over a female after all?

COUNT No, it's a political duel. And to some extent I'm the cause.

PRINCESS You?

COUNT My speech in Parliament.

PRINCESS You don't really think I've read it? I only read the ones of the Social Democrats.

COUNT Oh, if I had known that —

PRINCESS So this is how your political career is starting. With murder and mayhem!

COUNT Well —

PRINCESS But you'll be able to look at yourself in the mirror if some misfortune happens here. Such a nice young man.

COUNT Yes, he is that.

PRINCESS But — I can't leave Herr Kajetan standing here any longer. So, my dear Herr Kajetan, here I am.

KAJETAN Your Highness, the connecting text is finished. With your permission, I'd like to read it to you.

PRINCESS Is it very long, Herr Kajetan?

COUNT Don't let me disturb you, Priska, nothing will come of our ride anyway.

KAJETAN   Not very long. Average. Can be shortened or lengthened as needed.

PRINCESS   Rhymed?

KAJETAN   Pretty much. But can also be spoken so no one will notice.

PRINCESS   Well, go on and start, Herr Kajetan. May the Count hear it?

KAJETAN   A great honor. *He has taken the manuscript out of his briefcase.*
The Princess has taken a seat. The Count stands a little in back of her, continually absent-minded.

KAJETAN   *sits down and reads* First tableau. Paradise. After the painting by Lucas Cranach. Characters: Adam, Eve, the serpent, the apple.

PRINCESS   But that's not a character.

KAJETAN   It is with me. Beautiful role. Haha!

PRINCESS   But if you begin in paradise it'll take a bit long.

KAJETAN   Oh no, Your Highness. Big leaps. From paradise directly to Pericles. From Pericles to Nero. From Nero to the migration of the Germanic tribes, and so on. — So — *he interrupts himself* Yes, right, something comes even before paradise. The Prologue. He appears as Harlequin, a staff in his hand.

PRINCESS   But why?

KAJETAN   He needs it in order to point at the tableaux after.

PRINCESS   I see, — a little staff.

KAJETAN   So, Harlequin bows in all directions and speaks:
Since God, our Lord, created all,
And near and far to his stern call —

COUNT   Please forgive me for interrupting. Tell me, Priska, are you in the mood to see a duel?

PRINCESS   What do you mean?

COUNT   Surely you've never been to one. So, do you want to?

PRINCESS   What kind of joke is this?

COUNT   It would interest you, perhaps.

PRINCESS The duel between —

COUNT Between Fink and Fliederbusch. Yes. Perhaps Herr Kajetan will be kind enough to take us along in his carriage —

KAJETAN *disconcerted* His carriage? How come? Haha!

PRINCESS Read on, Herr Kajetan.

COUNT I'm not joking. We'll drive to the Fink-Fliederbusch duel. But if we want to get there in time we have to leave at once.

KAJETAN Excuse me, — duel isn't taking place until twelve.

COUNT A mistake. At ten-thirty. Take it from me, Herr Kajetan. If we don't leave right away we'll miss it. I have my sources too.

PRINCESS But tell me, seriously now, have you gone mad?

COUNT Not in the least. And I promise you that you will amuse yourself splendidly.

PRINCESS Say, what do you take me for?

KAJETAN Five shots each.

PRINCESS What?

KAJETAN Colossal bitterness. Strike here —

COUNT So, quickly, Priska.

PRINCESS *indicating her riding dress* Yes, but can one go to a duel like this?

COUNT Why not? Maybe it'll become the fashion.

PRINCESS *calling up* Lina, my coat, quickly!

COUNT And your text, Herr Kajetan, you'll read it to us at lunch, — for dessert. From Adam and Eve up to — this will surely be a trifle for you — up to the duel between Fink and Fliederbusch. That is where world history ends for the time being.

CHAMBERMAID *has brought the coat.*

PRINCESS *places it over her shoulders* OK, I'm ready.

COUNT So, forward!

Franz stands at the gate; he and the chambermaid look at each other in amazement as the Count, the Princess, and

Kajetan leave the park. One still sees Kajetan waving and hears the carriage roll up.

Quick scene change on the darkened stage without lowering the curtain. A meadow surrounded by woods. Small paths from different directions, the widest from the right. A beautiful spring day.

FLIEDERBUSCH, EGON, WÖBL, KUNZ

Kunz is thirty-five, elegant, wearing a top hat and a short yellow overcoat, has a pair of binoculars around his neck and is sitting on a tree stump to the left; Wöbl stands in front of him, Fliederbusch is walking up and down in the background, along the edge of the woods, occasionally glancing to the right. Egon further to the right, is standing still.

KUNZ *lecturing, in good humor* Think of it, gentlemen, even under terms such as these the likelihood of a fatal outcome is no higher than one in thirteen.

WÖBL Ah!

KUNZ The likelihood of a serious injury one in seven, a slight one, one in three and of a totally favorable outcome —

WÖBL Even up.

KUNZ One and a half to one.

EGON *looks at his watch* Ten-forty. The gentlemen keep us waiting.

FLIEDERBUSCH A glorious spring day! Don't you agree, gentlemen!? *He lights a cigarette.*

EGON *looks at him not without admiration.*

KUNZ *stands up, goes over to Fliederbusch, feels his pulse* With your permission, Herr Fink!

FLIEDERBUSCH Please!

KUNZ Eighty-two. Barely increased. The highest pulse rate I was able to diagnose just prior to a duel was a hundred and thirty two; the lowest fifty-four. One can characterize yours as downright average. *He writes something.*

FLIEDERBUSCH I assume you're working on a statistical study of the duel?

KUNZ You guessed it. It'll be an epoch-making work. Today is the hundred seventeenth I've been present at.

FLIEDERBUSCH And always with binoculars?

KUNZ Only if there's a horse race taking place that afternoon. By the way, gentlemen, Feverish Dream has gone lame.

WÖBL What? — This is really —

EGON Gentlemen, ten-fifty! I don't know whether it's even allowable —

FLIEDERBUSCH *has stretched out on the grass and is whistling to himself.*

EGON *looks at him, surprised.*

WÖBL *pointing at Fliederbusch* What do your statistics say, Herr Doctor?

KUNZ I've never yet seen one lying there like that beforehand.

WÖBL And — after?

KUNZ It's better not to speak of that.

EGON *listening* Gentlemen —

WÖBL Steps —

KUNZ No doubt.

FLIEDERBUSCH *gets up* Hmm —

WÖBL There they come!

FLIEDERBUSCH *goes slowly towards the back.*

EGON I see only two —

They all stand to the far left. From the other side, on the wood path, FÜLLMANN *and* OBENDORFER *appear.*

FÜLLMANN We're going the wrong way, I tell you.

OBENDORFER Impossible. — See, there they are. *About to go on.*

FÜLLMANN But where is Fliederbusch? Still no sign of him?

FLIEDERBUSCH *has moved back into the woods, remaining visible to the audience but not to the other characters.*

WÖBL They're stopping.

EGON Surely they must have seen us.

FÜLLMANN *to Obendorfer* We were not at all careful to trust this Herr Styx after Fliederbusch's strange behavior on the phone.

OBENDORFER What reason would Herr Styx have had —? And he did have the letter from Fliederbusch.

FÜLLMANN Which said nothing about his alleged mission.

EGON Most unusual —

FÜLLMANN I suggest we disappear again. It would be a disgrace, you know —

OBENDORFER Impossible. They've surely seen us already.

FLIEDERBUSCH *has come further to the front again, having stepped out of the little woods; stands fairly distant from all the others, exactly equidistant from both parties.*

OBENDORFER *sees him* There he is!

FLIEDERBUSCH *greets him stiffly, remains standing where he is.*

FÜLLMANN Right. But why doesn't he come closer?

OBENDORFER Forward, then! *Quickly to the center.*
    Egon and Wöbl likewise approach the middle.

FÜLLMANN You talk, Obendorfer.
    The seconds stand facing each other; they greet each other solemnly.

OBENDORFER Gentlemen, first of all, please excuse our slight delay. Our carriage took a wrong turn at the pavilion. But I think we can get to work now without further delay.

EGON I will only be so free as to point out that we are still not all here.

OBENDORFER How so?

KUNZ *who has come closer in the meantime, introducing himself* Doctor Kunz.

OBENDORFER Of course — We thought from a distance — So, Herr Fink hasn't shown up?

EGON Herr Fink is obviously present; but Herr Fliederbusch has thus far not —

OBENDORFER Excuse me — he's standing right there.

EGON Where? There —? If you please, Herr Fink!

FÜLLMANN *waving for him to come over* Fliederbusch!

FLIEDERBUSCH *has come forward and now stands between the two parties, greets each side in silence.*
Short pause of amazement.

EGON AND WÖBL Herr Fink! —

FÜLLMANN AND OBENDORFER Herr Fliederbusch! —

FLIEDERBUSCH *bowing* Fink — and Fliederbusch — with your permission, gentlemen!

EGON I don't rightly — understand.

OBENDORFER This would really —

FÜLLMANN You wrote — *at the top of his voice* both articles? Here and there — against yourself —?

WÖBL *who gradually understands* Well, this really is a sleazy trick!

OBENDORFER You presumed to make fools of us?

EGON *with composure* Sir — who are you?

OBENDORFER, FÜLLMANN AND WÖBL Who are you?

FLIEDERBUSCH *simply* The day before yesterday I was Fliederbusch, yesterday I was Fink, today I'm both — or perhaps neither.

EGON This is by no means a satisfactory explanation.

FLIEDERBUSCH I can't give you any other, unfortunately.

OBENDORFER What effrontery!

FÜLLMANN Today you write so — and yesterday so, — and you want to be a journalist? You're a pus bag, is what you are! Scum!

EGON Gentlemen, none of us, I think, has anything further to do with this gentleman. There is nothing left for us but to withdraw from this desecrated spot as quickly as possible and — *getting a liberating idea* to draw up a protocol!

OBENDORFER A protocol?

KUNZ *earnestly* Absolutely. This is and remains an affair of honor, gentlemen. We have a proper challenge, we have a proper acceptance, the seconds have appeared at the appointed place, the doctor and — both antagonists. That these are joined in one person is, to be sure, a rare occurrence — in my practice a unique one, even — but that changes nothing in the nature of the matter.

WÖBL *to Egon* Here comes your Papa!

OBENDORFER *to Füllmann* Leuchter!

EGON AND FÜLLMANN Styx!

STYX *enters from the right with Satan and Leuchter* We're at the spot, gentlemen, here is the battleground. *Greets the others* My respects. Good morning, Herr Fliederbusch, I've taken the liberty of inviting your bosses to your duel with yourself.

LEUCHTER AND SATAN What?

FLIEDERBUSCH You've managed this very well, Herr Styx.

STYX I have, haven't I?

FLIEDERBUSCH *to Leuchter and Satan* Good morning, gentlemen. *Short bow to Leuchter, pointing to himself* Fink! *To Satan, likewise* Fliederbusch!

LEUCHTER Excellent! *He laughs* But I thought right away it'd be something like this.

FÜLLMANN *to Obendorfer* He thought —!?

SATAN *to Fliederbusch* This really is interesting. Well, I congratulate you on its turning out so well.

EGON Papa! *Since Satan pays no attention to him* Papa! Surely you won't — with this gentleman —

SATAN How's that? Why? We have obligations, Egon! Count
Niederhof —

EGON Will give him a swift kick — it goes without saying!

LEUCHTER My compliments, Herr Fliederbusch.

FÜLLMANN *to Obendorfer* His compliments —?

LEUCHTER A capital joke, truly. *To Füllmann* Don't you
agree?

FÜLLMANN *turns away in anger.*

LEUCHTER *to Fliederbusch* Do you know what you've done?
You have carried something ad absurdum. True, I still don't
know exactly what, but you've done it.

SATAN *uneasy because Leuchter is apparently monopolizing
Fliederbusch, to Egon* Let me alone, son. *To Fliederbusch*
My dear Herr Fink — if you please, Herr Fink — I regard
this whole thing as a youthful prank, an ingenious youthful
prank. And I propose herewith that from the first of the
month you join our paper on a permanent basis at a salary of
seven hundred crowns.

STYX Ah!

LEUCHTER *to Obendorfer* What is it you want? We'll have
the laughers on our side. *To Fliederbusch* I greet you in the
spirit of our arrangement of yesterday as co-editor of the
"Times" with a monthly salary of eight hundred crowns.

SATAN Nine hundred, Herr Fink!

LEUCHTER A thousand, Herr Fliederbusch!

SATAN A thousand and fifty.

COUNT NIEDERHOF, PRINCESS *and* KAJETAN *enter.*

EGON Count Niederhof!

STYX Ah, the Princess, not bad.

KUNZ Of all the duels I've ever witnessed this one is at any
rate the best attended.

PRINCESS *to the Count* But not so close. If a bullet goes
  astray —

COUNT Have no fear! *He extends greetings to all sides.*

OBENDORFER You've come too late, Kajetan.

KAJETAN Too late, Kajetan, how come? Already over? Hi,
  Fliederbusch! Nothing happened? Congratulations! But
  where's the other one?

OBENDORFER Dead.

KAJETAN Dead? Bad luck! Can never meet him, this Fink.
  Desperado, — had to end up this way. Body removed
  already?

OBENDORFER Buried.

KAJETAN Ha, don't believe it.

PRINCESS *to Fliederbusch* You've really —

FLIEDERBUSCH Your Highness, my name is Fliederbusch!

PRINCESS But where is Herr Fink, then?

COUNT *to the Princess* You see here both of them joined in
  one person.

PRINCESS I'm not sure I understand — are you a double,
  maybe?

KAJETAN Ah, — Fink and Fliederbusch in one person, —
  splendid! Grist for my mill! More water glideth by the mill
  — Identity of opposites —

SATAN A thousand and fifty!

LEUCHTER Eleven hundred!

KUNZ Eleven hundred going once, going twice —

SATAN Eleven hundred and fifty!

KAJETAN What's the meaning of this?

PRINCESS What's being auctioned off here?

COUNT Our young friend, obviously. Maybe you'd like to join
  in the bidding?

LEUCHTER Twelve hundred.

KUNZ Going once, twice. —

FLIEDERBUSCH Enough.

LEUCHTER All the better! Agreed at twelve hundred. Come along, Fliederbusch.

FLIEDERBUSCH I didn't mean it that way.

SATAN Twelve hundred and fifty!

FLIEDERBUSCH Stop, gentlemen. You're both mistaken. I am in no position to accept your most honorable offers. My opinions are not for sale.

FÜLLMANN Oh, that's a good one.

FLIEDERBUSCH I must reserve the right to think and to write whatever I want every day! I cannot commit myself to any one conviction.

FÜLLMANN You dare to speak of convictions? — And change them from one day to the next!

KUNZ A respectable person needs at least a week for that!

LEUCHTER Who wants to pin you down, Herr Fliederbusch? We'll come to terms all right.

SATAN We have already come to terms! *With what strikes him as a fortunate idea* The Count is my witness. Our conversation yesterday — Isn't that so, Count?

COUNT Forgive me, my dearest Herr Satan, Herr Radlmann's conditions are not acceptable. My consortium is withdrawing.

SATAN Withdrawing?

STYX I could have predicted that.

COUNT On the other hand, I will hold you to your word, Herr Fink — and Fliederbusch.

FLIEDERBUSCH *looks at him.*

COUNT Our arrangements of this morning remain in force.

SATAN AND LEUCHTER Arrangements?

They approach each other; the seconds find each other as well.

COUNT *closer to Fliederbusch* The two of us will understand each other, I think!

FLIEDERBUSCH Will we?

COUNT The equation works out. *Softly* You have two convictions, I have none —

FLIEDERBUSCH Are you quite certain of that, Count? In the
end you might be disappointed — in both of us.

COUNT I've taken this possibility into account in my equation
as well. *Offers him his hand.*

FLIEDERBUSCH *does not take it yet; loudly again* And if I
make it a condition that you hire Herr Styx as well —

STYX What? You want to offer me patronage, Herr
Fliederbusch? This I call — audacity! I intend to publish a
paper on my own. I do not require your patronage, Herr
Fliederbusch!

COUNT Certainly not with me, Herr Styx. And it will be
nothing but a pleasure, my dear Baron, to resume our former
relationship on a new basis, one promising so much success.

STYX I could consider your proposal only if it were your
intention — to call an anarchist paper into being. Otherwise
I'll do it alone. Material I have enough, gentlemen, about all
of you, too!

COUNT Let's think it over. In any event, it would be a pity if
such a promising partnership were to miscarry on account of
small differences of opinion.

FÜLLMANN *to Obendorfer* A fine paper this will turn out to
be.

KAJETAN Reactionary — anarchistic — conservative-liberal!
— Stupendous! I'll telegraph to America! Future of the press
— identity of opposites! I've always said so!

EGON We are superfluous here, gentlemen. Let us go and draw
up our protocol. *To Satan* It must appear in the next issue of
"The Elegant World."

LEUCHTER The protocol of the duel? We have just as much
of a right to that, Füllmann, I'm making you responsible.

COUNT Gentlemen, this protocol, you should really save it for
the new paper, — instead of a platform!

EGON Let's go!

*They all salute each other and make as if to leave. The Count
and Fliederbusch are standing together.*

COUNT One moment, gentlemen! *They all stop* Acting on the
fortunately not erroneous hunch that the duel between Fink
and Fliederbusch would not have a bloody outcome, I took
the liberty of ordering a luncheon at the pavilion, and I ask
you all, gentlemen, to do me the honor of taking part as my
esteemed guests.

Embarrassed pause.

EGON For my part, Count —

SATAN *softly* Egon! — It is Count Niederhof who's inviting
us.

FÜLLMANN What are you going to do, Obendorfer?

OBENDORFER I think one can always eat lunch.

KUNZ Why are you hesitating, gentlemen? After all, the affair
has been concluded as chivalrously as possible. Maybe never
in all my hundred and seventeen cases —

FÜLLMANN Count, even if I have the honor today of being
your guest, — it will, of course not hinder me, when the
occasion arises, to proceed with all ruthlessness against your
paper —

COUNT I am counting on it. And now, gentlemen — peace —
or at least a cease-fire until after lunch. For dessert, however,
Herr Kajetan will —

KAJETAN Read my script for the gala.

COUNT Oh, I beg your pardon! I completely forgot about your
script. I meant — the obituaries!

KAJETAN Haha!

FLIEDERBUSCH Obituaries?

COUNT *to Fliederbusch* About you — and you!

KAJETAN *takes both manuscripts from his briefcase, one from
the right side one from the left* Here Fink! Here
Fliederbusch!

FLIEDERBUSCH Give me those! *Takes them and begins to
tear them.*

KAJETAN And without even reading them?

FLIEDERBUSCH I'm sure there's not a word of truth in them!

KAJETAN Word of truth about Fink and Fliederbusch?! Asking
too much!

FLIEDERBUSCH *tears the pages into small pieces* To the four
winds with them! And now, Addio, Fink and Fliederbusch!

FÜLLMANN And with that you find the matter settled?

FLIEDERBUSCH Oh, you pedant! Must everything, then, be
settled? Can anything at all be settled? Did I come into this
world to settle anything? There are others here for that!

COUNT Who in the end also only imagine they are. Give the
Princess your arm, you hero — and victim of the day!

*They've all begun gradually to move. Satan with Leuchter,
Wöbl with Obendorfer, Egon with Füllmann, Styx with the
Count, Kajetan with Kunz, Fliederbusch with the Princess, to
whom he offers his arm.*

The curtain falls

AFTERWORD

by Jeffrey B. Berlin

"For many years I have been conscious of the far reaching
concord which exists between your views and mine on
some psychological and erotic problems . . . . I have often
asked myself in amazement how you could possibly come
by the one or other secret piece of knowledge which I had
acquired only by painstaking investigation of the object;
and then I arrived at envying the writer whom I had
previously admired. You will now appreciate how pleased
and elated I feel on reading that you, too, have derived
some stimulation from my writings."[1]
      Sigmund Freud. Letter of 5 May 1906 to Schnitzler.

> "Truth lies somewhere in the middle?
> By no means. Only in the depths."

> "Whether truths in the highest sense
> exist, is questionable. At all events
> there are beliefs. These however are of
> greatly varying degree."[2]

                    Arthur Schnitzler

The present edition will be a welcome contribution to the
reader and connoisseur of great literature, because Schnitzler's
works continue to fascinate audiences around the world. At the

same time, it will be of special interest to the comparativist, since many of Schnitzler's works have frequently been likened to writings by, among others, Maupassant, Chekhov, Tolstoy, Ibsen, Strindberg, and Shaw—a truly remarkable literary heritage. Nevertheless, despite some rather obvious similarities and possible influences here, Schnitzler's writings are original and unique. Not only do they enjoy a permanent, undeniable place in the canon of world literature, but they insured their author's place as *the* representative chronicler of the last years of the Austro-Hungarian Empire. Indeed, it is Arthur Schnitzler who best captured the spirit of fin-de-siècle Vienna.

At the heart of Schnitzler's finest works we find an author who, with unrelenting honesty, methodically probed the conscious and unconscious behavior of individuals. In one work he properly characterized this special interest as an analysis of "the vast domain of the soul." Over and over again—from richly varied perspectives—this soul-searching became his chief focus.

In keeping with this search for understanding, Schnitzler and his characters often question the nature and meaning of truth, which always seemed illusory and ambiguous. But even though on an intellectual level he enjoyed philosophizing, Schnitzler remained first and foremost an observer of the perplexed, suffering mind. He was a trained, dedicated explorer of the mysterious workings of the human psyche—in short, a literary diagnostician whose interest was invariably sparked by human interaction, human behavior, and the complex of human emotions. In this regard, he created characters and placed them in situations reflective of basic, everyday experiences, maintaining that, "In a work of art, the point is never a problem itself, but always and only the working-out of that problem in a character; in the aesthetic sense, therefore, there are no old and no new problems. And it follows that there are no new and no old characters either, but only true and false characters" (*AuB* 473). In a like manner, he maintained: "It is never the problem you have chosen, never the imagination of your treatment, which will carry your work into the future; it is always the characters alone you have created and the atmosphere with which you have surrounded them" (*AuB* 103).

Although Schnitzler's primary concern is with individuals, i.e., characters and their weaknesses, he does not shrink from social criticism. However, he is not a problem solver, and the reader will look in vain for solutions to a sorry society. The works show Schnitzler to be analytical and penetrating in his scrutiny of individuals and society at large, but he often remains disheartened and discontented with what he sees. At the same time, his works are not restricted—as is sometimes still argued—to characterizations of the Vienna of his day; like many great writers, Arthur Schnitzler also writes about the nature of humanity.

Thematically, for example, Schnitzler's works speak about gradations of loneliness and marriage, ethics and morality, life and death, feelings and moods, cynicism and optimism, seriousness and play, appearance and reality, truth and falsehood, deception and loyalty, youth and old age, Jewishness and anti-Semitism, politics and language, nihilism and primitivism, free will and determinism, existential anguish and solace, fear and hope, freedom and entrapment, frivolity and solemnity, jealousy and trust, seduction and love, dreams and illusions, fate and chance. In pursuing these dichotomies as far as he could, Schnitzler drafted an emotional image of the personality caught at the extremes or between the shriek of anguished pain and ecstatic joy—or, to use his term again, "the vast domain of the soul."

Like every writer, Schnitzler too has a literary trademark, a characteristic style. But early in his career, various critics and literary historians came to regard his artistic stamp—partly, we should emphasize, for valid reasons—to be restricted to impressions of Vienna 1900. More specifically, among the dominant traits that were said to characterize his narratives and dramas, we find melancholy themes, witty and sometimes sparkling dialogue, somewhat risque settings, elements of lighthearted gaiety, little depth, and, often, impressionistic figures.

Because of these classifications Schnitzler continued to be associated with cliches such as poet of the sweet-girl (*das süße Mädel*), topographer of decadence, the Viennese Maupassant, precursor of Freud, the pleasure-seeking Anatol-prototype, skeptical ironist, and amoralist. While some of this stereotyping had a positive impact, bringing Schnitzler additional recognition and acclaim, viewed overall it appeared to be mostly undesirable, primarily because it incompletely and, therefore, unfairly defined his *oeuvre*.

Even as Schnitzler's literary productivity increased significantly in both quality and range, there was little or no effort on the part of some evaluators to revise the existing mindset. In short, the stereotyping was not easily discarded. Throughout his career, then, Schnitzler suffered at the pen of some who repeatedly misunderstood and misrepresented his literary accomplishments.

The ideas for the earliest stereotyping derived from Schnitzlerian works like *Anatol* (1893), *Sterben (Dying)* (1894), *Liebelei (Light-o'Love)* (1896), and *Reigen (Hands Around)* (1900). To the uninitiated, these (and a handful of other works) remained his insignia. Indeed, the gaiety and lightheartedness of Anatol's playful manner made it an instant theatrical success; and *Liebelei*, first produced on 9 October 1895 at Vienna's famous *Burgtheater*, while firmly establishing Schnitzler's literary reputation, also reinforced the stereotypes.

The private publication of *Reigen*—a dialogue in each of whose ten scenes each person switches partners until at the end they are reunited—caused an even greater critical outcry. To many, *Reigen* was scandalous and indecent, and Schnitzler was dubbed the dramatist of sexual intrigue—the author whose principal thematic interest was seduction (even though nothing sexual is explicitly stated by its author, who in appropriate places supplied a line of dashes, thereby letting the reader interpret the situation).

Schnitzler experienced a different type of stereotyping with the publication of *Sterben*. Now critics acted as if he were a disciple of Freud—an author who provides a "case study" under the guise of a story. However, the critics were not altogether wrong in this instance. At the beginning of his literary career Schnitzler had not always found the proper medium for expression of his psychological virtuosity, as his letter of 10 December 1903 to his colleague Hugo von Hofmannsthal illustrates: "It [*Sterben*] stems from the period when the case-study ["der Fall"] interested me more than people."[3] On the other hand, in both thematic arrangement and composition, *Sterben* is a work marked by excellence; it is undoubtedly more than an exemplification of an individual's response to impending death.

If we look beyond Schnitzler's so-called replication of Viennese bourgeois life, we see an artist who focused on an individual's thoughts and feelings. We witness, too, realistically and perfectly drawn characters. And we cannot but marvel at Schnitzler's insight and creativity. In this regard, he was the first German-language author to experiment with the interior monologue—that literary device by which a character gives unconscious expression to exactly what he or she feels or thinks—i.e., what Freud meant with his analytic technique of free association. Schnitzler's use of this narrative device was so successful that comparisons of his technique in his masterly *Leutnant Gustl* and *Fräulein Else* to that in Joyce's *Ulysses* are not uncommon.

Not surprisingly, then, thousands of audiences and readers have been intrigued and entertained by the variations in theme, form, style, diction and originality of Schnitzler's genuinely classic works. And frequently we are offered—in a scrambled order as befits the imitation of real life—a character's psychological profile; that is to say, Schnitzler challenges us to collect and analyze the contributing conscious and unconscious thoughts and feelings for each figure. By doing so, we may determine the emotional wealth or poverty of the fictional Schnitzlerian soul.

The above process, which is analogous in some ways to Strindberg's technique of unmasking and, in others, reminiscent of the moment in Ibsen's dramas when the life-lie is revealed, is discernible in the three plays offered here in G. J. Weinberger's exciting, new, and refreshing translations. At the same time, just as the thematic matter of Schnitzler's writings can be universally appreciated, so too do we realize that his works are timeless. They remain as truly relevant today as when they first were published. Following this, there is every reason to believe that Weinberger's translations will bring continued enjoyment and cultural enrichment to many thousands of readers.

Arthur Schnitzler spent his entire career in Vienna, that famous capital and cultural city of Europe, where he was born in 1862 and died in 1931. His father, a distinguished professor of laryngology at the University of Vienna, maintained an extensive private practice where many of his patients were important theater personages. As a result, the younger Schnitzler had the opportunity to visit the theater with some frequency from an early age and thus made his earliest acquaintance with the conflict between illusion and reality.

At the same time, Schnitzler lived in a period that witnessed historical and cultural developments unlike those of any other age. In particular, turn-of-the-century Vienna enriched us with its outstanding contributions in art, music, design, architecture, philosophy and literature. Like many of his famous Viennese colleagues, such as Hofmannsthal, Kraus, Beer-Hofmann, Adolf Loos, Kokoschka, Mahler, Schoenberg, Klimt, Schiele, Berg, Stefan Zweig, and Freud (*The Interpretation of Dreams* appeared in 1900), Schnitzler also reaped accolades acknowledging his place as a respected, innovative and distinguished creative individual.

Throughout his career Schnitzler established many significant and exciting relationships. But perhaps none is so special as his unusual interaction with Sigmund Freud, who lived only a short tram ride away from him. Like Freud, Schnitzler used various lenses of the microscope of psychology to explore the private thoughts of individuals. His style lends itself well to comparisons with ideas in Freud's theoretical writings. And regarding this last point, Schnitzler's own response to Theodor Reik's 1913 psychoanalytic treatment of his works (Reik's book was the first of its kind on Schnitzler)[4] is noteworthy:

> I have scruples about the onesidedness of the psychoanalytical method practiced by him and other students of Freud, regardless of the very interesting and sometimes even correct results if may lead to. . . . Reik draws attention to something that certain professional critics usually ignore: namely, my depiction of non-erotic human relationships as between siblings, parents and children, and friends. He also points out various deeper psychological connections. . . . In the future he will look upon Freud's methods of interpretation (regardless of the depth of knowledge of human nature from which the basic ideas might originally have emerged) not as the sole and only path to salvation, but as one among many that leads to the secret of poetic creation, at times, however, into vagueness or error.[5]

Schnitzler, who like Freud was a physician, abandoned his successful practice early in his career and directed his talent and effort to creative writing. Nevertheless, he always regarded himself as a "medical man." He once remarked: "He who has been a medical man can never cease to be one. For medicine entails a view of the world." His medical background and his writing activities were, to him, two sides of the same coin. "I write diagnoses," he declared, and he spoke of the "physiology of (his) creation."[6]

The signal feature of the Schnitzler/Freud relationship is that Freud himself once termed Schnitzler his "double" and even voiced a fear to meet his literary counterpart. So it happened that on 14 May 1922, Freud wrote to Schnitzler on the occasion of the latter's sixtieth birthday:

> I want to make a confession which, out of consideration for me, I would ask you to keep to yourself. . . . I have tormented myself with the question why in all these years I have never attempted to seek social intercourse and strike up a conversation with you. . . . The answer contains the confession which appears to me as too intimate. I think I have avoided you from a kind of shyness in the face of my own double ("aus einer Art Doppelgängerscheu"). Not that I am easily inclined to identify myself with another or that I mean to overlook the difference in talent that separates me from you but time and again when I get deeply absorbed in your beautiful creations I seem to find beneath their poetic surface the very presuppositions, interests and conclusions which I know to be my own. Your determination as well as your skepticism—what people call pessimism—your preoccupation ("Ergriffenheit") with the truths of the unconscious, of the instinctual drives in man, your dissection of the cultural and conventional certainties of our society, the dwelling of your thoughts on the polarity of love and death—all this moves me with an uncanny sense of familiarity. . . . Thus I have formed the impression that you know through intuition—or rather in consequence of subtle self-observation—everything that I have discovered by laborious work on other people. Indeed, I believe that fundamentally you are a depth-psychologist, as honestly impartial and undaunted as any; and if you were not that, your artistic abilities, your linguistic art and your creative power would have had free rein and would have made you into a writer of far greater appeal to the masses.

Invariably, Freud's document is fascinating both to the specialist and the general reader. To hear a "tormented" Freud's "confession" that he rates Schnitzler's talent above his own, recognizing Schnitzler as a depth psychologist of the highest order, considering Schnitzler a "Doppelgänger" figure—such accolades Freud bestowed upon few.

As concerns the "Doppelgänger" issue, during the course of my own correspondence with Anna Freud I once asked in what way she might summarize what her father meant in the famous May 1922 letter cited above. Her answer, in a letter of 11 July 1971 to me, was the following:

There is no difficulty in explaining what my father meant when he used the word Doppelgänger. He often spoke about the fact that poets and writers in their own way come to the same conclusions about human nature as he had to fight for in his painstaking analytical work with patients. In this sense the novelist is the Doppelgänger of the analyst.[7]

Finally, let us address the dramas in this volume. In so doing, we hope briefly to sketch out some additional topics that most concerned Schnitzler; at the same time, the discussion permits us to demonstrate how Schnitzler approached the concept of truth within a dramatic text.

While all gradations of truth were of concern to Schnitzler, language as a barrier between individuals and truth especially disturbed him. As he said:

The steep path has parched the lips and the hearts,
But finally there is the reward of delightful success:
The temple of truth towers in a sacred place.
Yet a voice comes roaring out of the darkness: Recede!
No Mortal will force his way in here.
A giant keeps watch by the fate: the Word. (*AuB* 9)

In *The Hour of Recognition* and *The Big Scene*, for example, we find that some of the principal characters act as if they knew the truth. In actuality, these same characters labor under semantically induced misapprehensions. They speak and listen to words that are ostensibly unmistakable, but the words are, as Schnitzler once stated, "treacherous and elusive."[8] And Schnitzler noted:

> What are words? Whoever raises this question never had the right to initiate a discussion. Certainly words do not express everything. There is always something between the words, beyond the words—but this inexpressible something derives its meaning only from the fact that words do exist, and from the varying distance, the diverse relationship that it has to those words. (*AuB* 337)

One central problem in these one-act plays is that truth becomes difficult to realize because of the characters' dependence upon a medium which can be unreliable and unrevealing. To put it differently, these works tell us that words do not reveal our innermost thoughts and may give support to intentionally misleading statements. This tendency inevitably results in the communication of untruths. When Schnitzlerian characters seek the truth, then, time and again their efforts to learn it are thwarted because of their dependence upon an unreliable and unrevealing medium of expression.

While Schnitzler is angered at individuals who blatantly disseminate only portions of the truth, he realizes that the problem is a deep one. It may even be bottomless—for the issue extends beyond the thoughts and deeds of any single category of people. It is rooted in language itself—in words. Like his Café Griensteidl colleagues and many other writers, again and again Schnitzler shows that words deceive—they hide the truth—that is, they allow the speaker to misrepresent his intent. As Schnitzler remarked: "Regarding the Word: Perhaps our entire morality consists only in making something better out of this imprecise material, language, which makes lying so easy, so irresponsible, so culpable. To lie with words as little as possible."[9]

In *Fink and Fliederbusch*, which appears in this volume for the first time in English translation (it was first published in

1917), we are also permitted to examine aspects of Schnitzler's attitude toward the concept of truth in relation to language. Because the play has heretofore not been available to English-language readers, it is appropriate here to address it in more detailed fashion.

First of all, Schnitzler's achievement in *Fink and Fliederbusch* rests not only on the creation of the interesting Fink/Fliederbusch character, but also on his penetrating analysis of the two rival newspapers and its journalists. It is here, within their respective private offices, that Schnitzler shocks us by exposing the truth, attempting to raise our and society's consciousness, much in the way of Ibsen and other great writers. Among other things, he wants us, almost as if we shared his own scientific training, to probe, to question, to doubt, to challenge, to criticize. And Schnitzler's criticism in *Fink and Fliederbusch* is powerful, so powerful that it raised the eyebrows of more than one critic at the time of its publication.

Although the many humorous situations and characters seem to detract from the seriousness of the play, Schnitzler's humor and sarcasm should not be underrated. It is precisely because of the comedic aspect that Schnitzler is able to make his point. Had he been didactic rather than comic, *Fink and Fliederbusch* would have been a less effective play.

The fact that Fink/Fliederbusch is taken seriously demonstrates the ease with which a person may deceive society. Because Fink/Fliederbusch writes for a "responsible" newspaper, the unsuspecting reader, who anticipates the dissemination of truth, is duped, at least temporarily. This is not to suggest, however, that either the utterances of Fink *or* Fliederbusch are not supported with real facts. But failure to present all the facts, and, thus, the whole truth, or a willingness to manipulate or slant the facts, brings with it deception—untruth. Indeed, until the conclusion of the play both newspapers are also victims.

According to Schnitzler, journalists are excessively wont to draw immediate inferences from a situation and to pass judgment on it, frequently from a partisan standpoint. After all, the newspaper is waiting to be printed! But when events are deceptively taken out of context, and when half-truths are accepted as whole truths, the real truth is all too often distorted. Sensational stories may be gripping and engaging, but misleading and spellbinding lines can only contribute to flawed understanding.

To Schnitzler, the misrepresentation of information is equivalent to blatant lying. As he remarked in one aphoristic notation, "A so-called half-truth, in whatever guise, will never become a whole truth. Indeed, if we look at it closely enough we shall realize that such a 'half-truth' has been a lie from the outset" (*AuB* 51). At the same time, he posited: "The truth that someone expresses cannot give us real pleasure if we fell that this person might not have expressed it if he had considered it more advantageous to suppress it" (*AuB* 252).

Fink and Fliederbusch also prompts us to ask whether we should excuse journalists for the inadequacy of the tools of their craft. Is the blame, rather, to fall upon language? Does a newspaper guild render journalists immune from responsibility? What about principles, ethics, morals? Schnitzler does not absolve journalists of their crimes. While language may certainly exacerbate a problem, it is, as *Fink and Fliederbusch* shows, the given journalist's unethical behavior that significantly causes the problem in the first place. According to Schnitzler, these newspaper reporters and editors disregard facts and intentionally misuse words. They ignore and distort truth when it serves their purpose. Of course we should make clear that it is not journalists or politicians alone who misuse language. Schnitzler's *opus* provides a host of figures either guilty of or plagued by linguistic deceptiveness.

While the scenario of Schnitzler's play is pessimistic, it is not nihilistic. Even though genuine sincerity is lacking in Fliederbusch's response to Fink's articles, opposition exists. Fink does not control the reporting of news on any large scale. At the same time, though still minimal and not yet effective, elements of refutation of the Finkian viewpoint are present in the newspaper's editorial office. Ever skeptical that human motivation and language will change, Schnitzler still imagines that one day truth shall prevail. But dreams, reflection and mere thought, Schnitzler holds, are insufficient. Unlike Bernhardi, Schnitzler knew that only action and exposure bring on change. Perhaps this helps explain why he might have written both works. As Schnitzler once wrote: "Belief and doubt have nothing to do with progress and development. Only the man of action advances the world; and, since both the believer and the doubter can be active, it will be best to leave each in that state of mind which promotes his activity" (*AuB* 23).

In *Fink and Fliederbusch*, then, Schnitzler chronicles the motivation of a few groups of individuals and suggests the ripple effect that their actions have on the community at large. And he knew that *Fink and Fliederbusch* as well as *Professor Bernhardi* would generate some alarm. On 12 December 1917 he wrote to Richard Charmatz:

> . . . I have to be just as prepared with "F. and Fl." for the least worthy journalists to react most wildly, as I had to expect the wrath of similar elements on the appearance of "Leutnant Gustl," or a like reaction with "Bernhardi" on the part of certain medical circles. And yet. . . my satire was as harmless as could be desired. Look at the few characters I've tried more or less successfully to stage in "F. and Fl," and you'll find that they all present more or less honest (which is not the same as decent), even if in some cases ridiculous, examples of their type.
>
> (*Briefe 1913-1931* 154)

In *Professor Bernhardi* we have a drama which has remained controversial since its appearance in 1912. In considering this play—and without giving away too much of the plot—one may justifiably suggest that if an individual wishes to remain a member of society, he or she must become actively involved in it. When faced with opposition, one must fight for what he takes to be just. In the play, Bernhardi insists that his only consideration is his patient's best interests. However, judgment must in some cases go beyond the purely medical and scientific and be of a moral and ethical nature relative to societal conditions and expectations.

As director of the Elisabethinum, Professor Bernhardi is responsible for protecting the rights of both his patients and the institute itself. This he does, but in a limited fashion because he finds politics scandalous and wishes no part of it. When removed from office, more for political-religious reasons than for any crime, Bernhardi desires to remain silent; that is, he refuses to avail himself of any legal or other self-clarifying opportunities. He maintains that his position is known and participation in a political game unnecessary. Because Bernhardi is unwilling to defend himself the supposed truth becomes distorted.

Bernhardi is trapped in a serious situation where not to react is equivalent to taking action. He attempts to face his problem by ignoring everything and accepting the jail sentence. Such an attitude has the function of incriminating him. In short, the truth of the situation has not been established because the human element—Bernhardi's reaction—comes to dominate the action.

One useful approach to the play is to examine the contrasting figures of Professor Bernhardi and the priest. Each character, ostensibly responsible for his own behavior, is actually being manipulated. Schnitzler's depiction of the destructive ramifications of political maneuvering, religious pressure and the resultant distortion of truth may be better understood by elucidating their effect on these two antagonists.

That Schnitzler recognized their confrontation as a major element is reinforced by his own draft notes—available among his unpublished posthumous papers at the Cambridge University Library in England—on the priest and Bernhardi:

The priest and Bernhardi talk past each other. Of course, my dears, this is precisely the meaning of this dialogue. Each man says exactly what he must say in accordance with his nature. If they understood each other completely, they would be identical. But even if each were the most perfect human being of his kind as far as personal cast of thought and philosophy are concerned, they still would never solve the great question that lies dormant at the bottom of this dialogue, the question of free will and causality. If they had not talked past each other, one would have had to convince the other; in the end one man would stand where the other man stood in the beginning, and the whole story could start all over again. But someone who had solved the problem once and for all would no longer be a poet but the creator of the world.[10]

To be sure, the clash between Bernhardi and the priest serves to erupt into a situation never contemplated by either of them. Neither Bernhardi nor the priest knows how to proceed without offending the other. At best, they can only use their intuition and make judgments. But such judgments take them within the realm of value decisions. In the case at hand, Bernhardi's judgment does not satisfy all the individuals involved. It is with these comments in mind that the reader is challenged to interpret Schnitzler's poignant masterpiece, *Professor Bernhardi*.

Holy Family College

NOTES

1. See "Sigmund Freud: Briefe an Arthur Schnitzler," ed. Heinrich Schnitzler," *Neue Rundschau* 66.1 (1955). All translations in this afterword are my own.

2. Arthur Schnitzler, *Gesammelte Werke: Aphorismen und Betrachtungen*, ed. Robert O. Weiss (Frankfurt a.M.: S. Fischer Verlag, 1967) 327 and 344, respectively. Future references to this volume appear in the text with the abbreviation *AuB* and the page number.

3. *Hugo von Hofmannsthal/Arthur Schnitzler Briefwechsel*, ed. Therese Nickl and Heinrich Schnitzler (Frankfurt a.M.: S. Fischer Verlag, 1964) 179.

4. It is a pleasure to acknowledge my gratitude to Theodor Reik's son, Mr. Arthur Reik, for discussing with me on several occasions the time period as well as Freud's circle of colleagues.

5. Letter of 2 April 1914 to Hans Henning. In Arthur Schnitzler, *Briefe 1913-1931*, ed. Peter Michael Braunwarth, et al. (Frankfurt a.M.: S. Fischer Verlag, 1984) 37-38.

6. I am indebted to Schnitzler's son, the late Professor Heinrich Schnitzler, for this information.

7. The original of Anna Freud's letter is in German and reads as follows: "Was mein Vater mit dem 'Doppelgänger' meinte, ist nicht schwer zu sagen. Er hat oft davon gesprochen, dass Dichter und Schriftsteller auf dem ihnen eigenen Weg zu denselben Schlüssen über die menschliche Natur kommen, die er mühsam in der analytischen Arbeit an Patienten erkämpfen

musste. In diesem Sinn ist also der Novelist der Doppelgänger des Analytikers." Quoted with permission from Anna Freud.

8. Statement in an interview with George S. Viereck. See Viereck, *Glimpses of the Great* (New York: Macaulay, 1930) 409.

9. Arthur Schnitzler, *Das Wort*, ed. Kurt Bergel (Frankfurt a.M.: S. Fischer Verlag, 1966) 27.

10. Arthur Schnitzler, "Zu den eigenen Werken." I wish to express my appreciation to the Cambridge University Library as well as the International Arthur Schnitzler Research Association for courtesies extended to me on several occasions.